NAUSICAÄ
Of The Valley Of The Wind

2

HAYAO MIYAZAKI

Nausicaä of the Valley of the Wind
Volume 2

STORY & ART BY HAYAO MIYAZAKI

Translation/David Lewis and Toren Smith [Studio Proteus]
Translation Assist — Editor's Choice Edition/ Kaori Inoue & Joe Yamazaki
Touch-up Art & Lettering/Walden Wong
Design/Izumi Evers

Editor — 1st Edition/Annette Roman
Editor — Editor's Choice Edition/Elizabeth Kawasaki

Managing Editor/Masumi Washington
Editor-in-Chief/William Flanagan
Production Manager/Noboru Watanabe
Sr. Director of Licensing & Acquisitions/Rika Inouye
Vice President of Marketing/Liza Coppola
Sr. Vice President of Editorial/Hyoe Narita
Publisher/Seiji Horibuchi

Printed in Canada

Published by VIZ, LLC
P.O. Box 77010
San Francisco CA 94107

Editor's Choice Edition

10 9 8 7 6 5 4 3 2 1

First printing, March 2004
First English edition, May 1995

www.viz.com

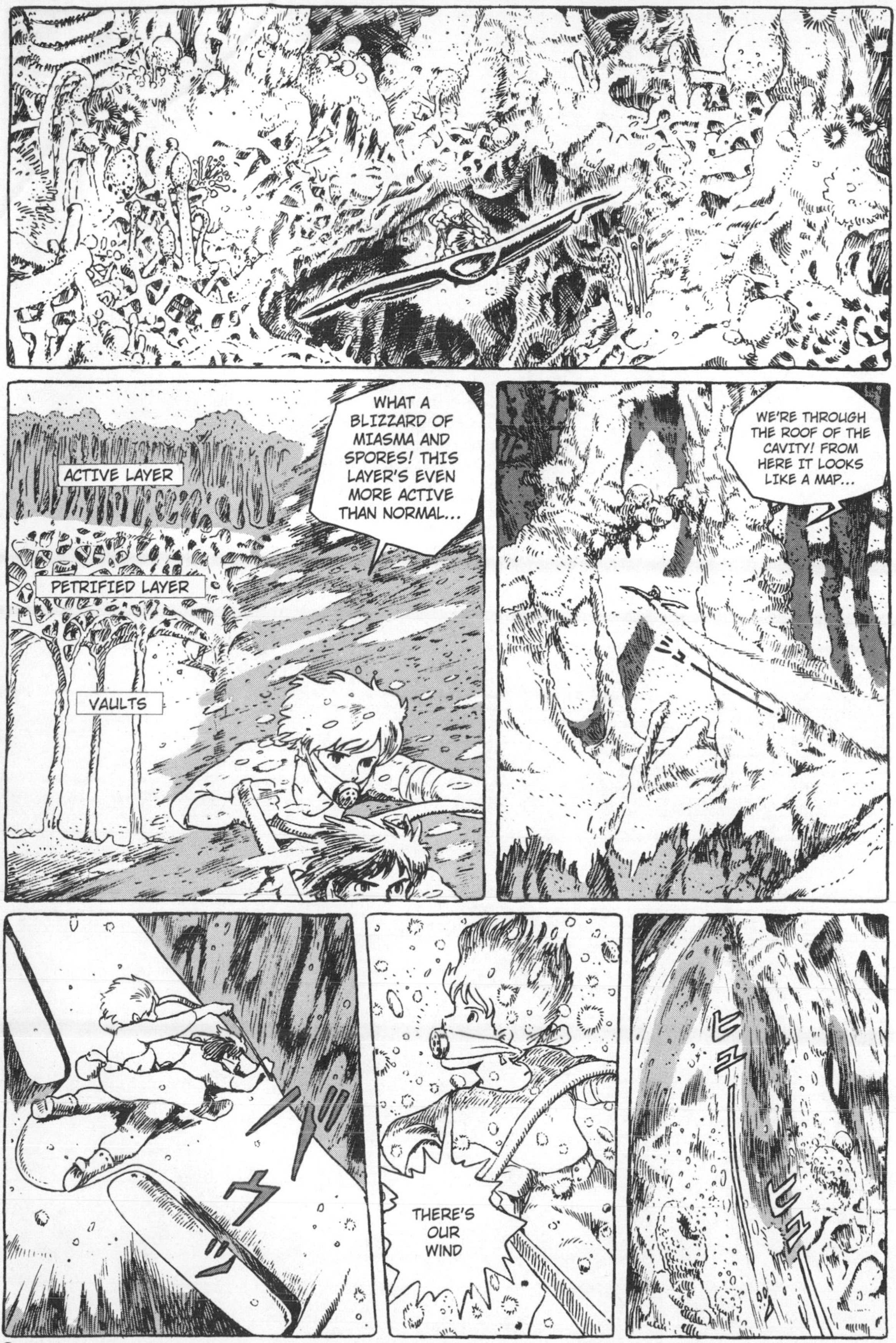
WE'RE THROUGH THE ROOF OF THE CAVITY! FROM HERE IT LOOKS LIKE A MAP...
WHAT A BLIZZARD OF MIASMA AND SPORES! THIS LAYER'S EVEN MORE ACTIVE THAN NORMAL...
ACTIVE LAYER
PETRIFIED LAYER
VAULTS
THERE'S OUR WIND

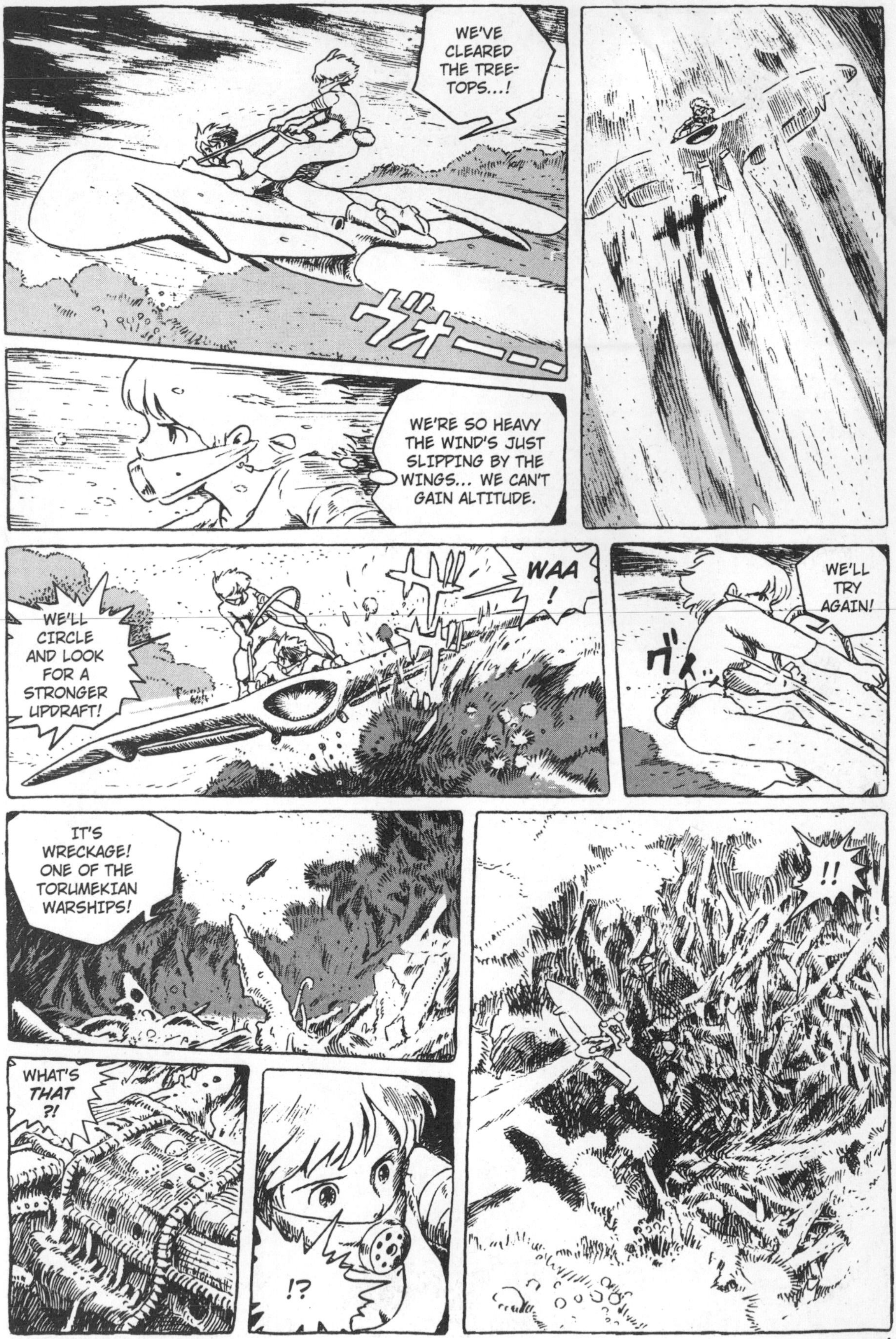
WE'VE CLEARED THE TREE-TOPS...!
ヴォーーー
WE'RE SO HEAVY THE WIND'S JUST SLIPPING BY THE WINGS... WE CAN'T GAIN ALTITUDE.
WE'LL TRY AGAIN!
WAA!
WE'LL CIRCLE AND LOOK FOR A STRONGER UPDRAFT!
!!
IT'S WRECKAGE! ONE OF THE TORUMEKIAN WARSHIPS!
!?
WHAT'S *THAT* ?!

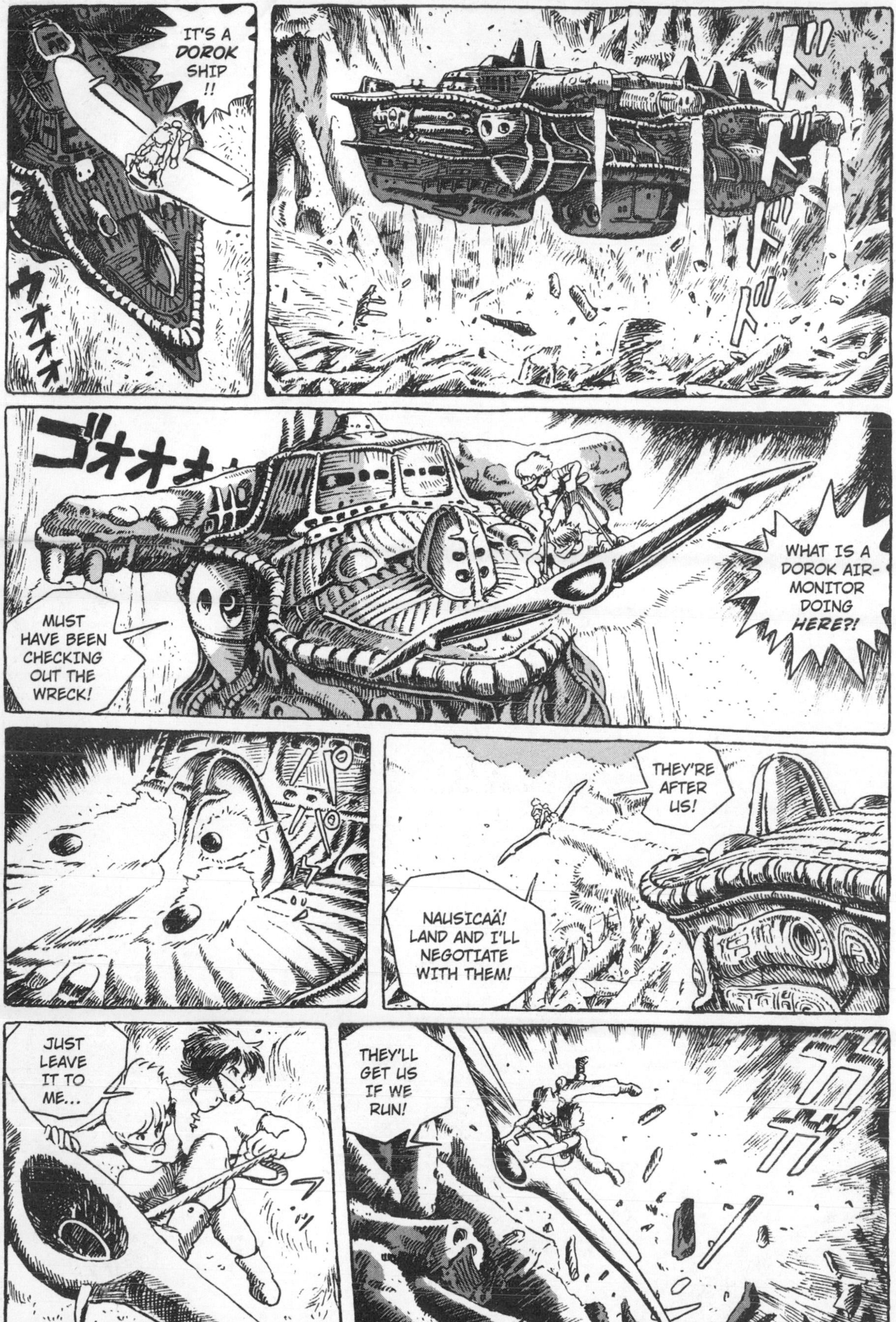
IT'S A DOROK SHIP !!
ゴオオオ
WHAT IS A DOROK AIR-MONITOR DOING HERE?!
MUST HAVE BEEN CHECKING OUT THE WRECK!
THEY'RE AFTER US!
NAUSICAÄ! LAND AND I'LL NEGOTIATE WITH THEM!
THEY'LL GET US IF WE RUN!
JUST LEAVE IT TO ME...

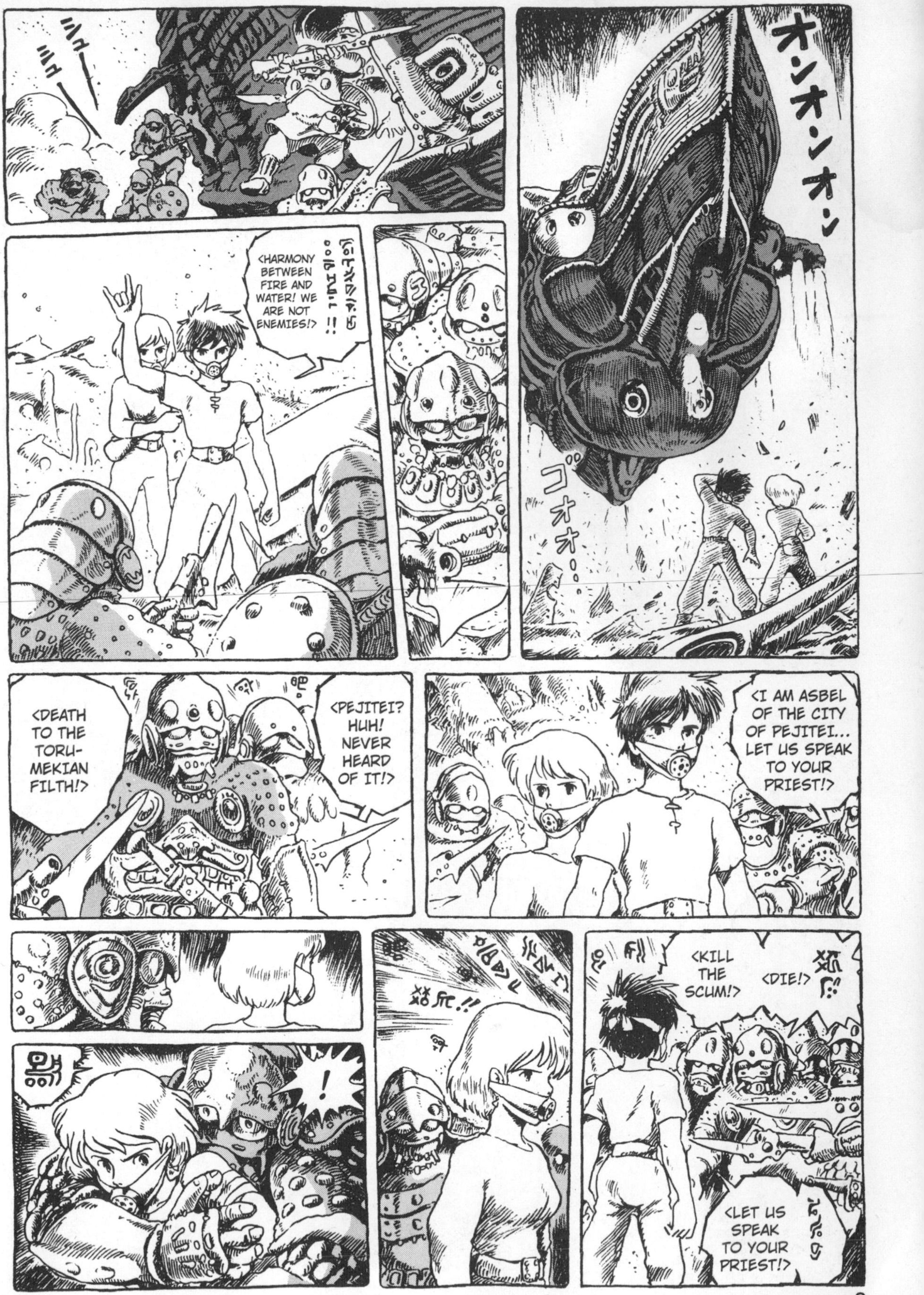
オンオンオンオン
ゴォオォ…
シュー
シュー
<HARMONY BETWEEN FIRE AND WATER! WE ARE NOT ENEMIES!>
<I AM ASBEL OF THE CITY OF PEJITEI... LET US SPEAK TO YOUR PRIEST!>
<PEJITEI? HUH! NEVER HEARD OF IT!>
<DEATH TO THE TORU-MEKIAN FILTH!>
<DIE!>
<KILL THE SCUM!>
<LET US SPEAK TO YOUR PRIEST!>
!

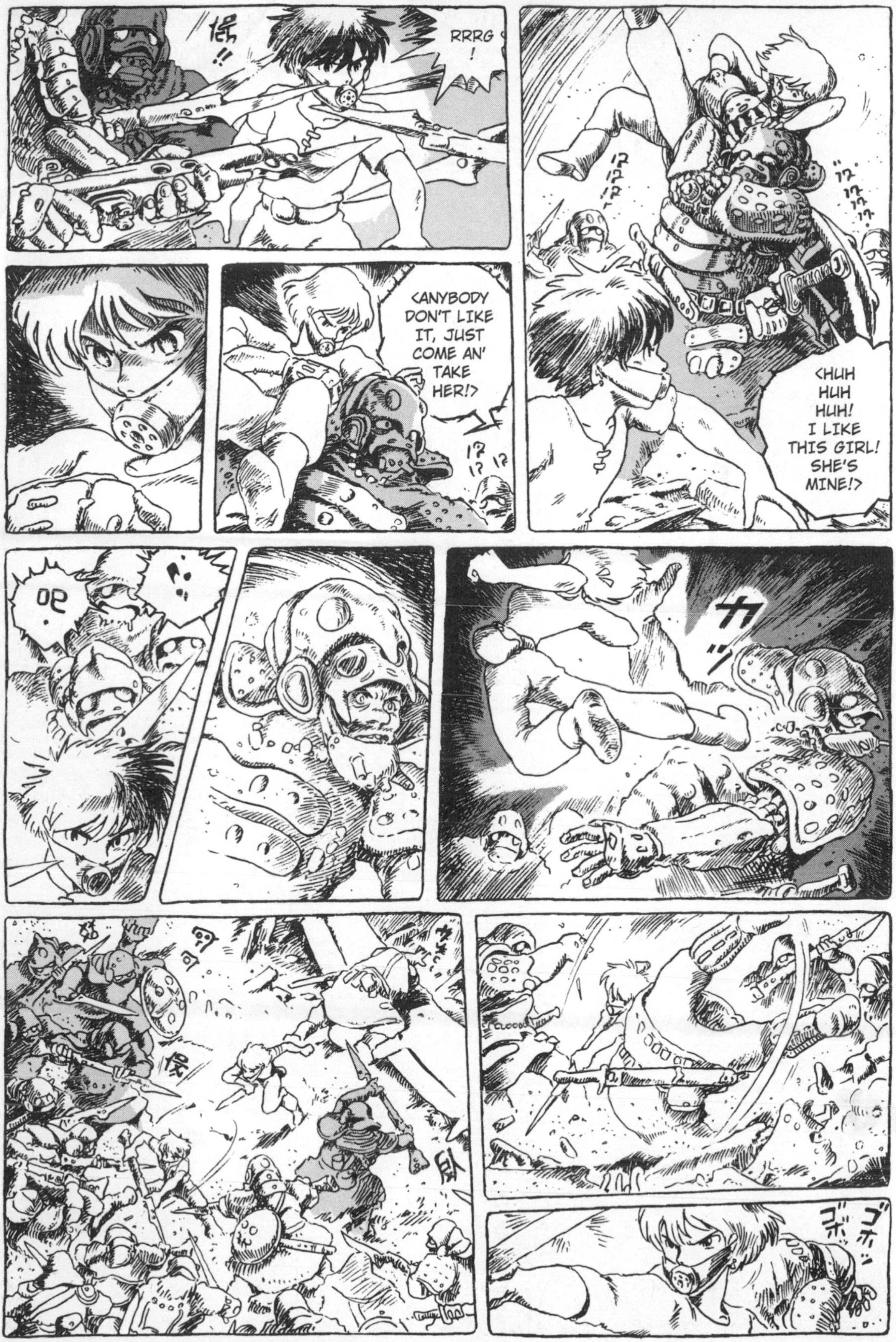
<HUH HUH HUH! I LIKE THIS GIRL! SHE'S MINE!>
RRRG !
<ANYBODY DON'T LIKE IT, JUST COME AN' TAKE HER!>

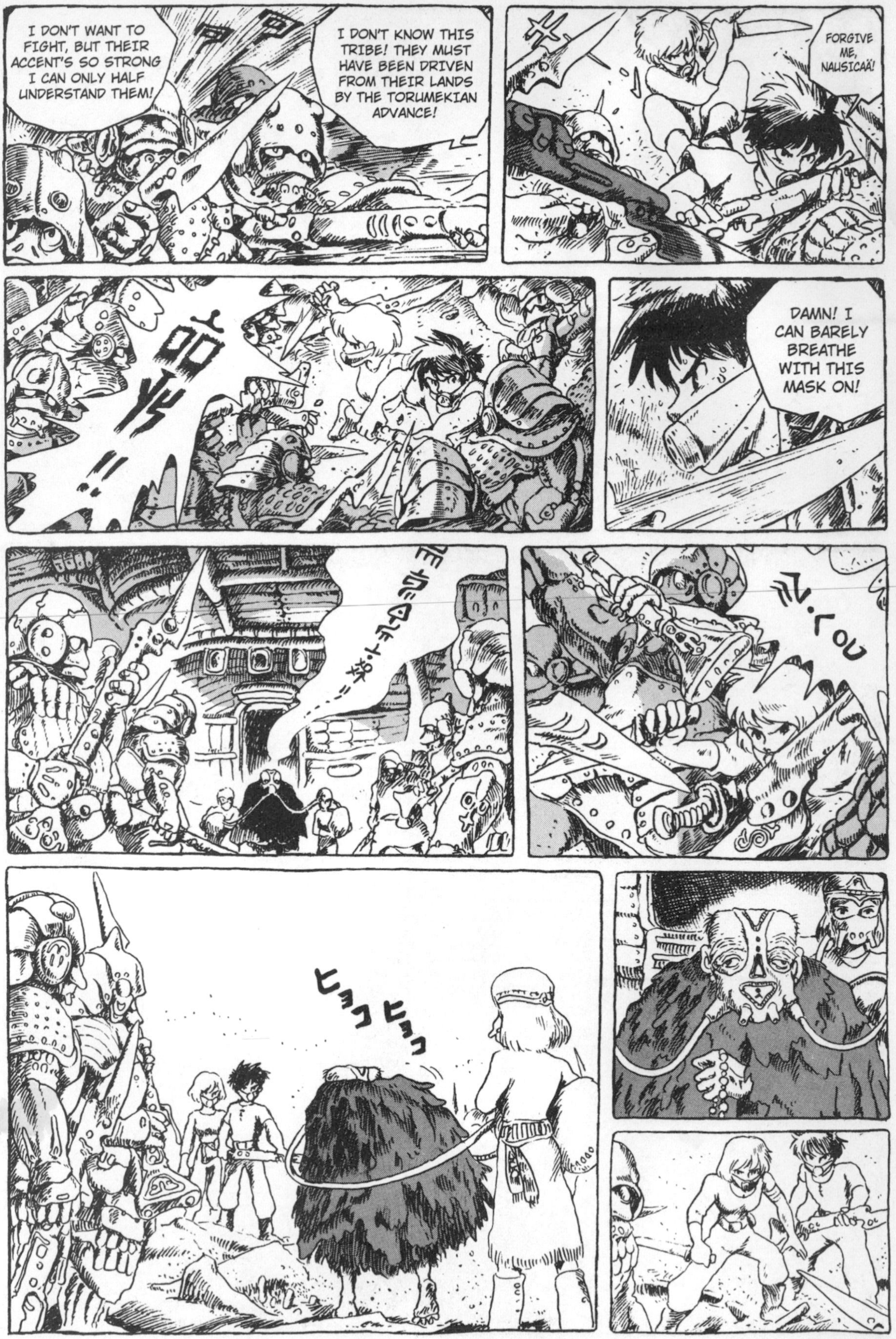
FORGIVE ME, NAUSICAÄ!
I DON'T KNOW THIS TRIBE! THEY MUST HAVE BEEN DRIVEN FROM THEIR LANDS BY THE TORUMEKIAN ADVANCE!
I DON'T WANT TO FIGHT, BUT THEIR ACCENT'S SO STRONG I CAN ONLY HALF UNDERSTAND THEM!
DAMN! I CAN BARELY BREATHE WITH THIS MASK ON!
ヒョコ ヒョコ

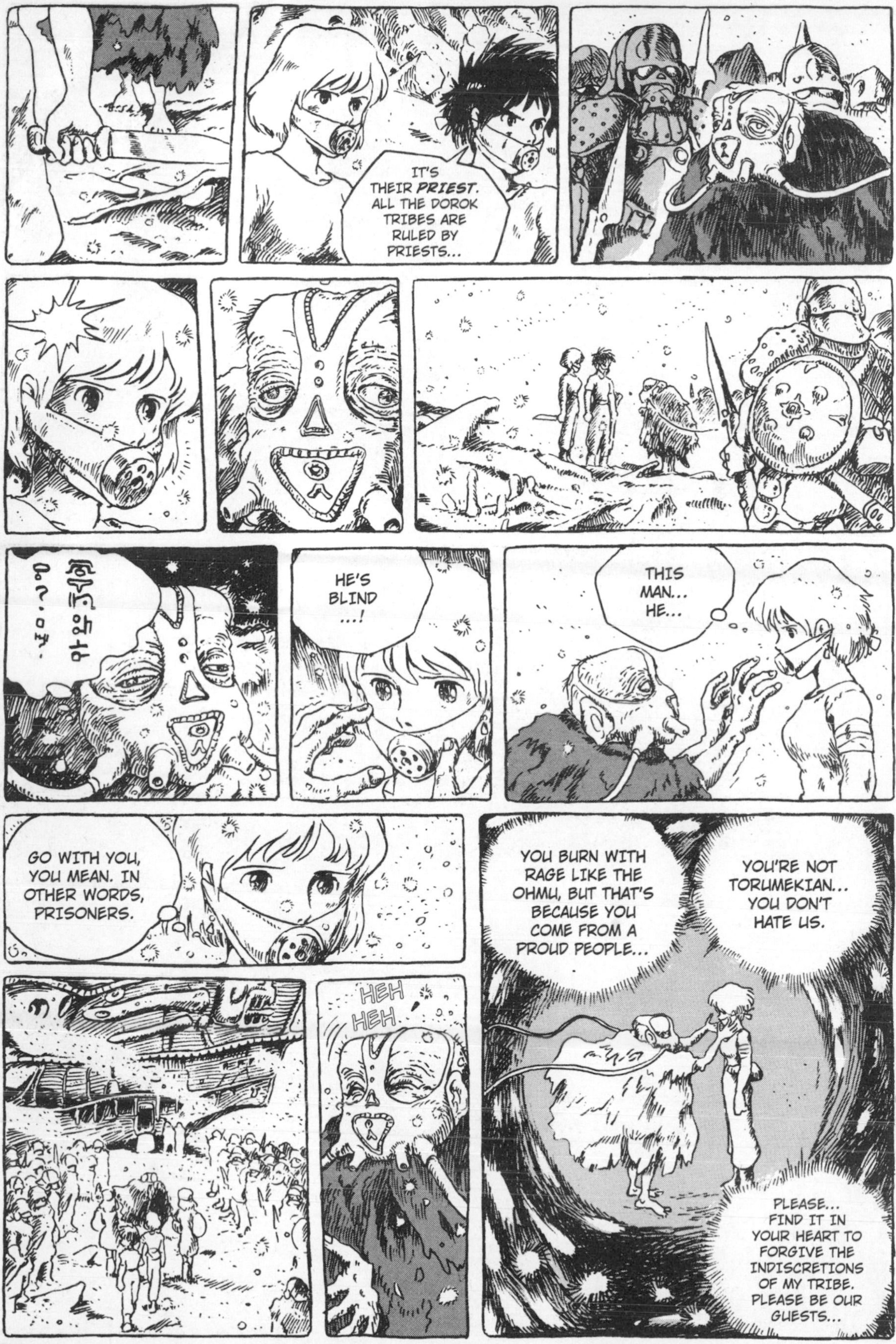
IT'S THEIR PRIEST. ALL THE DOROK TRIBES ARE RULED BY PRIESTS...
THIS MAN... HE...
HE'S BLIND ...!
YOU'RE NOT TORUMEKIAN... YOU DON'T HATE US.
YOU BURN WITH RAGE LIKE THE OHMU, BUT THAT'S BECAUSE YOU COME FROM A PROUD PEOPLE...
PLEASE... FIND IT IN YOUR HEART TO FORGIVE THE INDISCRETIONS OF MY TRIBE. PLEASE BE OUR GUESTS...
GO WITH YOU, YOU MEAN. IN OTHER WORDS, PRISONERS.
HEH HEH

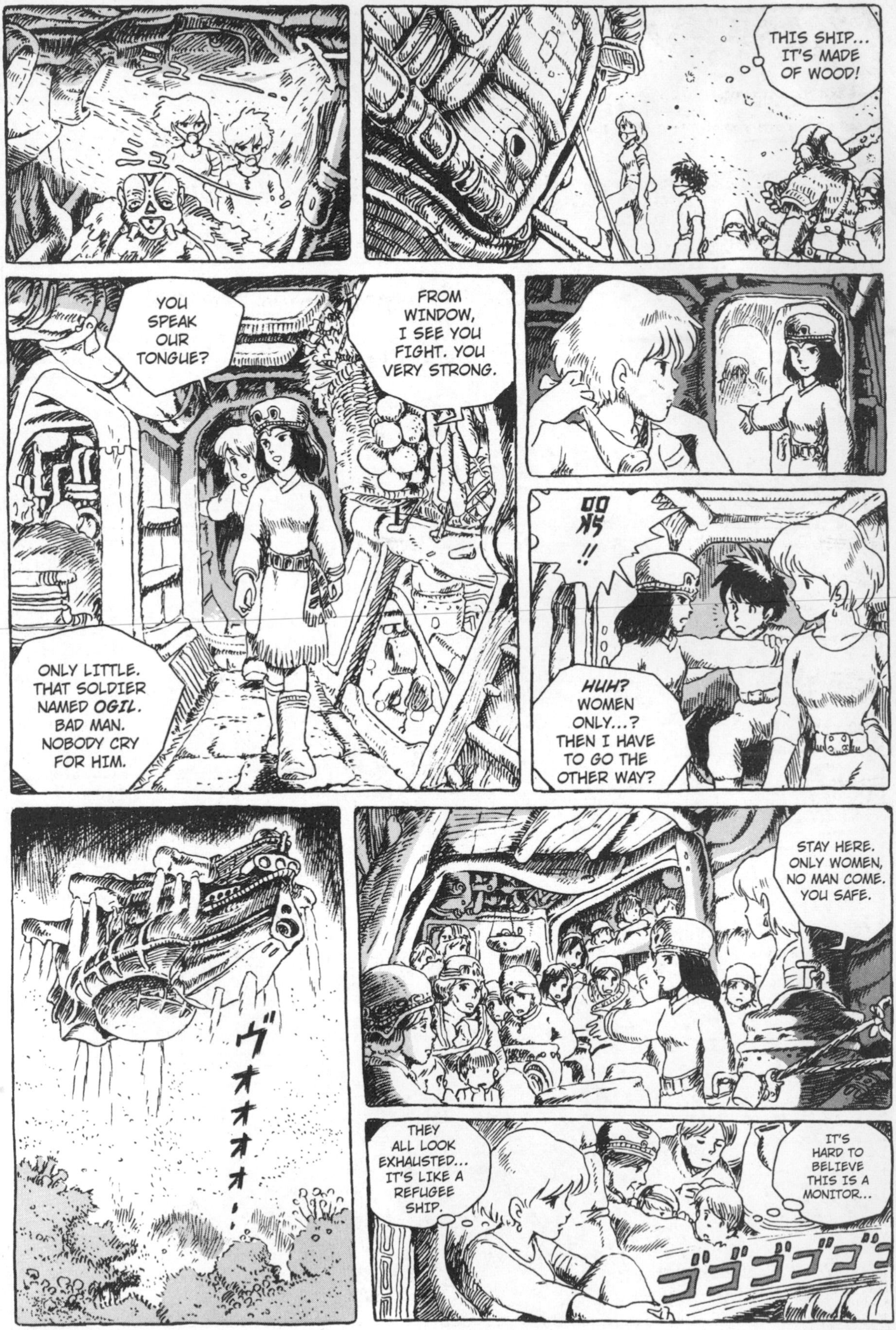
THIS SHIP... IT'S MADE OF WOOD!
ニュー
ニュ
DOKS!!
HUH? WOMEN ONLY...? THEN I HAVE TO GO THE OTHER WAY?
FROM WINDOW, I SEE YOU FIGHT. YOU VERY STRONG.
YOU SPEAK OUR TONGUE?
ONLY LITTLE. THAT SOLDIER NAMED OGIL. BAD MAN. NOBODY CRY FOR HIM.
STAY HERE. ONLY WOMEN, NO MAN COME. YOU SAFE.
IT'S HARD TO BELIEVE THIS IS A MONITOR...
THEY ALL LOOK EXHAUSTED... IT'S LIKE A REFUGEE SHIP.
ゴゴゴゴゴ
ヴォオオオー

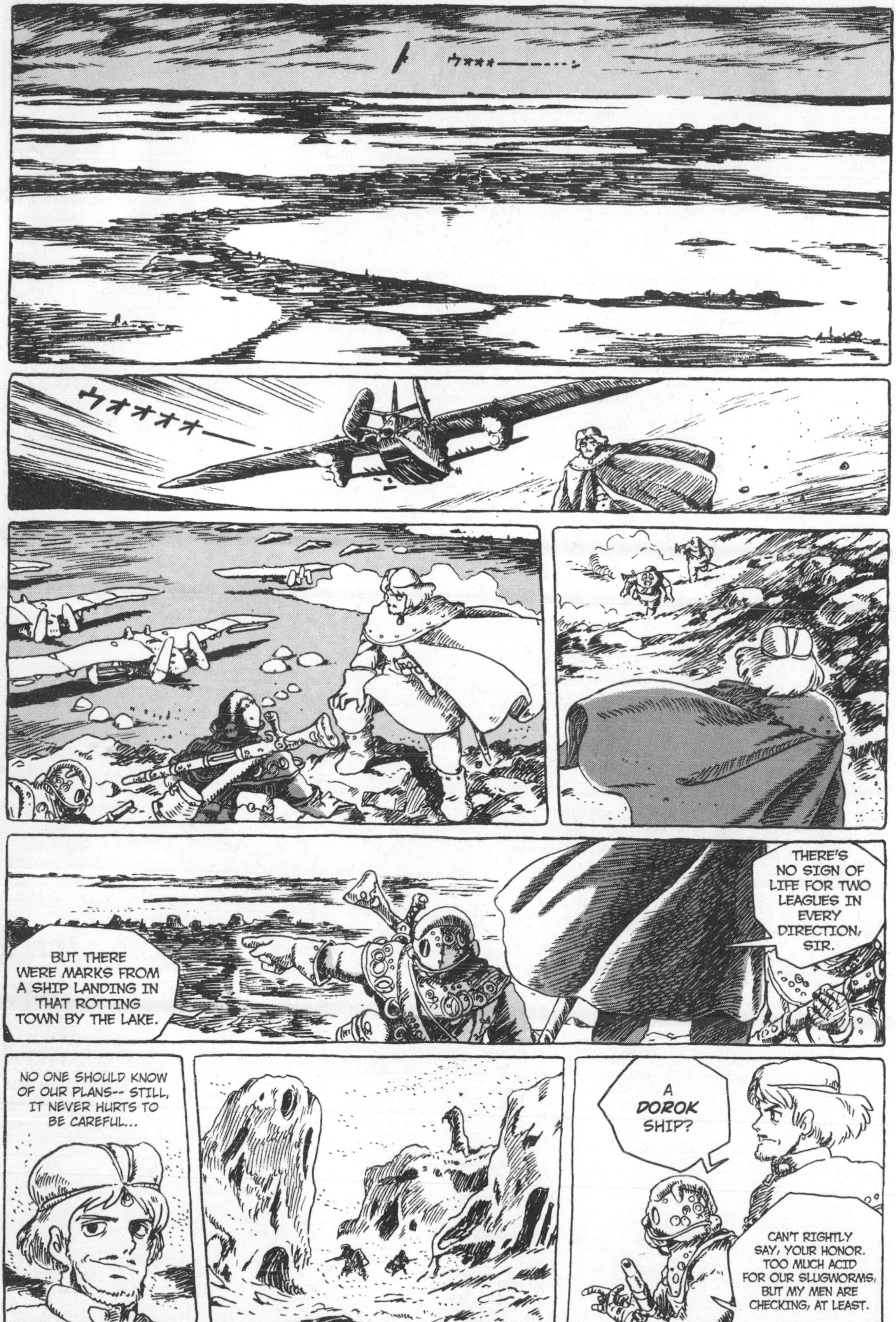
ウォォォーーー・・・ン
ウオオオオオー
THERE'S NO SIGN OF LIFE FOR TWO LEAGUES IN EVERY DIRECTION, SIR.
BUT THERE WERE MARKS FROM A SHIP LANDING IN THAT ROTTING TOWN BY THE LAKE.
A **DOROK** SHIP?
CAN'T RIGHTLY SAY, YOUR HONOR. TOO MUCH ACID FOR OUR SLUGWORMS, BUT MY MEN ARE CHECKING, AT LEAST.
NO ONE SHOULD KNOW OF OUR PLANS-- STILL, IT NEVER HURTS TO BE CAREFUL...

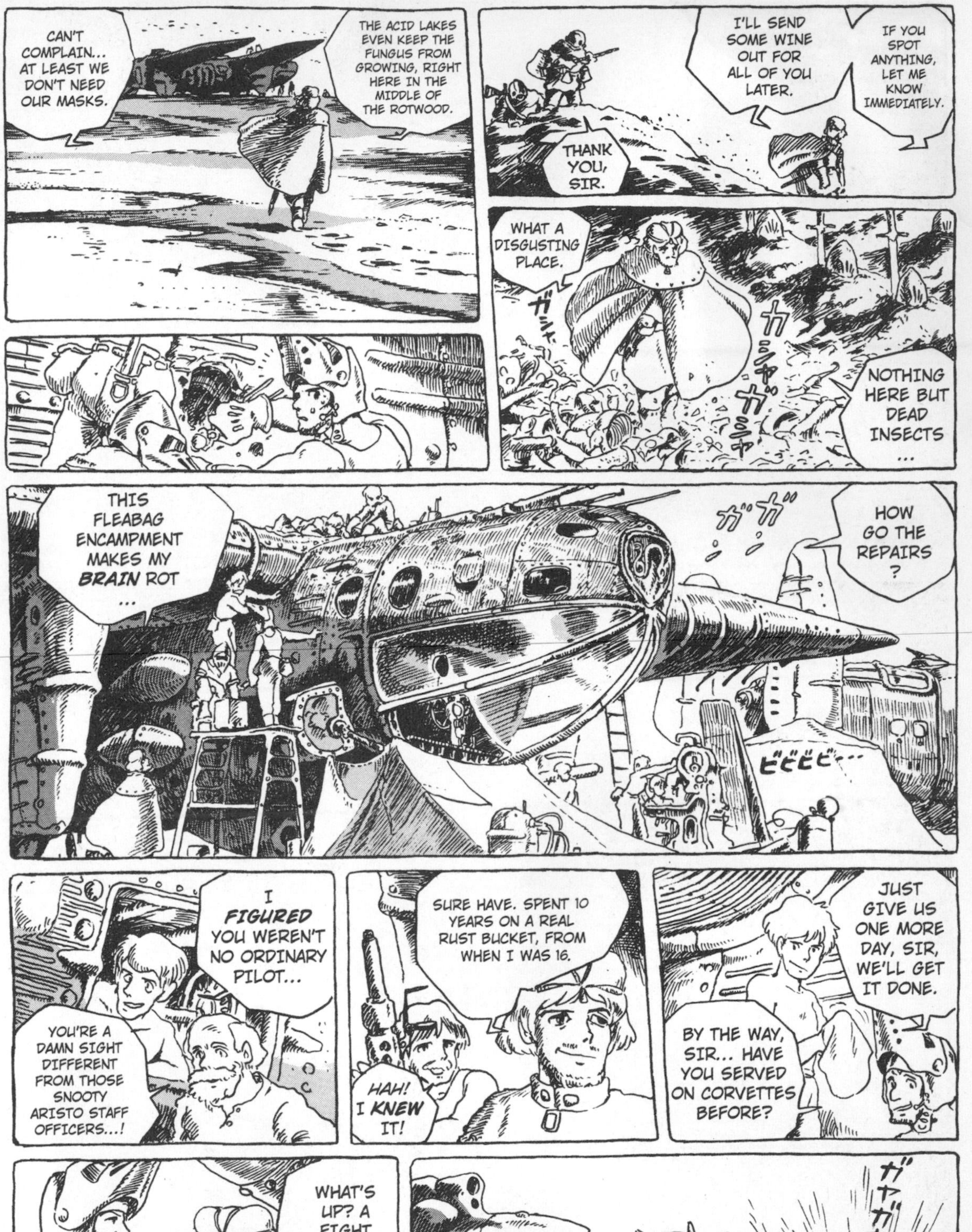
IF YOU SPOT ANYTHING, LET ME KNOW IMMEDIATELY.
I'LL SEND SOME WINE OUT FOR ALL OF YOU LATER.
THANK YOU, SIR.
THE ACID LAKES EVEN KEEP THE FUNGUS FROM GROWING, RIGHT HERE IN THE MIDDLE OF THE ROTWOOD.
CAN'T COMPLAIN... AT LEAST WE DON'T NEED OUR MASKS.
WHAT A DISGUSTING PLACE.
ガシャ
カシャガシャ
NOTHING HERE BUT DEAD INSECTS ...
HOW GO THE REPAIRS ?
ガガ
THIS FLEABAG ENCAMPMENT MAKES MY **BRAIN** ROT ...
ビビビビ...
JUST GIVE US ONE MORE DAY, SIR, WE'LL GET IT DONE.
BY THE WAY, SIR... HAVE YOU SERVED ON CORVETTES BEFORE?
SURE HAVE. SPENT 10 YEARS ON A REAL RUST BUCKET, FROM WHEN I WAS 16.
HAH! I ***KNEW*** IT!
I ***FIGURED*** YOU WEREN'T NO ORDINARY PILOT...
YOU'RE A DAMN SIGHT DIFFERENT FROM THOSE SNOOTY ARISTO STAFF OFFICERS...!
ガヤガヤ
WHAT'S UP? A FIGHT ...?
NO, SIR. IT'S THE TROOPERS FROM THE VALLEY OF THE WIND. THEY'VE BEEN IN AN UPROAR SINCE THIS MORNING.

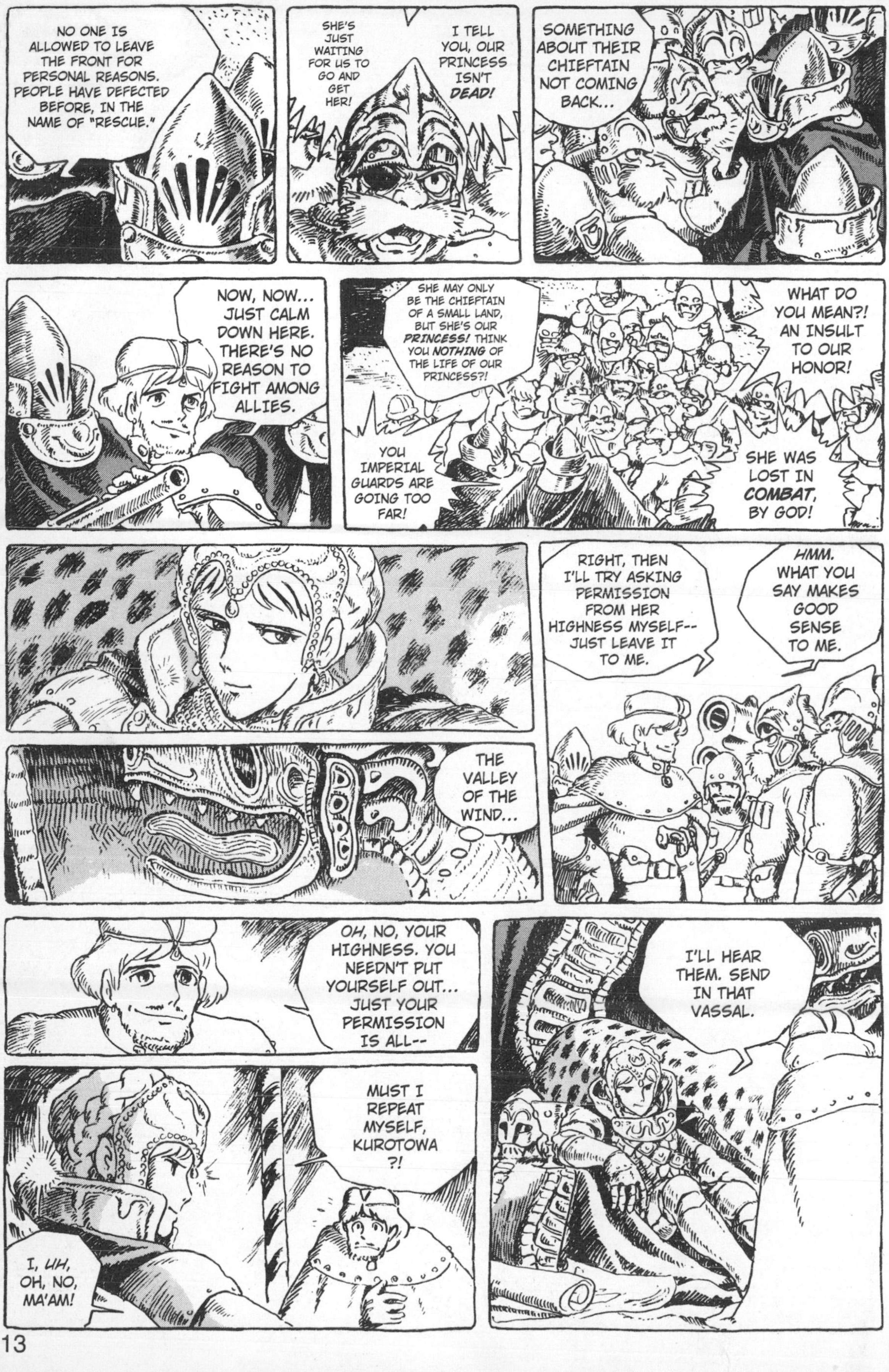
SOMETHING ABOUT THEIR CHIEFTAIN NOT COMING BACK...
I TELL YOU, OUR PRINCESS ISN'T *DEAD!*
SHE'S JUST WAITING FOR US TO GO AND GET HER!
NO ONE IS ALLOWED TO LEAVE THE FRONT FOR PERSONAL REASONS. PEOPLE HAVE DEFECTED BEFORE, IN THE NAME OF "RESCUE."
WHAT DO YOU MEAN?! AN INSULT TO OUR HONOR!
SHE MAY ONLY BE THE CHIEFTAIN OF A SMALL LAND, BUT SHE'S OUR *PRINCESS!* THINK YOU *NOTHING* OF THE LIFE OF OUR PRINCESS?!
SHE WAS LOST IN *COMBAT*, BY GOD!
YOU IMPERIAL GUARDS ARE GOING TOO FAR!
NOW, NOW... JUST CALM DOWN HERE. THERE'S NO REASON TO FIGHT AMONG ALLIES.
HMM. WHAT YOU SAY MAKES GOOD SENSE TO ME.
RIGHT, THEN I'LL TRY ASKING PERMISSION FROM HER HIGHNESS MYSELF-- JUST LEAVE IT TO ME.
THE VALLEY OF THE WIND...
I'LL HEAR THEM. SEND IN THAT VASSAL.
OH, NO, YOUR HIGHNESS. YOU NEEDN'T PUT YOURSELF OUT... JUST YOUR PERMISSION IS ALL--
MUST I REPEAT MYSELF, KUROTOWA ?!
I, *UH*, OH, NO, MA'AM!

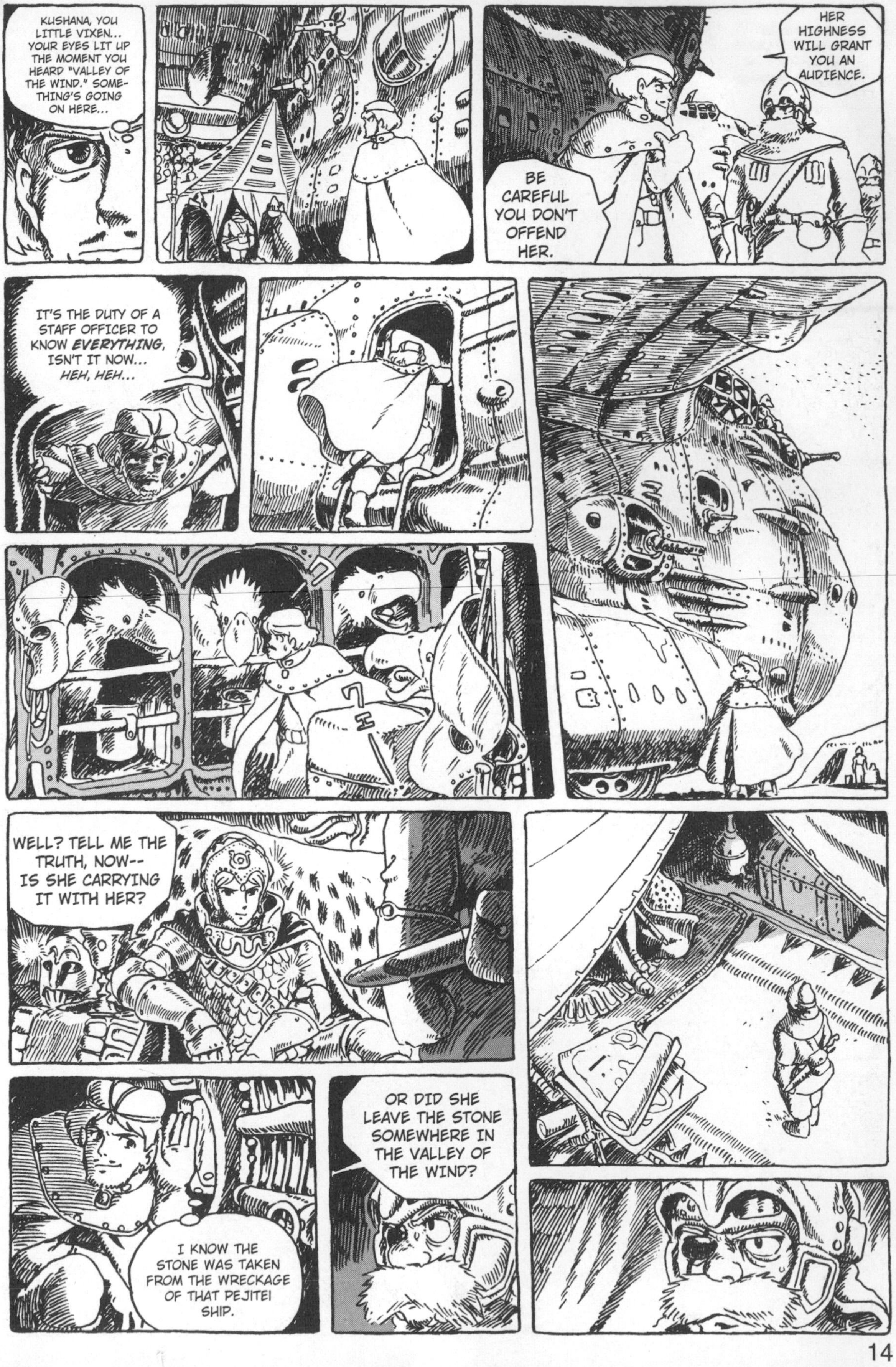
HER HIGHNESS WILL GRANT YOU AN AUDIENCE.
BE CAREFUL YOU DON'T OFFEND HER.
KUSHANA, YOU LITTLE VIXEN... YOUR EYES LIT UP THE MOMENT YOU HEARD "VALLEY OF THE WIND." SOME-THING'S GOING ON HERE...
IT'S THE DUTY OF A STAFF OFFICER TO KNOW *EVERYTHING*, ISN'T IT NOW... *HEH, HEH...*
WELL? TELL ME THE TRUTH, NOW-- IS SHE CARRYING IT WITH HER?
OR DID SHE LEAVE THE STONE SOMEWHERE IN THE VALLEY OF THE WIND?
I KNOW THE STONE WAS TAKEN FROM THE WRECKAGE OF THAT PEJITEI SHIP.

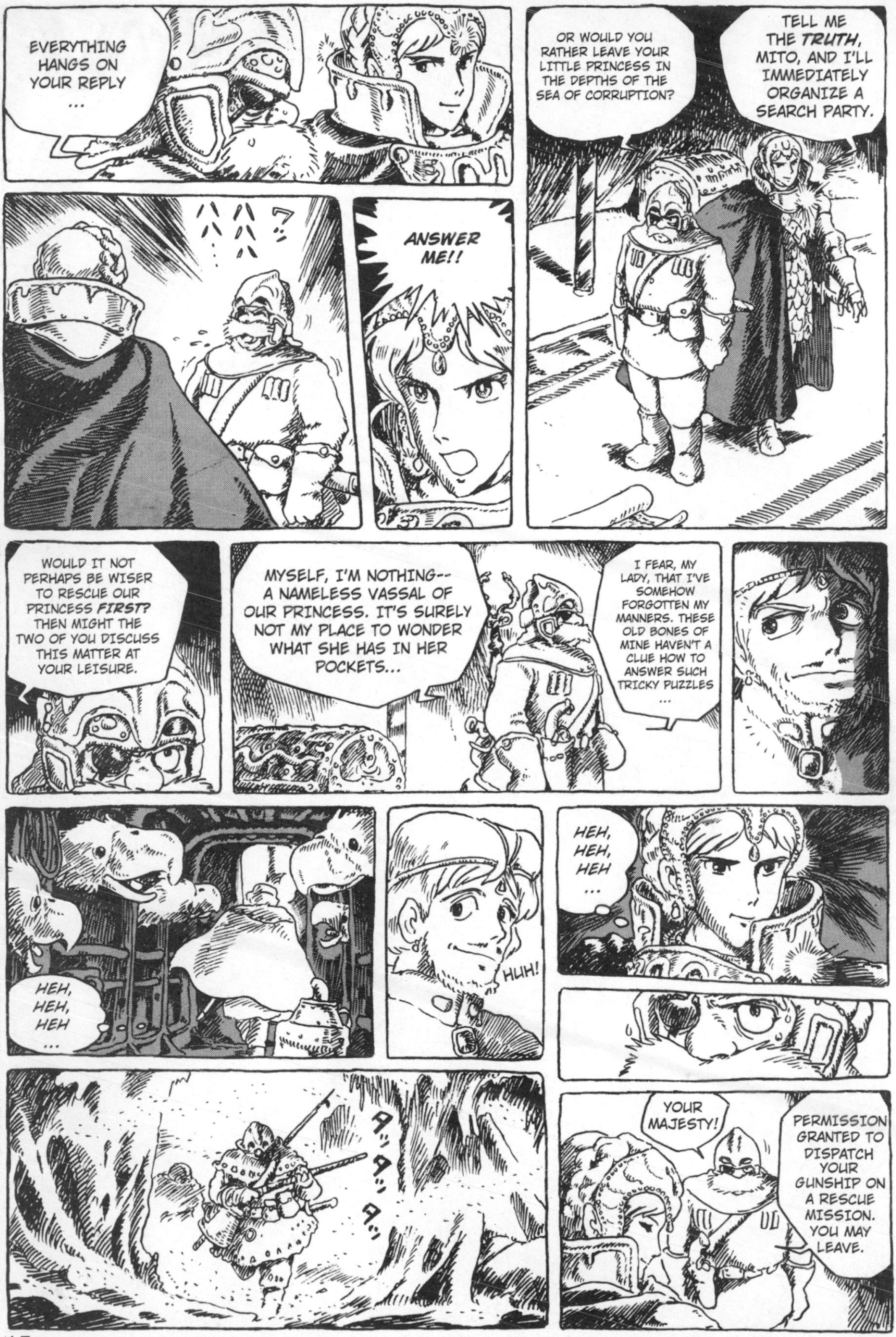
TELL ME THE *TRUTH*, MITO, AND I'LL IMMEDIATELY ORGANIZE A SEARCH PARTY.
OR WOULD YOU RATHER LEAVE YOUR LITTLE PRINCESS IN THE DEPTHS OF THE SEA OF CORRUPTION?
EVERYTHING HANGS ON YOUR REPLY ...
ANSWER ME!!
I FEAR, MY LADY, THAT I'VE SOMEHOW FORGOTTEN MY MANNERS. THESE OLD BONES OF MINE HAVEN'T A CLUE HOW TO ANSWER SUCH TRICKY PUZZLES ...
MYSELF, I'M NOTHING-- A NAMELESS VASSAL OF OUR PRINCESS. IT'S SURELY NOT MY PLACE TO WONDER WHAT SHE HAS IN HER POCKETS...
WOULD IT NOT PERHAPS BE WISER TO RESCUE OUR PRINCESS *FIRST?* THEN MIGHT THE TWO OF YOU DISCUSS THIS MATTER AT YOUR LEISURE.
HEH, HEH, HEH ...
HUH!
HEH, HEH, HEH ...
PERMISSION GRANTED TO DISPATCH YOUR GUNSHIP ON A RESCUE MISSION. YOU MAY LEAVE.
YOUR MAJESTY!

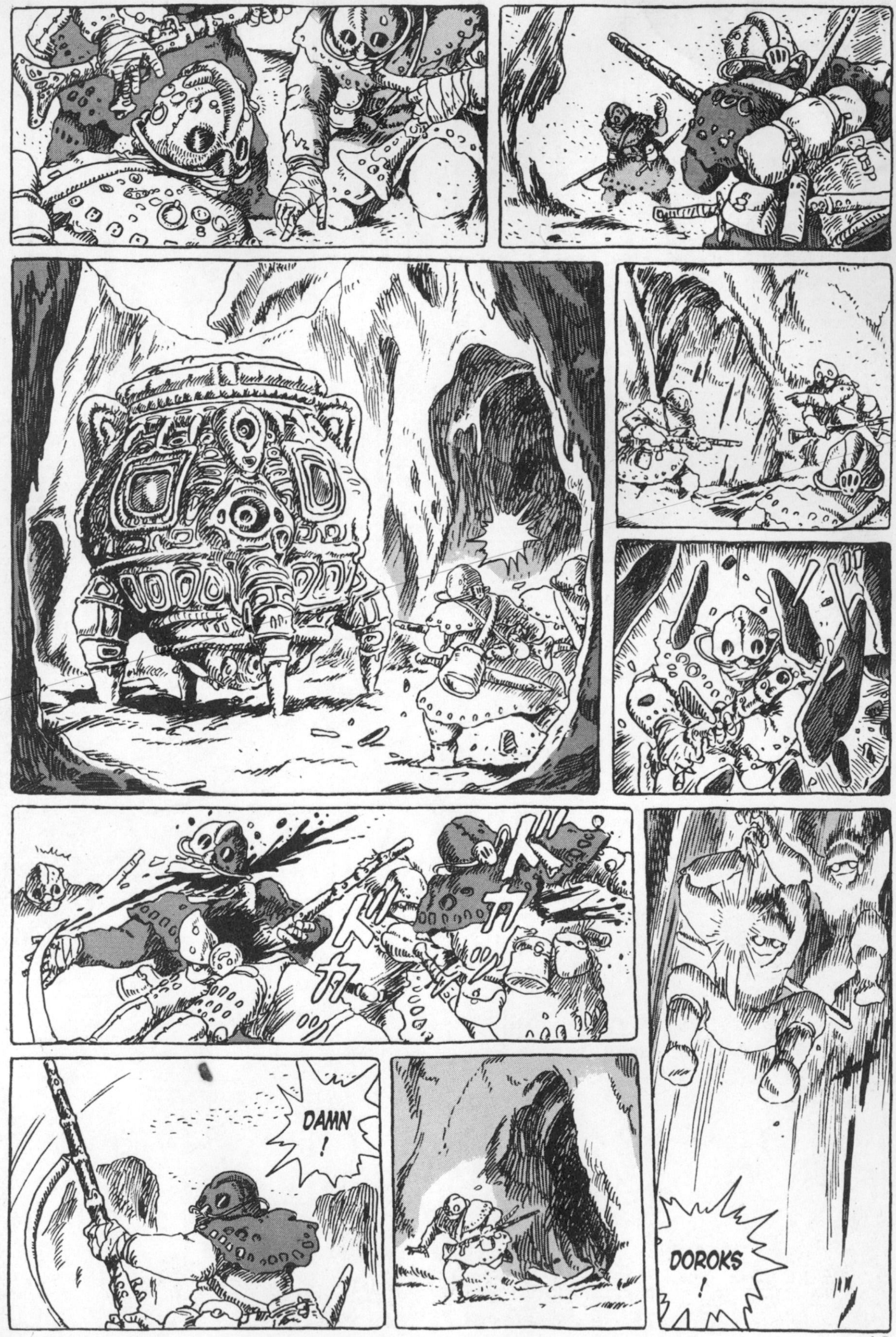
DOROKS !
DAMN !

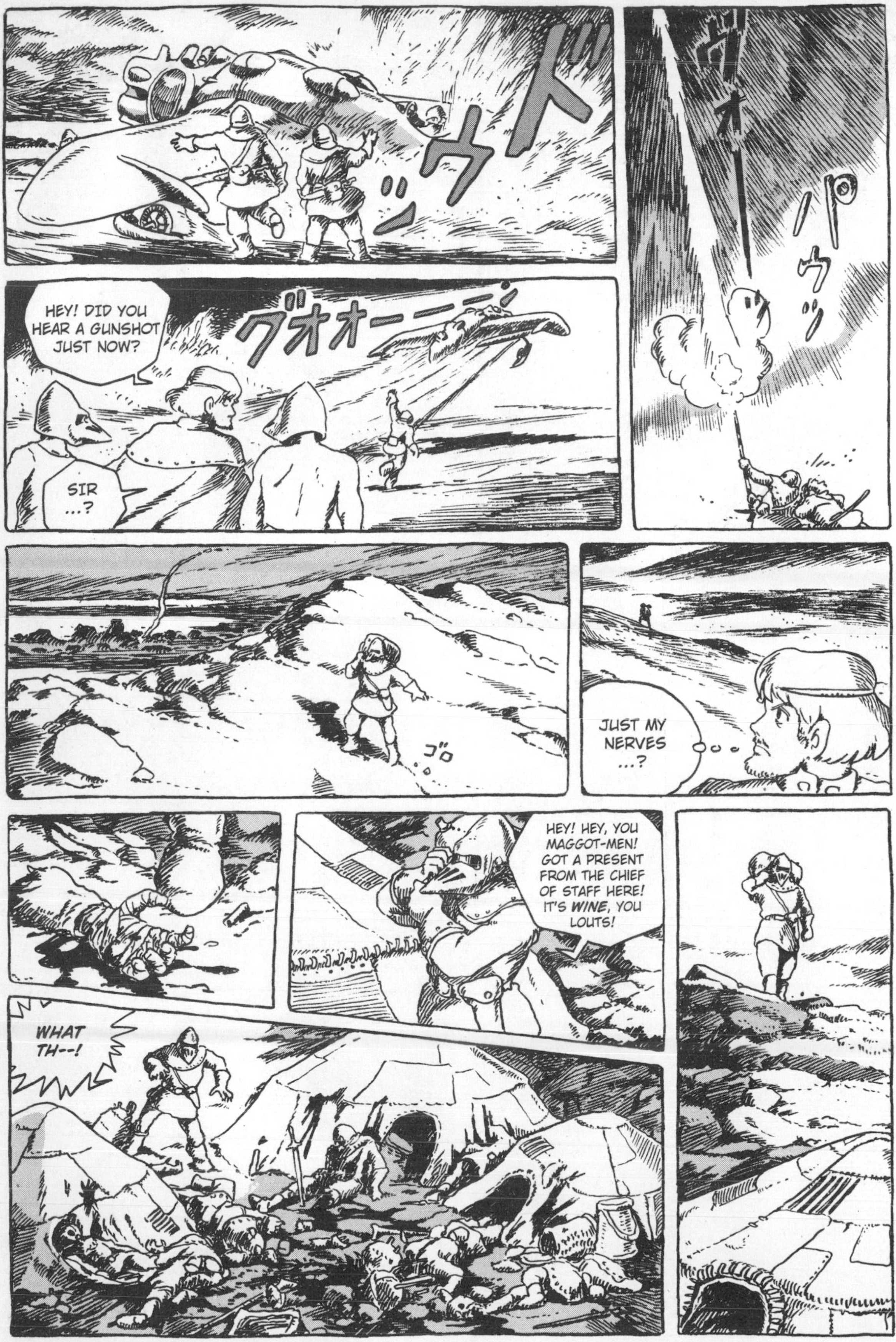

パウッ
HEY! DID YOU HEAR A GUNSHOT JUST NOW?
グオオーーー
SIR ...?
JUST MY NERVES ...?
ゴロ
HEY! HEY, YOU MAGGOT-MEN! GOT A PRESENT FROM THE CHIEF OF STAFF HERE! IT'S *WINE*, YOU LOUTS!
WHAT TH--!

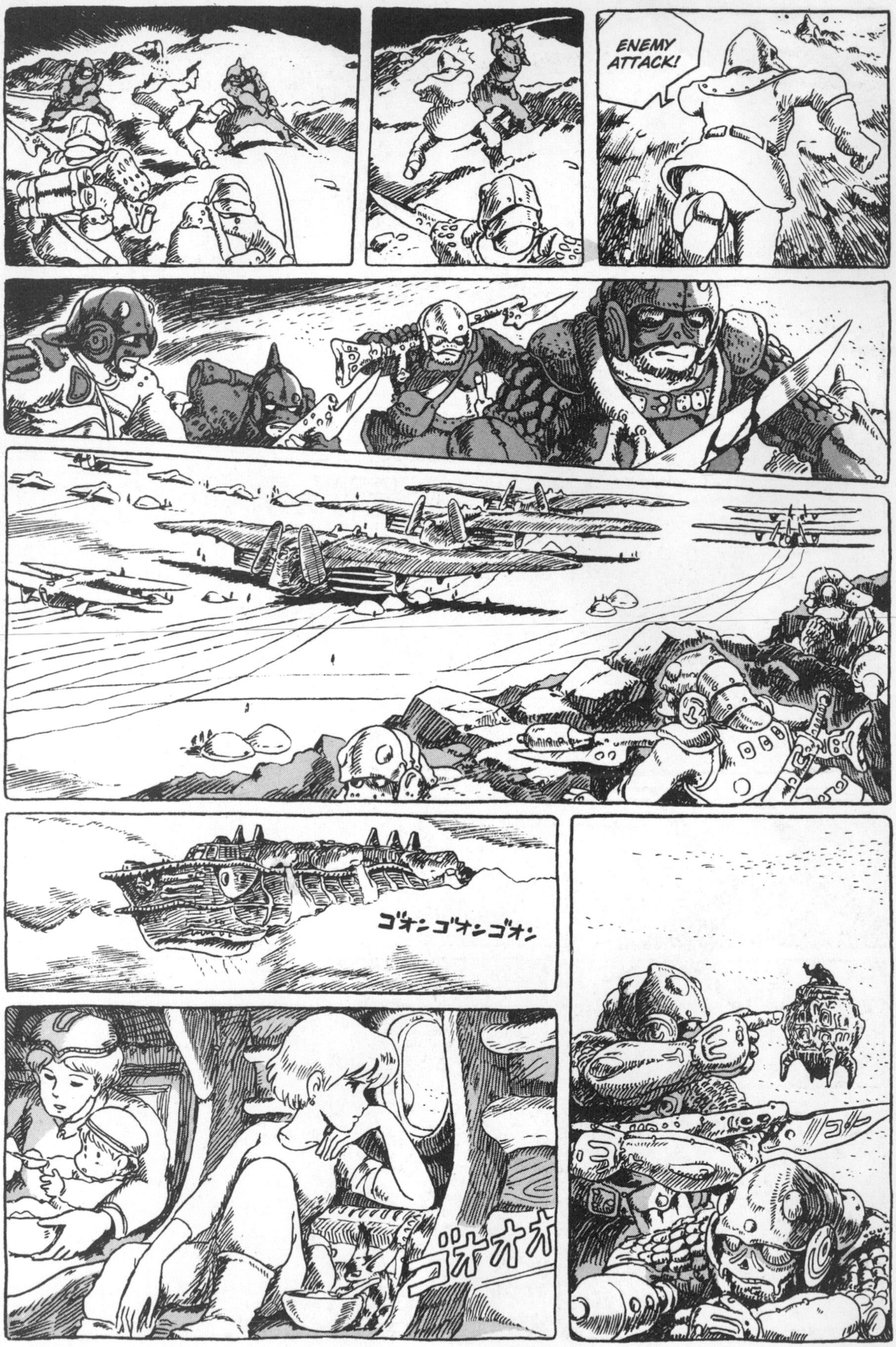
ENEMY ATTACK!
ゴオンゴオンゴオン
ゴオオオ

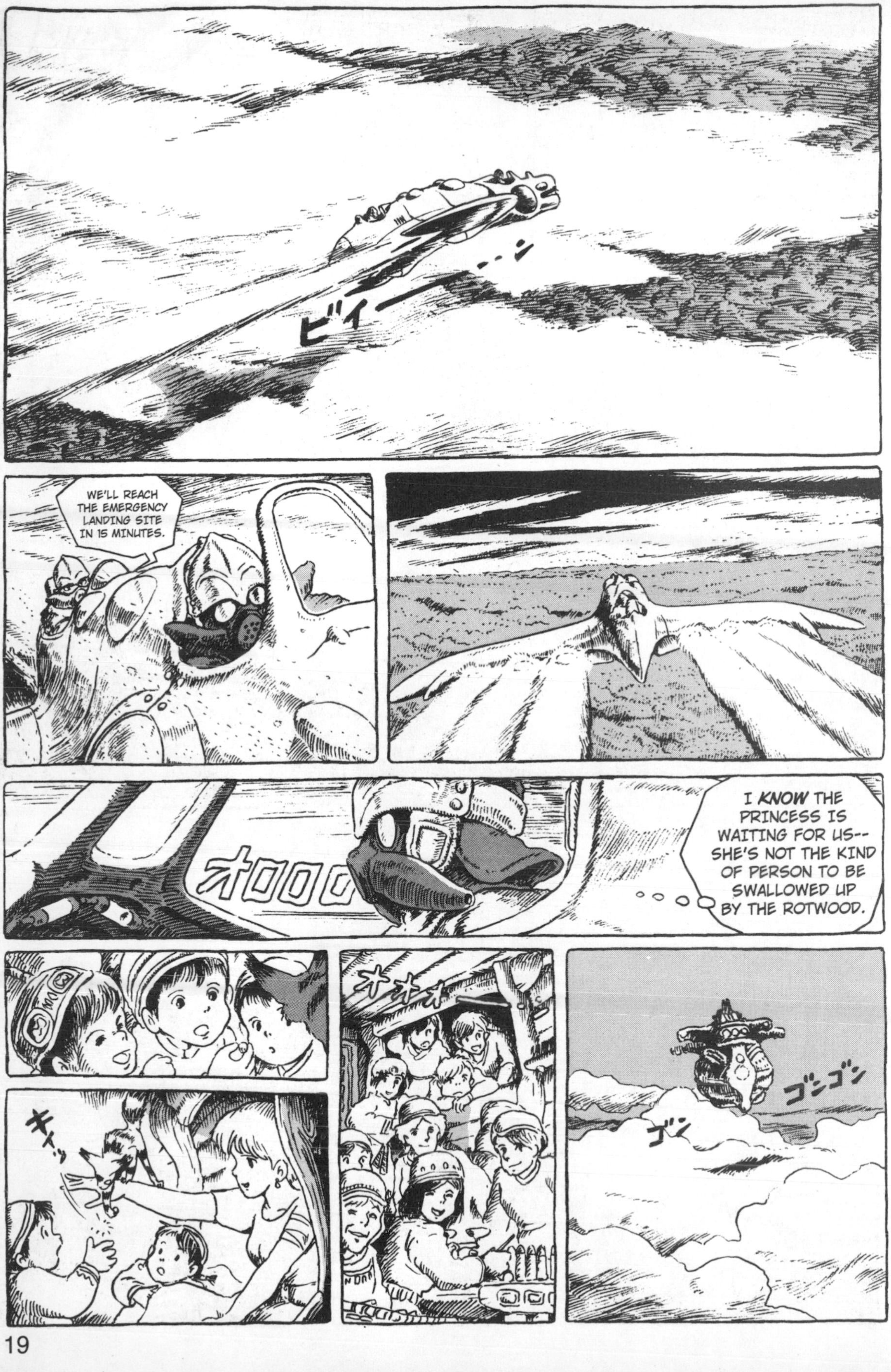
ビィーーン
WE'LL REACH THE EMERGENCY LANDING SITE IN 15 MINUTES.
I *KNOW* THE PRINCESS IS WAITING FOR US--SHE'S NOT THE KIND OF PERSON TO BE SWALLOWED UP BY THE ROTWOOD.
ゴンゴン
ゴン

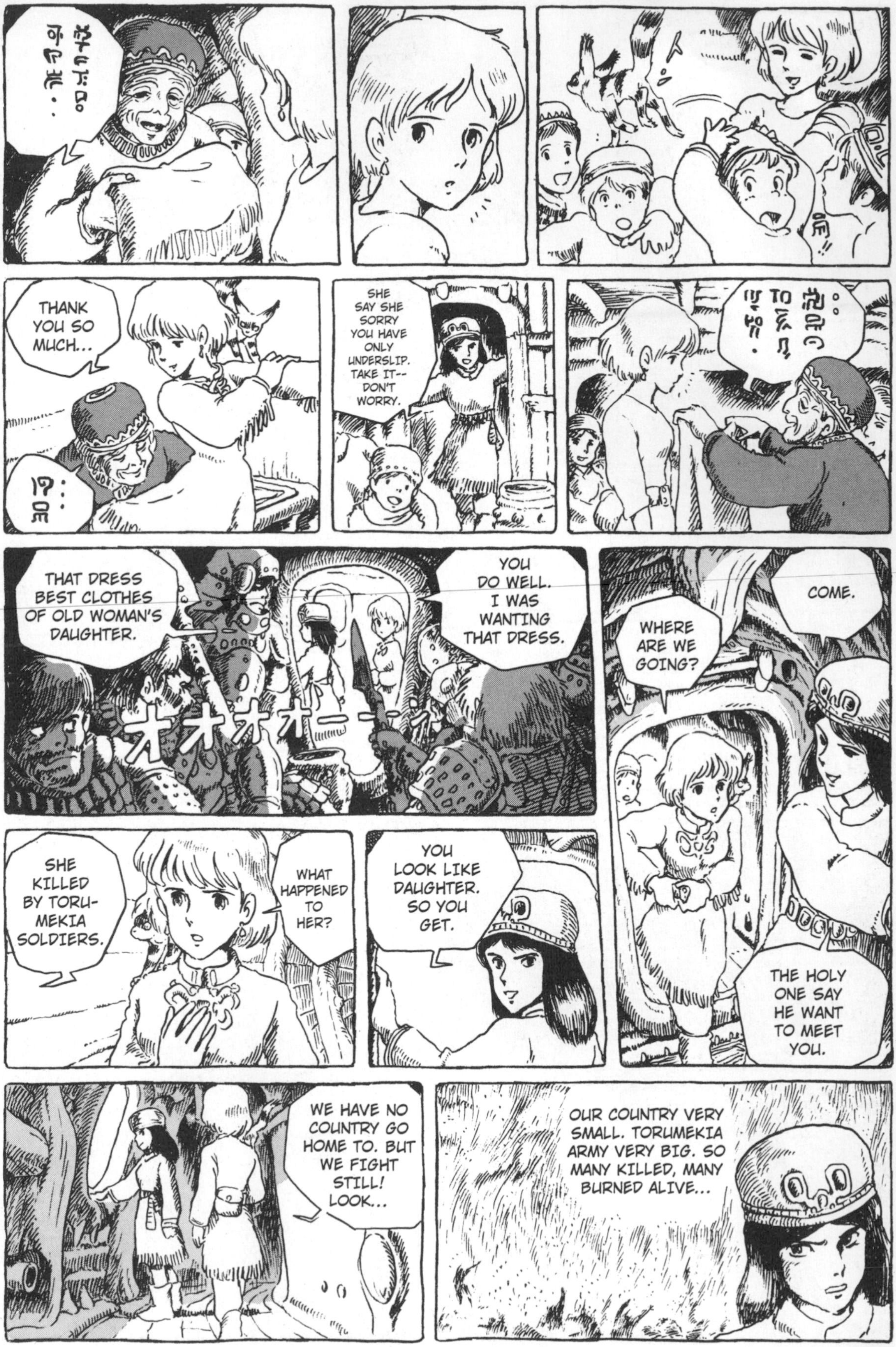
SHE SAY SHE SORRY YOU HAVE ONLY UNDERSLIP. TAKE IT-- DON'T WORRY.
THANK YOU SO MUCH...
COME.
WHERE ARE WE GOING?
THE HOLY ONE SAY HE WANT TO MEET YOU.
YOU DO WELL. I WAS WANTING THAT DRESS.
THAT DRESS BEST CLOTHES OF OLD WOMAN'S DAUGHTER.
オオオオーー
YOU LOOK LIKE DAUGHTER. SO YOU GET.
WHAT HAPPENED TO HER?
SHE KILLED BY TORU-MEKIA SOLDIERS.
OUR COUNTRY VERY SMALL. TORUMEKIA ARMY VERY BIG. SO MANY KILLED, MANY BURNED ALIVE...
WE HAVE NO COUNTRY GO HOME TO. BUT WE FIGHT STILL! LOOK...

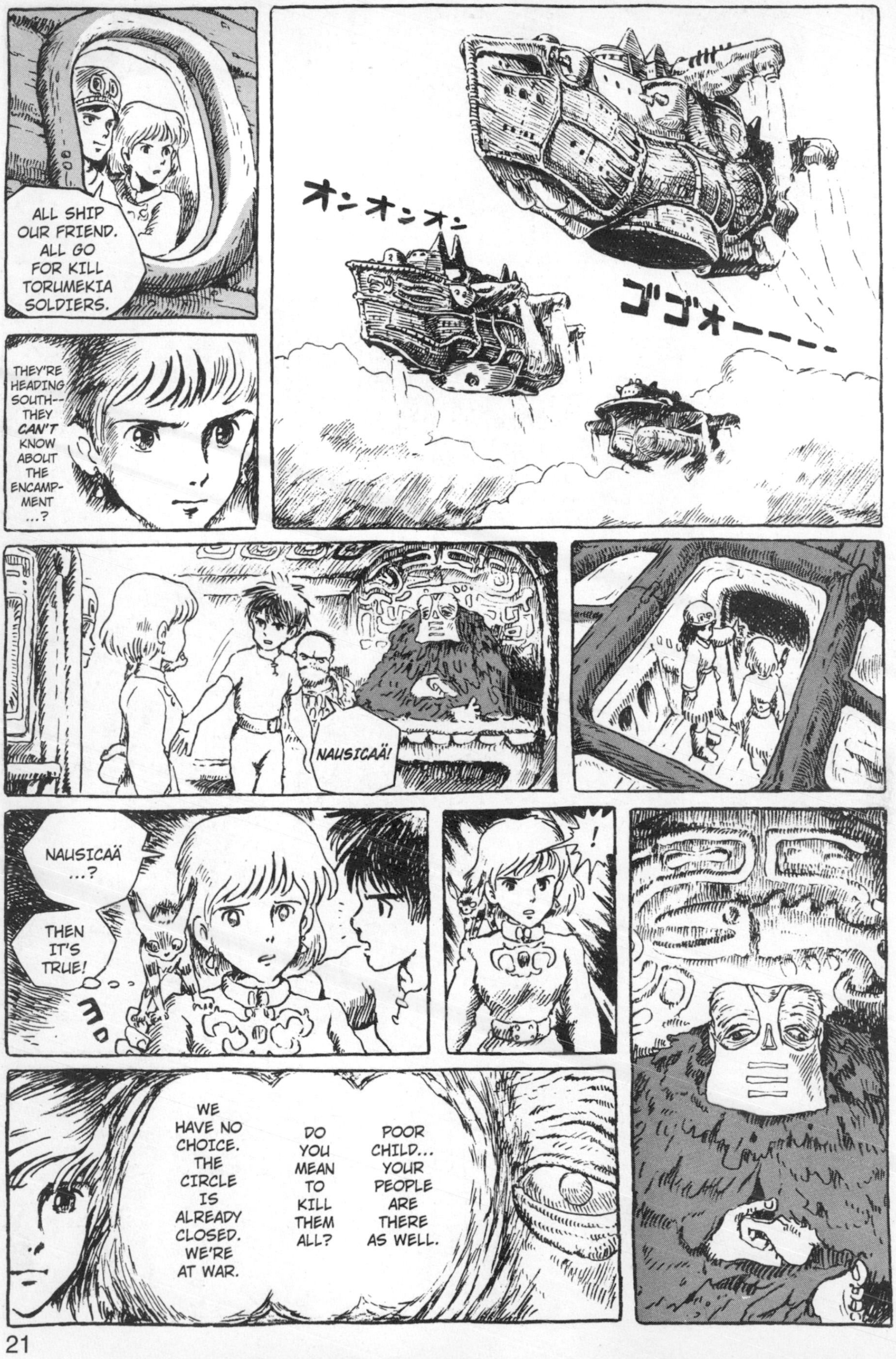

オンオンオン
ゴゴオーーーー
ALL SHIP OUR FRIEND. ALL GO FOR KILL TORUMEKIA SOLDIERS.
THEY'RE HEADING SOUTH-- THEY *CAN'T* KNOW ABOUT THE ENCAMPMENT ...?
NAUSICAÄ!
!
NAUSICAÄ ...?
THEN IT'S TRUE!
ヨロ
POOR CHILD... YOUR PEOPLE ARE THERE AS WELL.
DO YOU MEAN TO KILL THEM ALL?
WE HAVE NO CHOICE. THE CIRCLE IS ALREADY CLOSED. WE'RE AT WAR.

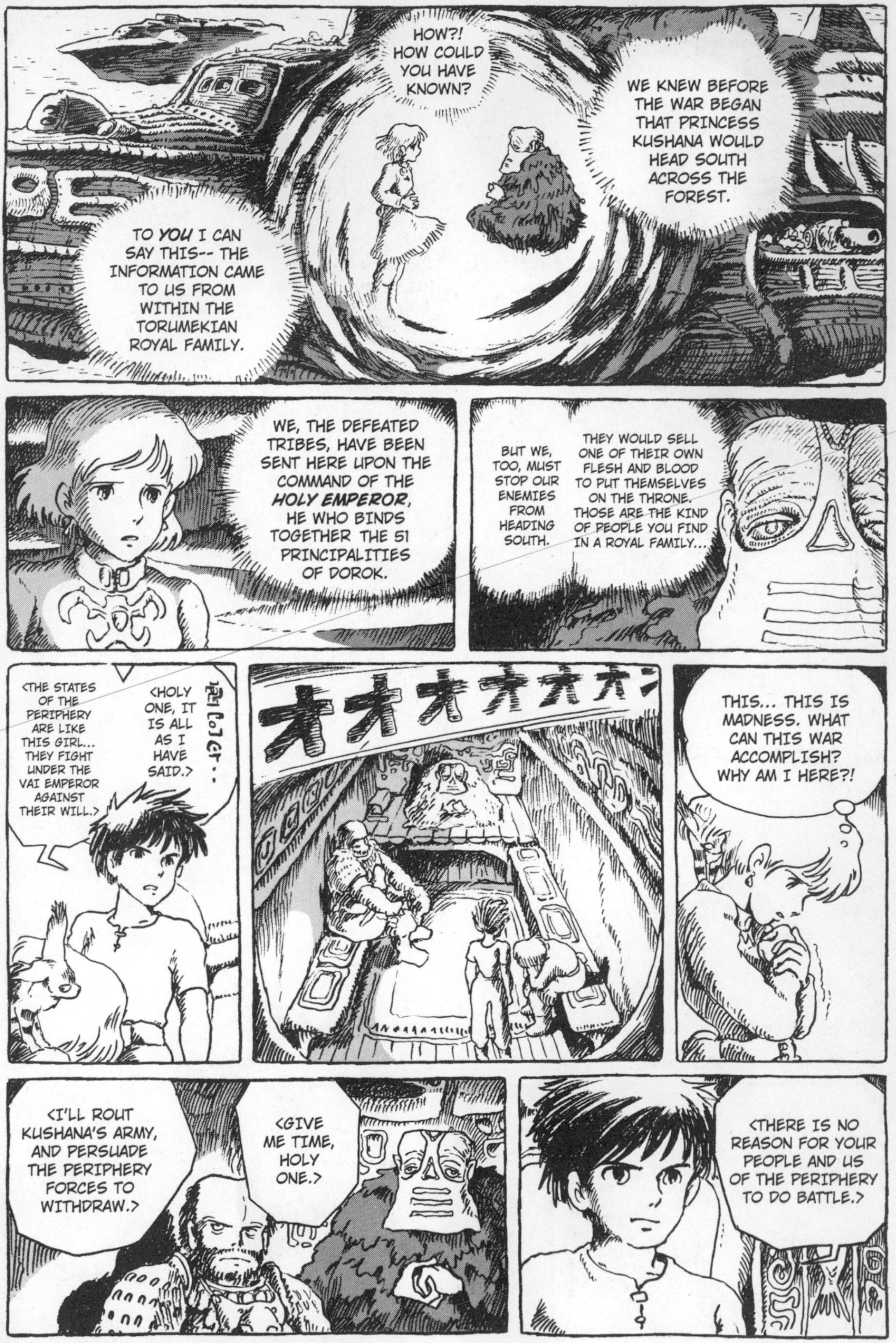
HOW?! HOW COULD YOU HAVE KNOWN?
WE KNEW BEFORE THE WAR BEGAN THAT PRINCESS KUSHANA WOULD HEAD SOUTH ACROSS THE FOREST.
TO *YOU* I CAN SAY THIS-- THE INFORMATION CAME TO US FROM WITHIN THE TORUMEKIAN ROYAL FAMILY.
THEY WOULD SELL ONE OF THEIR OWN FLESH AND BLOOD TO PUT THEMSELVES ON THE THRONE. THOSE ARE THE KIND OF PEOPLE YOU FIND IN A ROYAL FAMILY...
BUT WE, TOO, MUST STOP OUR ENEMIES FROM HEADING SOUTH.
WE, THE DEFEATED TRIBES, HAVE BEEN SENT HERE UPON THE COMMAND OF THE ***HOLY EMPEROR***, HE WHO BINDS TOGETHER THE 51 PRINCIPALITIES OF DOROK.
THIS... THIS IS MADNESS. WHAT CAN THIS WAR ACCOMPLISH? WHY AM I HERE?!
オオオオオオン
<HOLY ONE, IT IS ALL AS I HAVE SAID.>
<THE STATES OF THE PERIPHERY ARE LIKE THIS GIRL... THEY FIGHT UNDER THE VAI EMPEROR AGAINST THEIR WILL.>
<THERE IS NO REASON FOR YOUR PEOPLE AND US OF THE PERIPHERY TO DO BATTLE.>
<GIVE ME TIME, HOLY ONE.>
<I'LL ROUT KUSHANA'S ARMY, AND PERSUADE THE PERIPHERY FORCES TO WITHDRAW.>

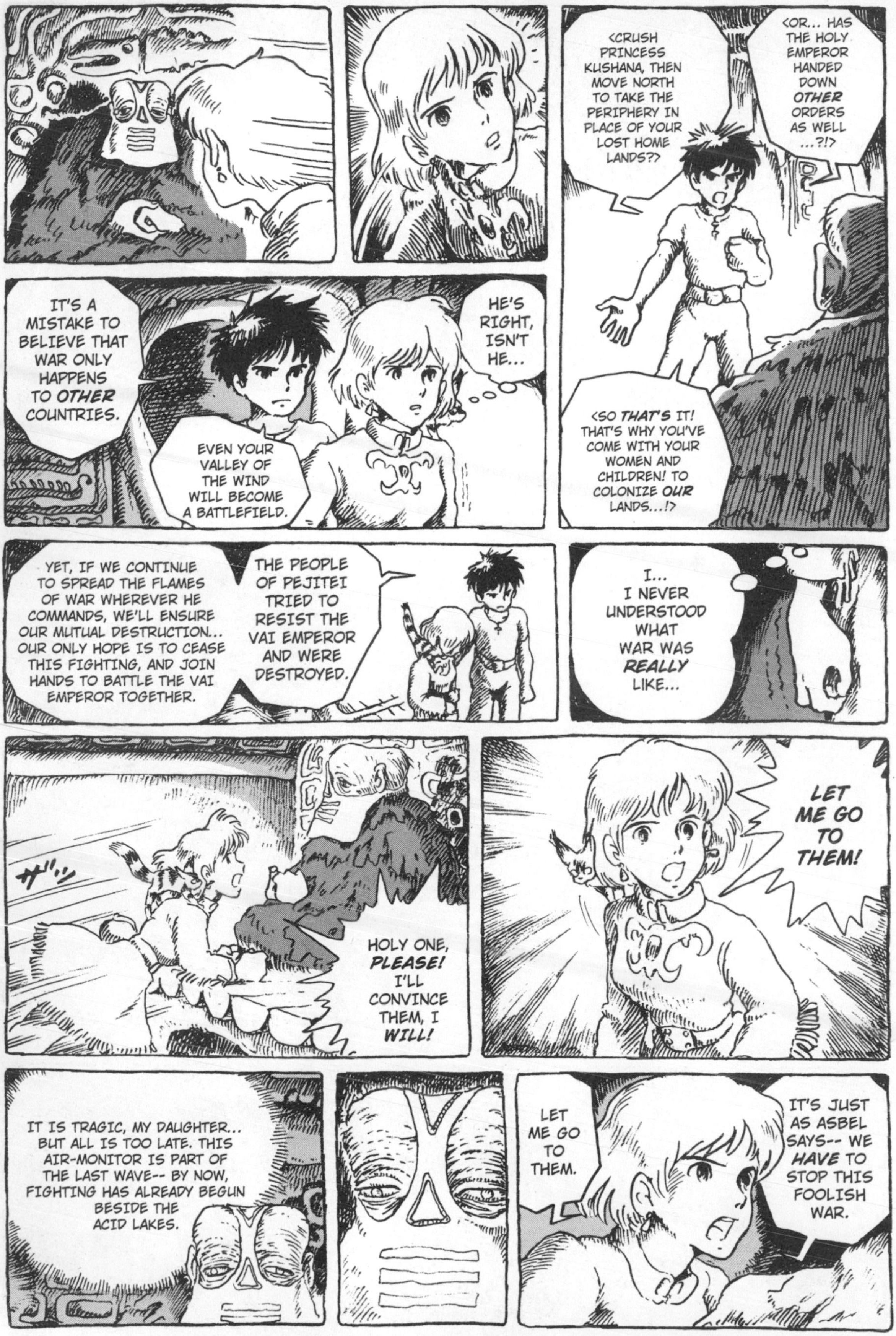

<CRUSH PRINCESS KUSHANA, THEN MOVE NORTH TO TAKE THE PERIPHERY IN PLACE OF YOUR LOST HOME LANDS?>
<OR... HAS THE HOLY EMPEROR HANDED DOWN *OTHER* ORDERS AS WELL ...?!>
<SO *THAT'S* IT! THAT'S WHY YOU'VE COME WITH YOUR WOMEN AND CHILDREN! TO COLONIZE *OUR* LANDS...!>
IT'S A MISTAKE TO BELIEVE THAT WAR ONLY HAPPENS TO *OTHER* COUNTRIES.
EVEN YOUR VALLEY OF THE WIND WILL BECOME A BATTLEFIELD.
HE'S RIGHT, ISN'T HE...
YET, IF WE CONTINUE TO SPREAD THE FLAMES OF WAR WHEREVER HE COMMANDS, WE'LL ENSURE OUR MUTUAL DESTRUCTION... OUR ONLY HOPE IS TO CEASE THIS FIGHTING, AND JOIN HANDS TO BATTLE THE VAI EMPEROR TOGETHER.
THE PEOPLE OF PEJITEI TRIED TO RESIST THE VAI EMPEROR AND WERE DESTROYED.
I... I NEVER UNDERSTOOD WHAT WAR WAS *REALLY* LIKE...
HOLY ONE, *PLEASE!* I'LL CONVINCE THEM, I *WILL!*
LET ME GO TO THEM!
IT IS TRAGIC, MY DAUGHTER... BUT ALL IS TOO LATE. THIS AIR-MONITOR IS PART OF THE LAST WAVE-- BY NOW, FIGHTING HAS ALREADY BEGUN BESIDE THE ACID LAKES.
LET ME GO TO THEM.
IT'S JUST AS ASBEL SAYS-- WE *HAVE* TO STOP THIS FOOLISH WAR.

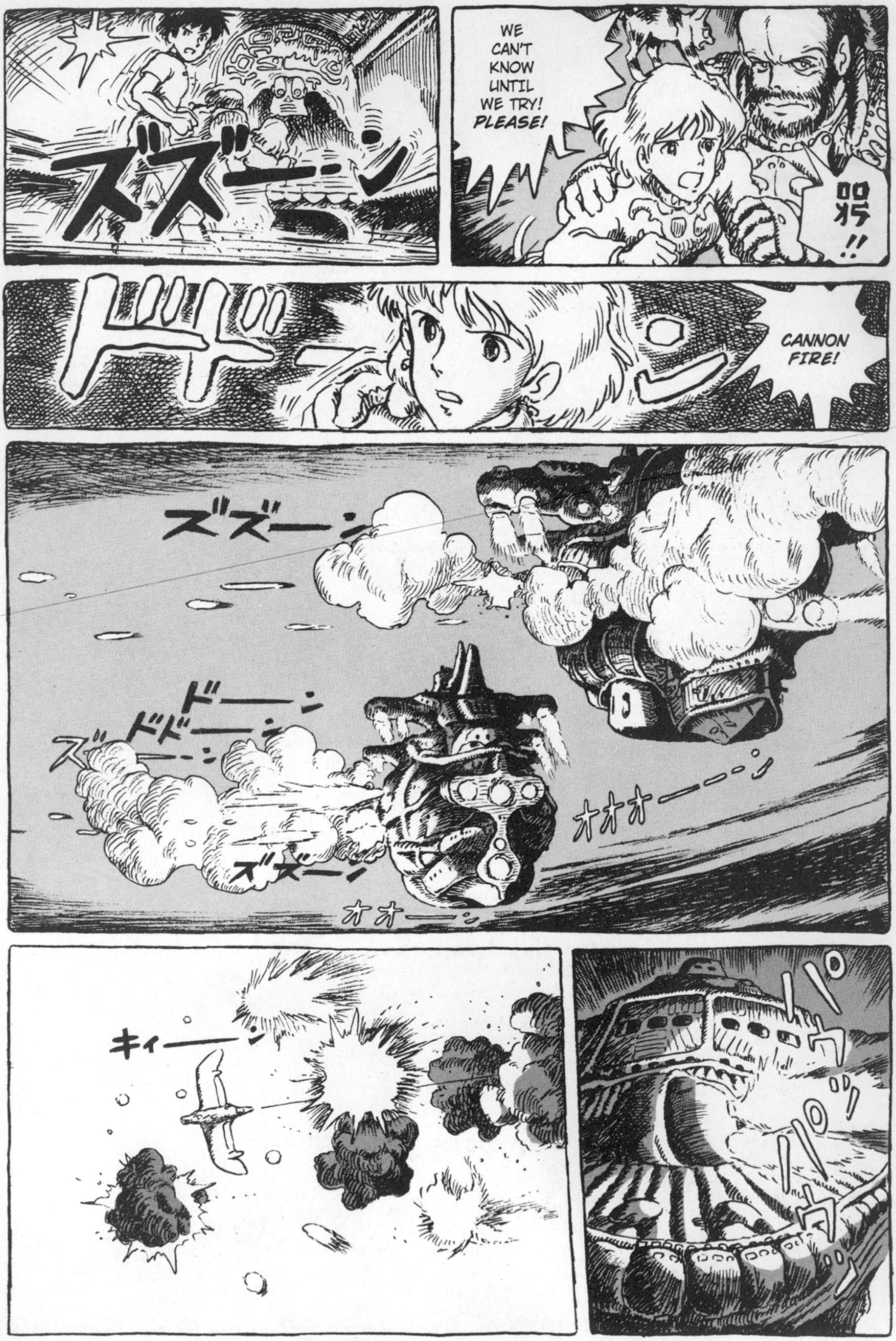
WE CAN'T KNOW UNTIL WE TRY! PLEASE!
CANNON FIRE!

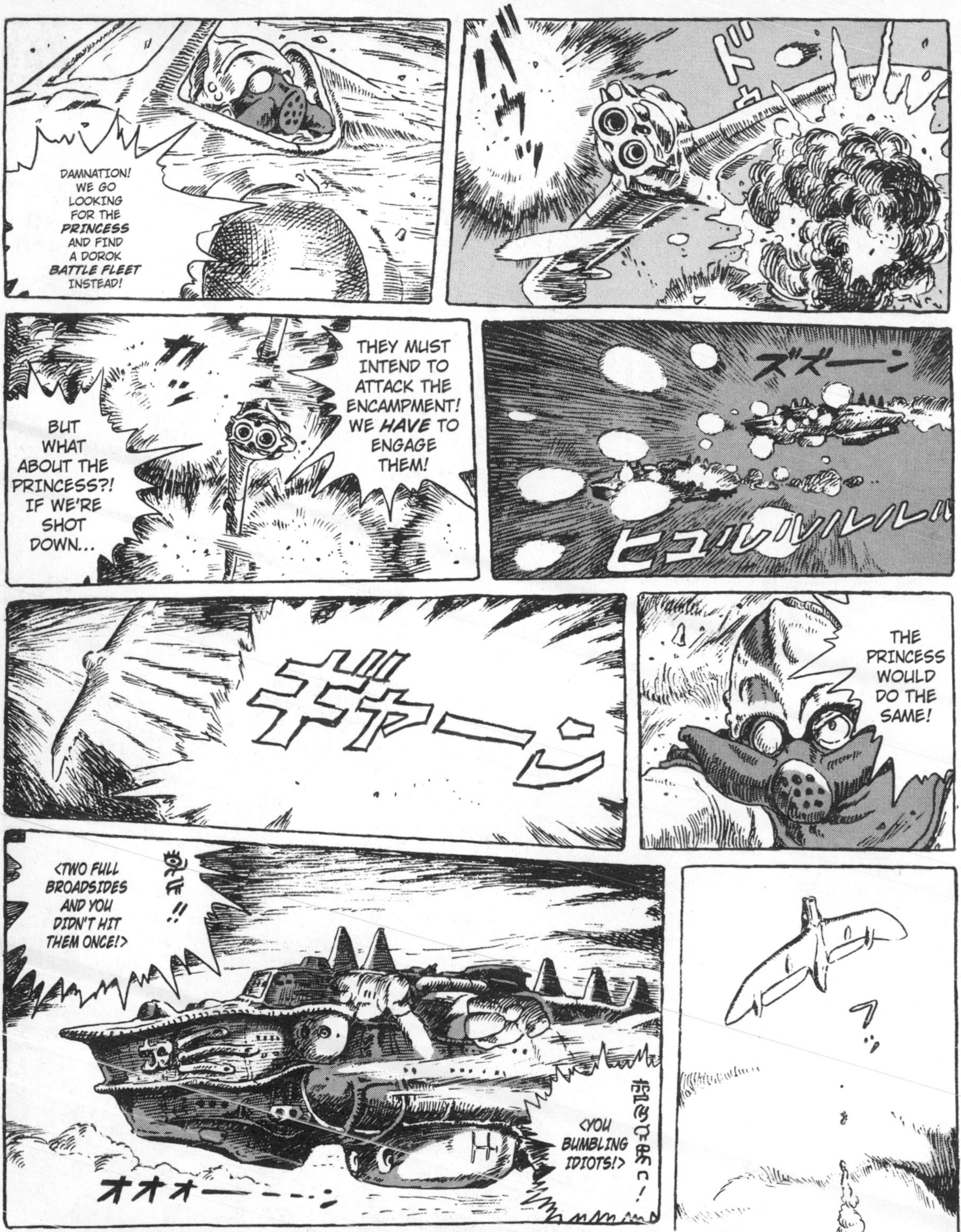
DAMNATION! WE GO LOOKING FOR THE ***PRINCESS*** AND FIND A DOROK ***BATTLE FLEET*** INSTEAD!
ズズーン
ヒュルルルルル
THEY MUST INTEND TO ATTACK THE ENCAMPMENT! WE ***HAVE*** TO ENGAGE THEM!
BUT WHAT ABOUT THE PRINCESS?! IF WE'RE SHOT DOWN...
THE PRINCESS WOULD DO THE SAME!
ギャーン
<TWO FULL BROADSIDES AND YOU DIDN'T HIT THEM ONCE!>
<YOU BUMBLING IDIOTS!>
オオオー
<HOLY ONE, PLEASE COME TO THE BRIDGE!>

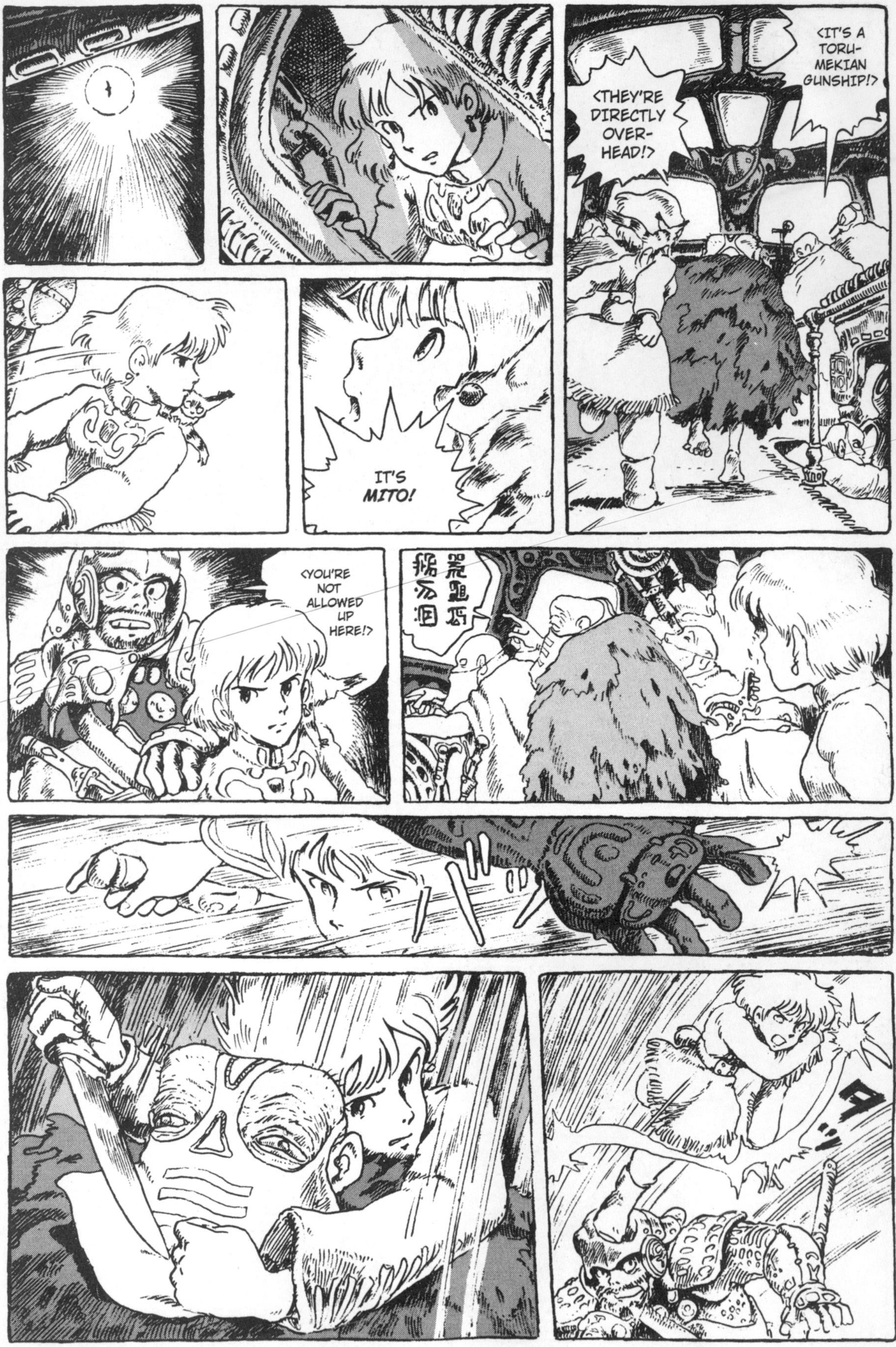
<IT'S A TORU-MEKIAN GUNSHIP!>
<THEY'RE DIRECTLY OVER-HEAD!>
IT'S MITO!
<YOU'RE NOT ALLOWED UP HERE!>
タッ

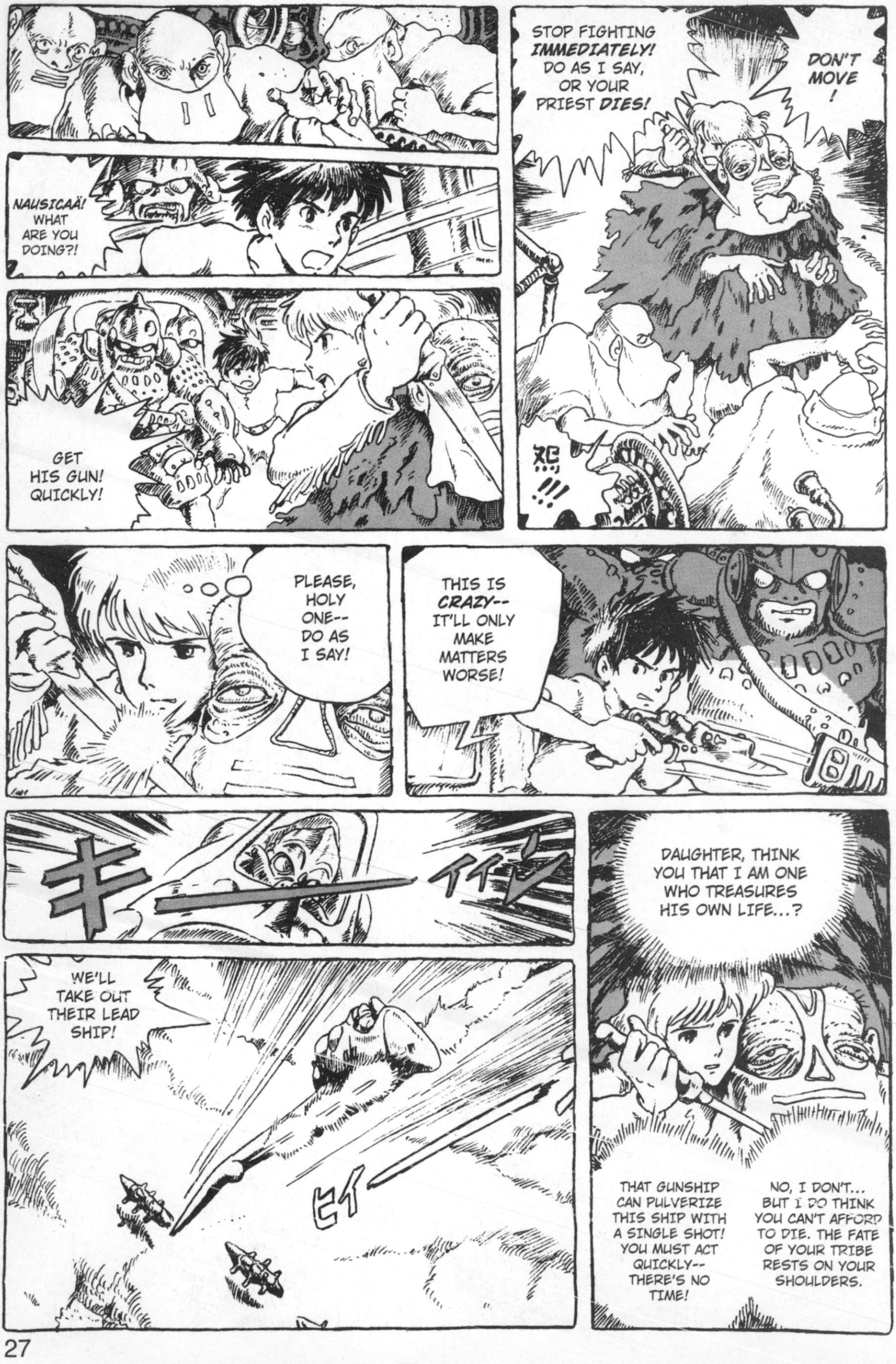

STOP FIGHTING *IMMEDIATELY!* DO AS I SAY, OR YOUR PRIEST *DIES!*
DON'T MOVE !
!!!
NAUSICAÄ! WHAT ARE YOU DOING?!
GET HIS GUN! QUICKLY!
THIS IS *CRAZY--* IT'LL ONLY MAKE MATTERS WORSE!
PLEASE, HOLY ONE-- DO AS I SAY!
DAUGHTER, THINK YOU THAT I AM ONE WHO TREASURES HIS OWN LIFE...?
NO, I DON'T... BUT I DO THINK YOU CAN'T AFFORD TO DIE. THE FATE OF YOUR TRIBE RESTS ON YOUR SHOULDERS.
THAT GUNSHIP CAN PULVERIZE THIS SHIP WITH A SINGLE SHOT! YOU MUST ACT QUICKLY-- THERE'S NO TIME!
WE'LL TAKE OUT THEIR LEAD SHIP!
ヒイ

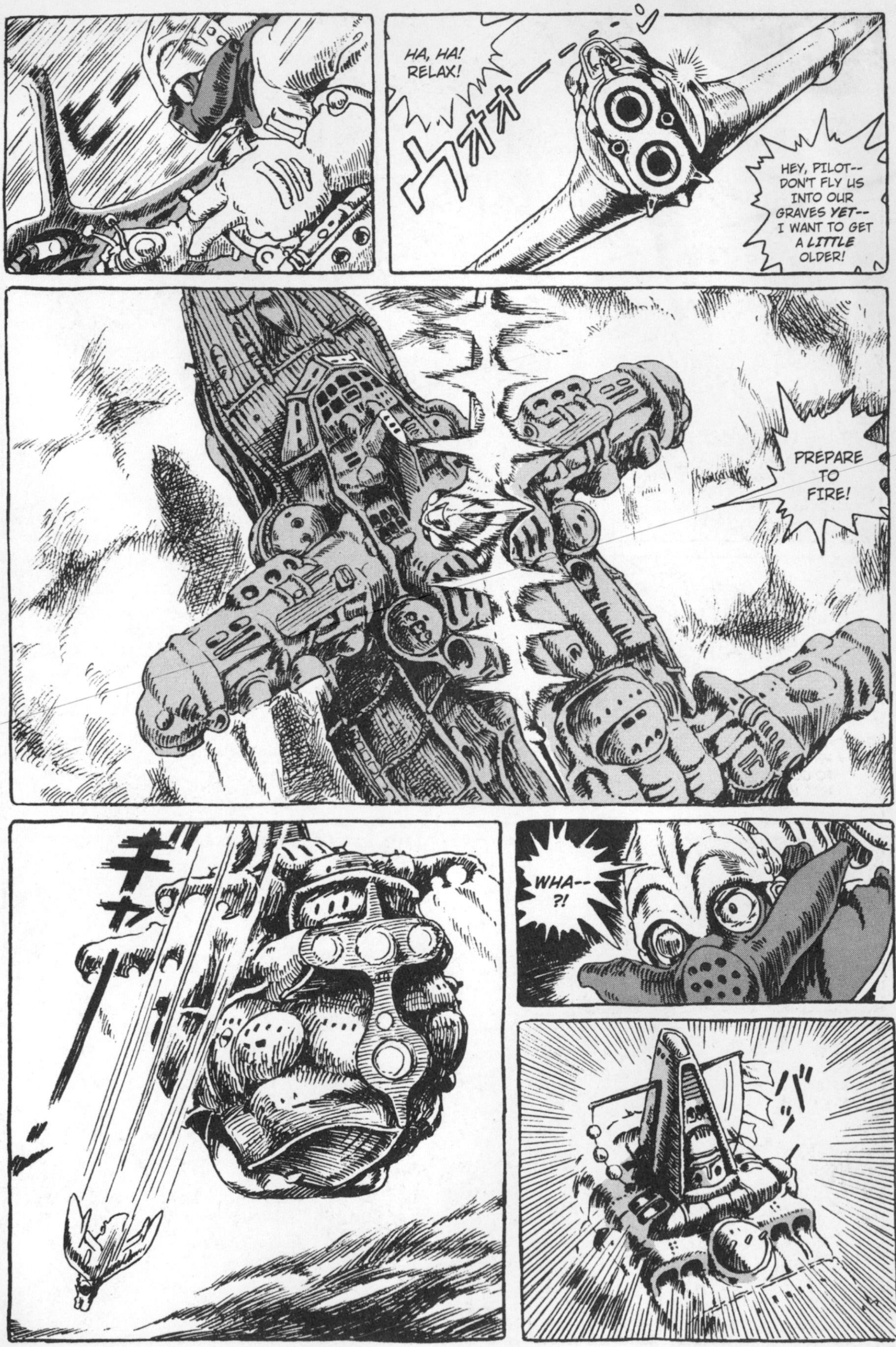
HA, HA! RELAX!
ウォオー
HEY, PILOT-- DON'T FLY US INTO OUR GRAVES *YET*-- I WANT TO GET A *LITTLE* OLDER!
PREPARE TO FIRE!
WHA-- ?!
バッ

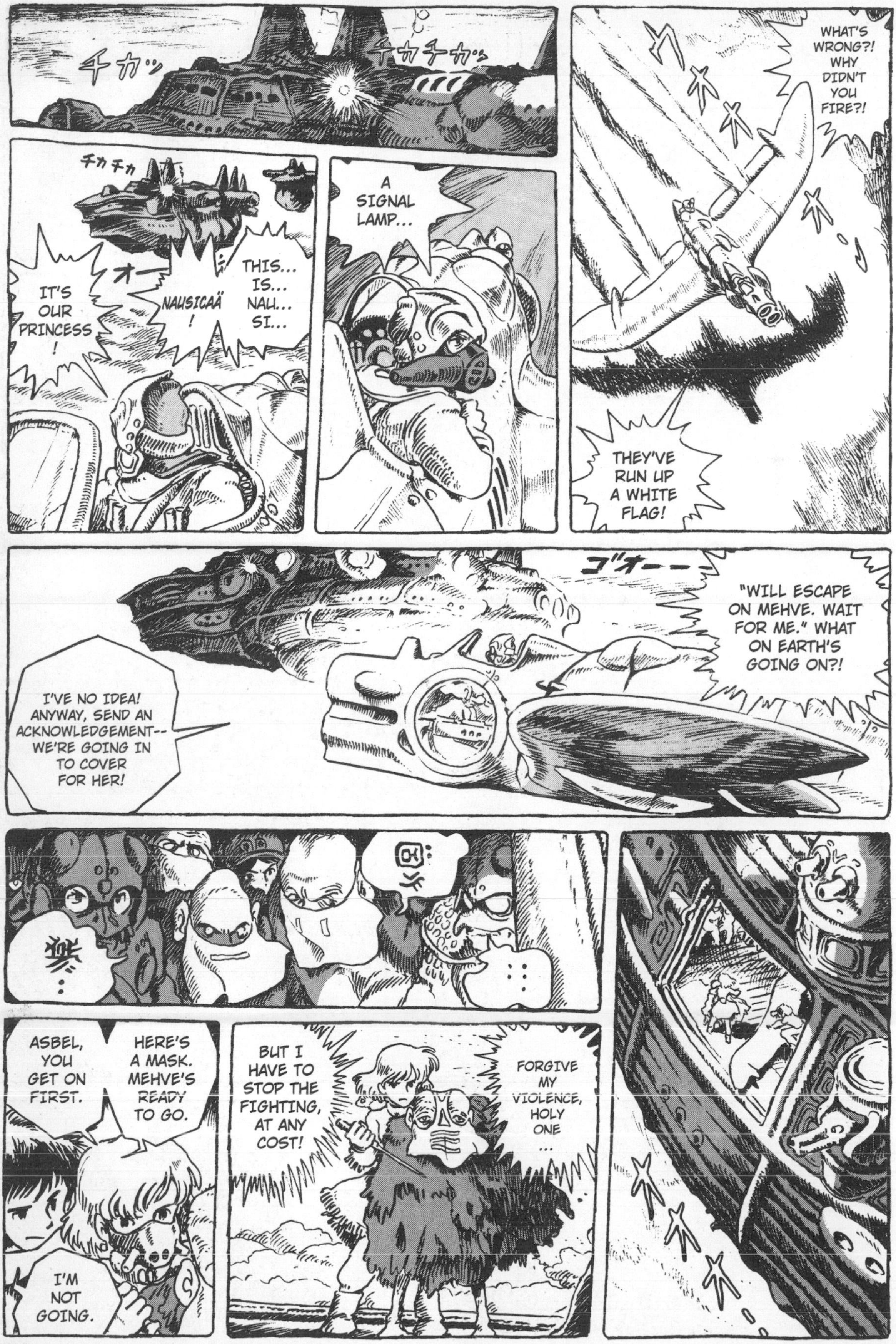
WHAT'S WRONG?! WHY DIDN'T YOU FIRE?!
THEY'VE RUN UP A WHITE FLAG!
A SIGNAL LAMP...
THIS... IS... NAU... SI...
NAUSICAÄ!
IT'S OUR PRINCESS!
"WILL ESCAPE ON MEHVE. WAIT FOR ME." WHAT ON EARTH'S GOING ON?!
I'VE NO IDEA! ANYWAY, SEND AN ACKNOWLEDGEMENT-- WE'RE GOING IN TO COVER FOR HER!
FORGIVE MY VIOLENCE, HOLY ONE ...
BUT I HAVE TO STOP THE FIGHTING, AT ANY COST!
HERE'S A MASK. MEHVE'S READY TO GO.
ASBEL, YOU GET ON FIRST.
I'M NOT GOING.

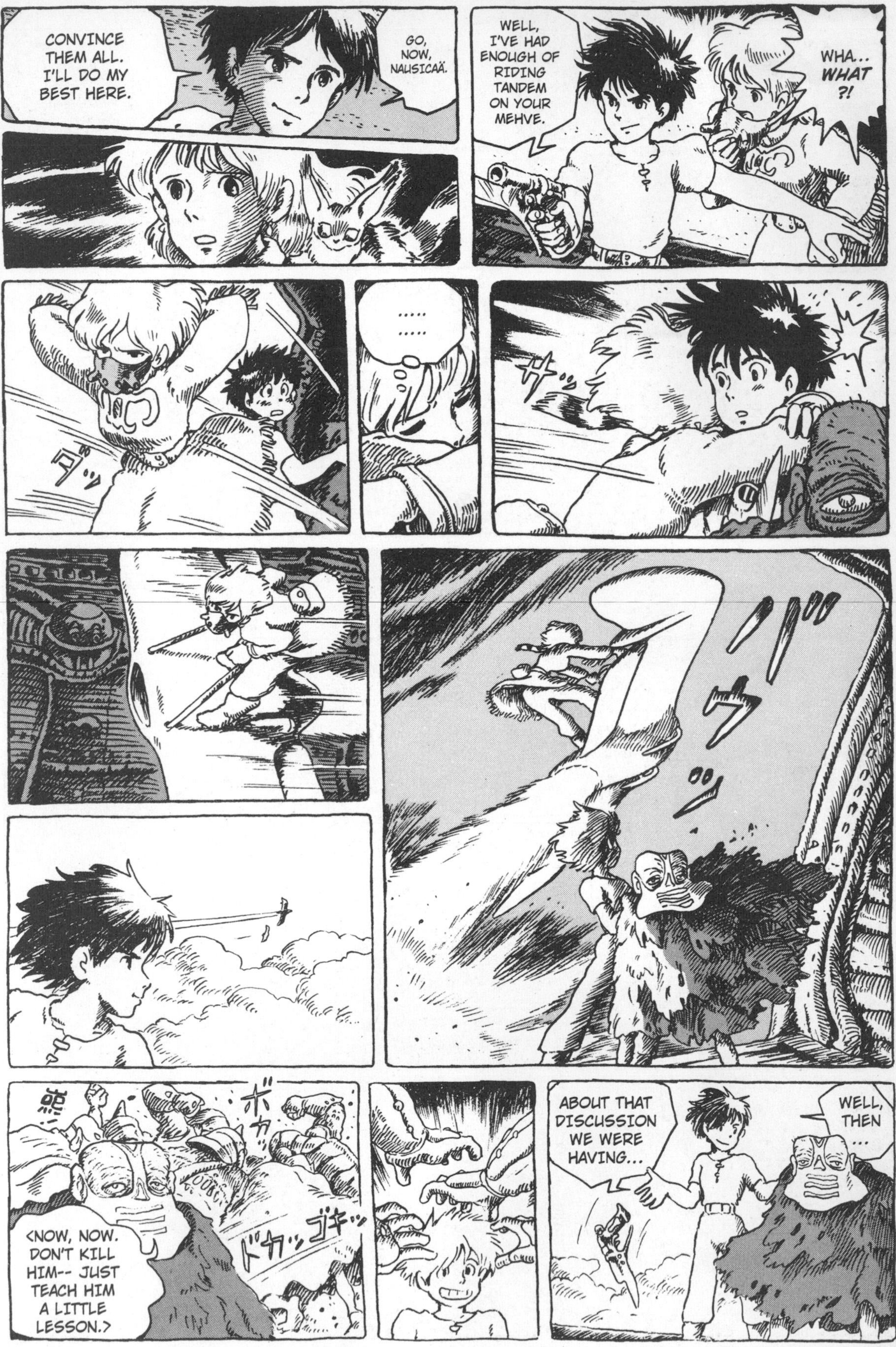
WELL, I'VE HAD ENOUGH OF RIDING TANDEM ON YOUR MEHVE.
WHA... WHAT?!
GO, NOW, NAUSICAÄ.
CONVINCE THEM ALL. I'LL DO MY BEST HERE.
.....
.....
ダッ
ABOUT THAT DISCUSSION WE WERE HAVING...
WELL, THEN ...
ドカッ ゴキッ
<NOW, NOW. DON'T KILL HIM-- JUST TEACH HIM A LITTLE LESSON.>

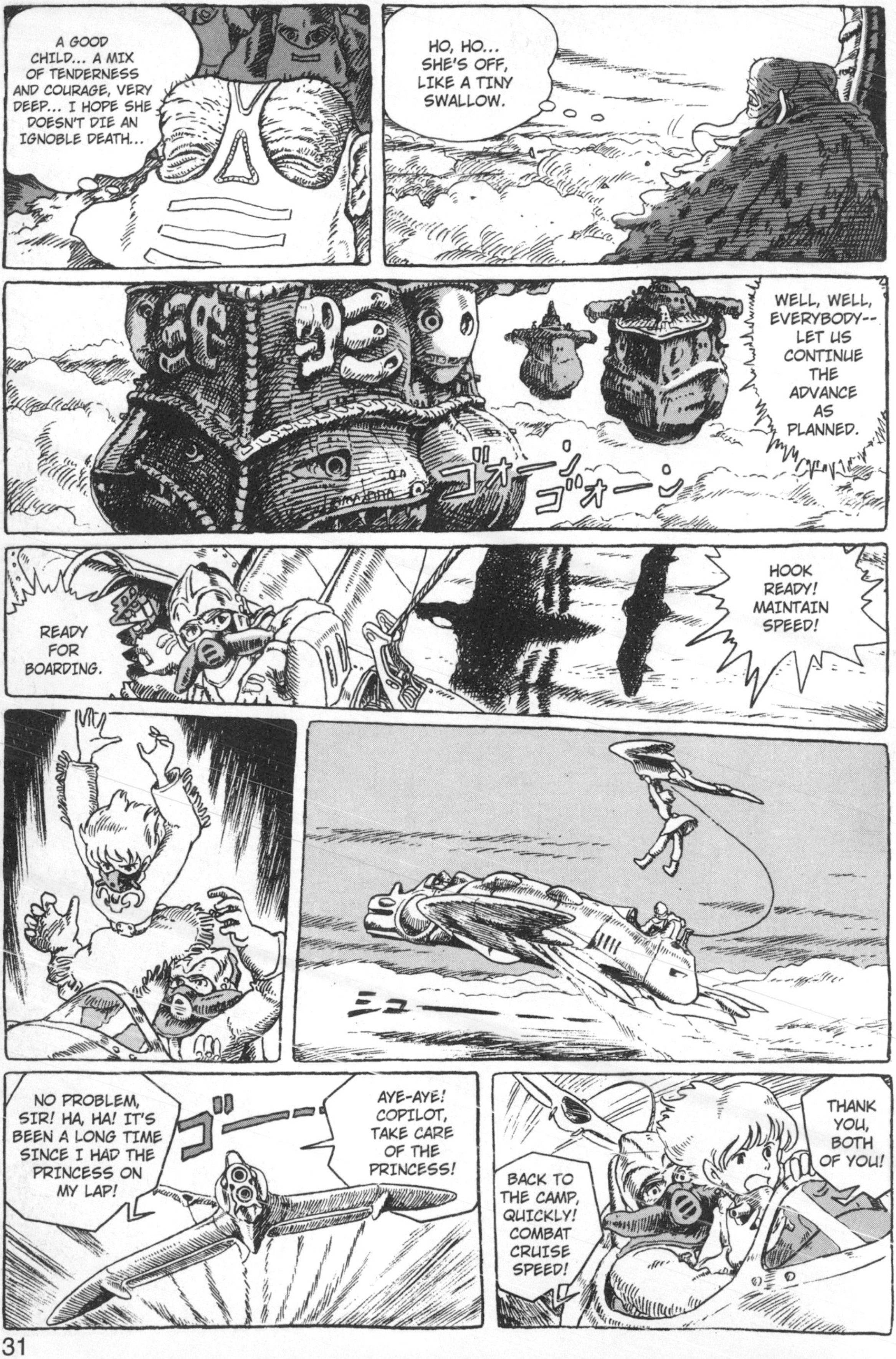
HO, HO... SHE'S OFF, LIKE A TINY SWALLOW.
A GOOD CHILD... A MIX OF TENDERNESS AND COURAGE, VERY DEEP... I HOPE SHE DOESN'T DIE AN IGNOBLE DEATH...
WELL, WELL, EVERYBODY-- LET US CONTINUE THE ADVANCE AS PLANNED.
ゴォーン
ゴォーン
HOOK READY! MAINTAIN SPEED!
READY FOR BOARDING.
シュー
THANK YOU, BOTH OF YOU!
BACK TO THE CAMP, QUICKLY! COMBAT CRUISE SPEED!
AYE-AYE! COPILOT, TAKE CARE OF THE PRINCESS!
NO PROBLEM, SIR! HA, HA! IT'S BEEN A LONG TIME SINCE I HAD THE PRINCESS ON MY LAP!
ゴー

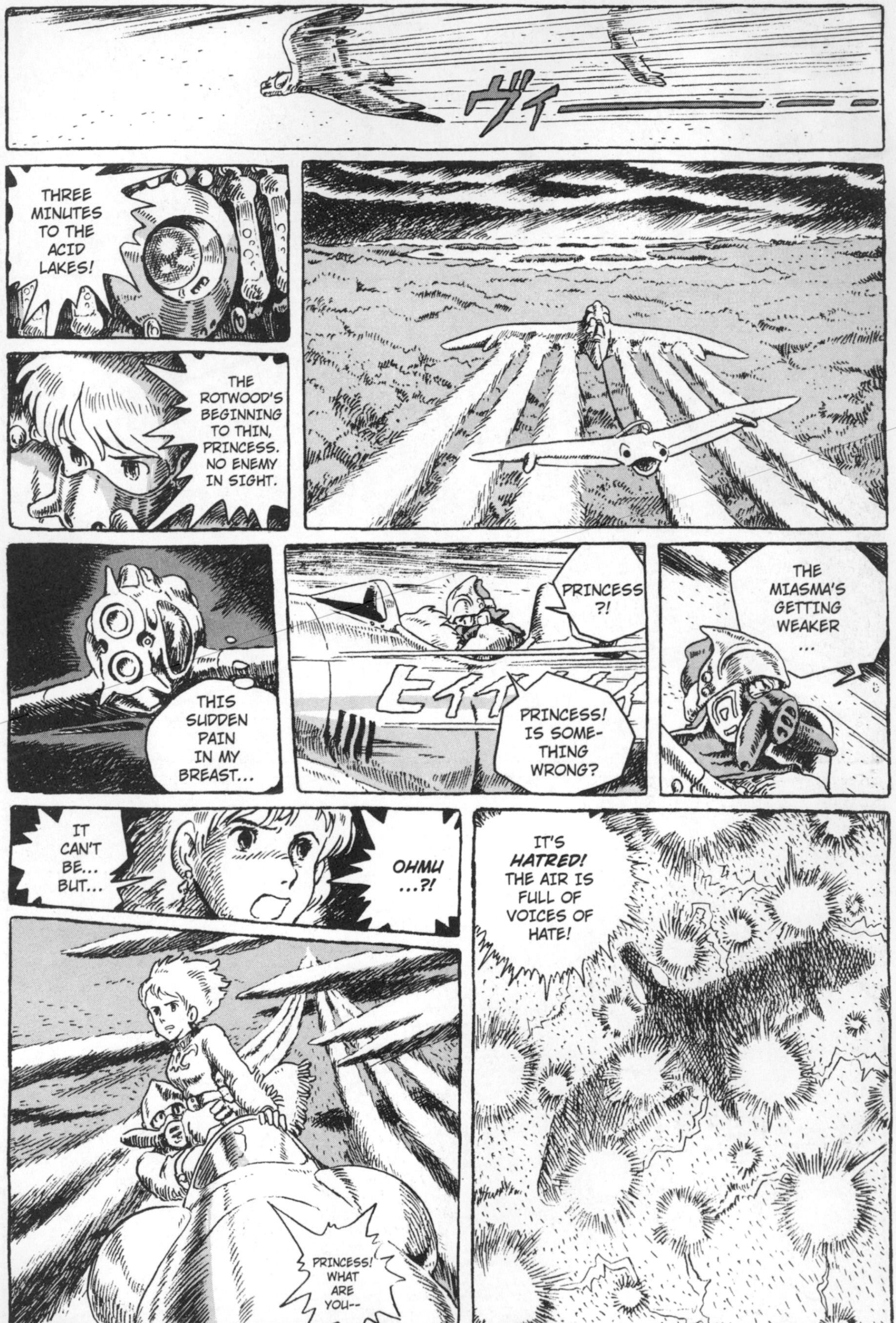
ヴィーーー
THREE MINUTES TO THE ACID LAKES!
THE ROTWOOD'S BEGINNING TO THIN, PRINCESS. NO ENEMY IN SIGHT.
THE MIASMA'S GETTING WEAKER ...
PRINCESS ?!
PRINCESS! IS SOMETHING WRONG?
THIS SUDDEN PAIN IN MY BREAST...
IT'S ***HATRED!*** THE AIR IS FULL OF VOICES OF HATE!
IT CAN'T BE... BUT...
OHMU ...?!
PRINCESS! WHAT ARE YOU--

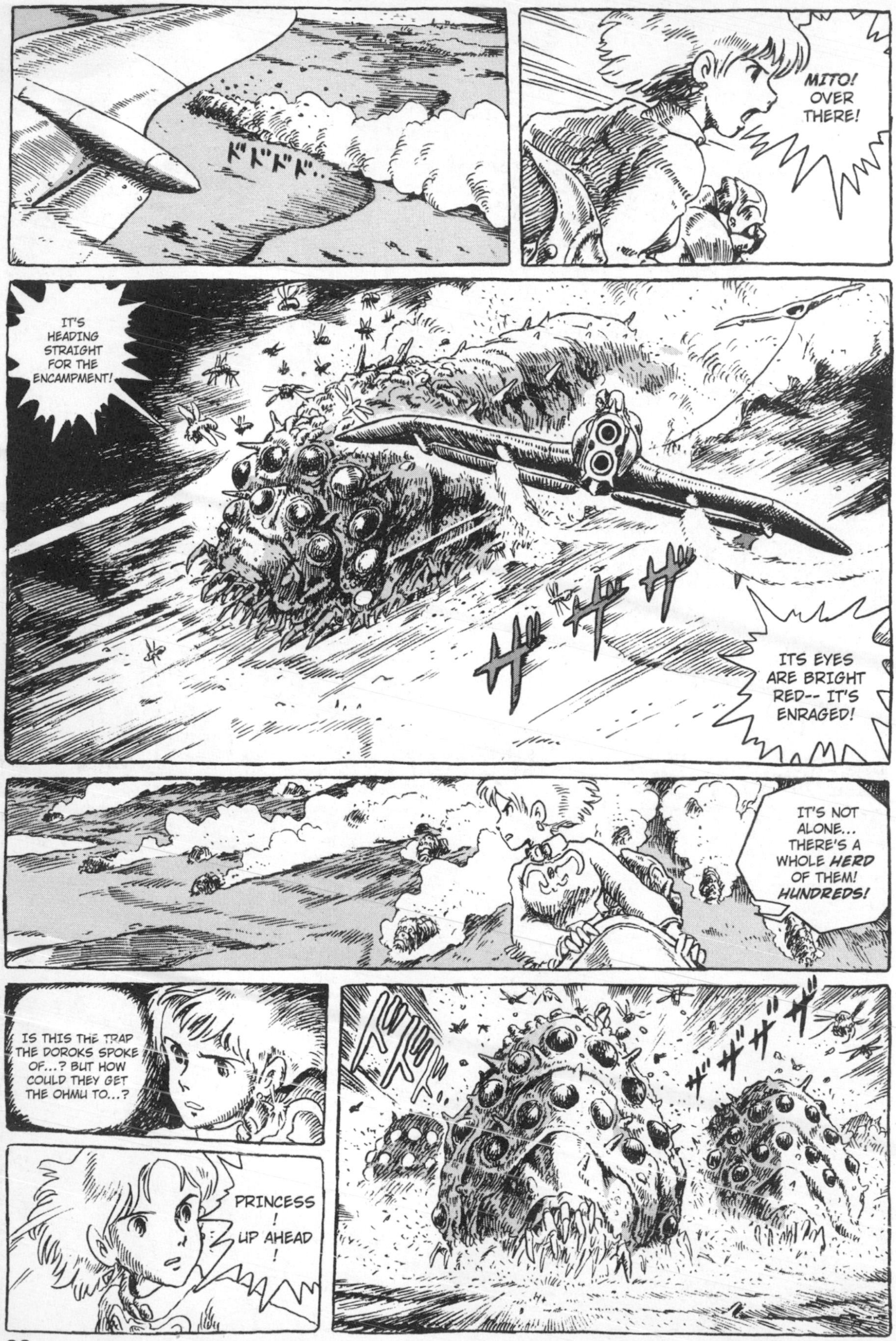
ドドドド・・
MITO! OVER THERE!
IT'S HEADING STRAIGHT FOR THE ENCAMPMENT!
ザザザザ
ITS EYES ARE BRIGHT RED-- IT'S ENRAGED!
IT'S NOT ALONE... THERE'S A WHOLE HERD OF THEM! HUNDREDS!
IS THIS THE TRAP THE DOROKS SPOKE OF...? BUT HOW COULD THEY GET THE OHMU TO...?
PRINCESS!
UP AHEAD!
ドドドド
ザザザザ

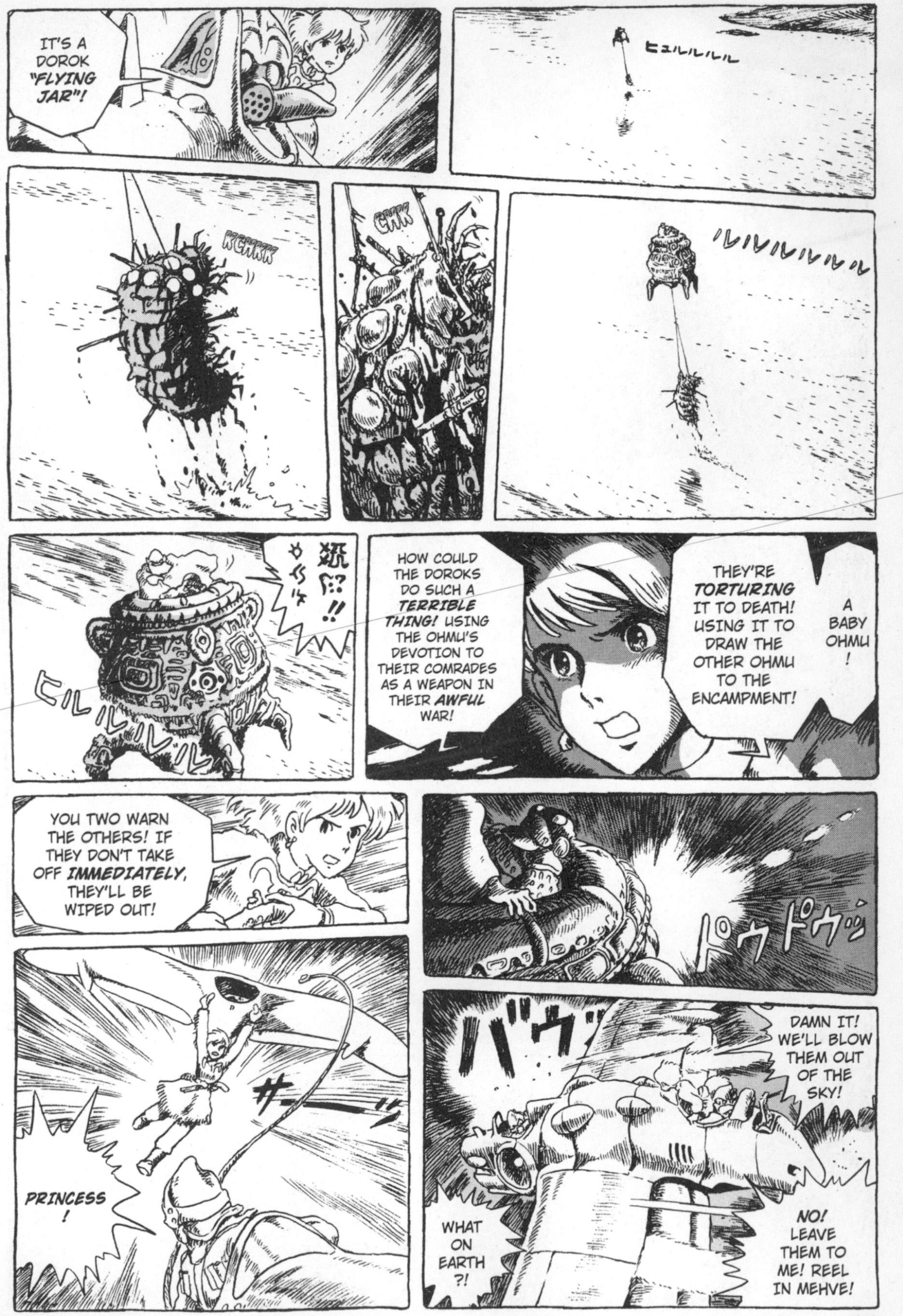
IT'S A DOROK "FLYING JAR"!
A BABY OHMU!
THEY'RE TORTURING IT TO DEATH! USING IT TO DRAW THE OTHER OHMU TO THE ENCAMPMENT!
HOW COULD THE DOROKS DO SUCH A TERRIBLE THING! USING THE OHMU'S DEVOTION TO THEIR COMRADES AS A WEAPON IN THEIR AWFUL WAR!
YOU TWO WARN THE OTHERS! IF THEY DON'T TAKE OFF IMMEDIATELY, THEY'LL BE WIPED OUT!
DAMN IT! WE'LL BLOW THEM OUT OF THE SKY!
NO! LEAVE THEM TO ME! REEL IN MEHVE!
WHAT ON EARTH?!
PRINCESS!

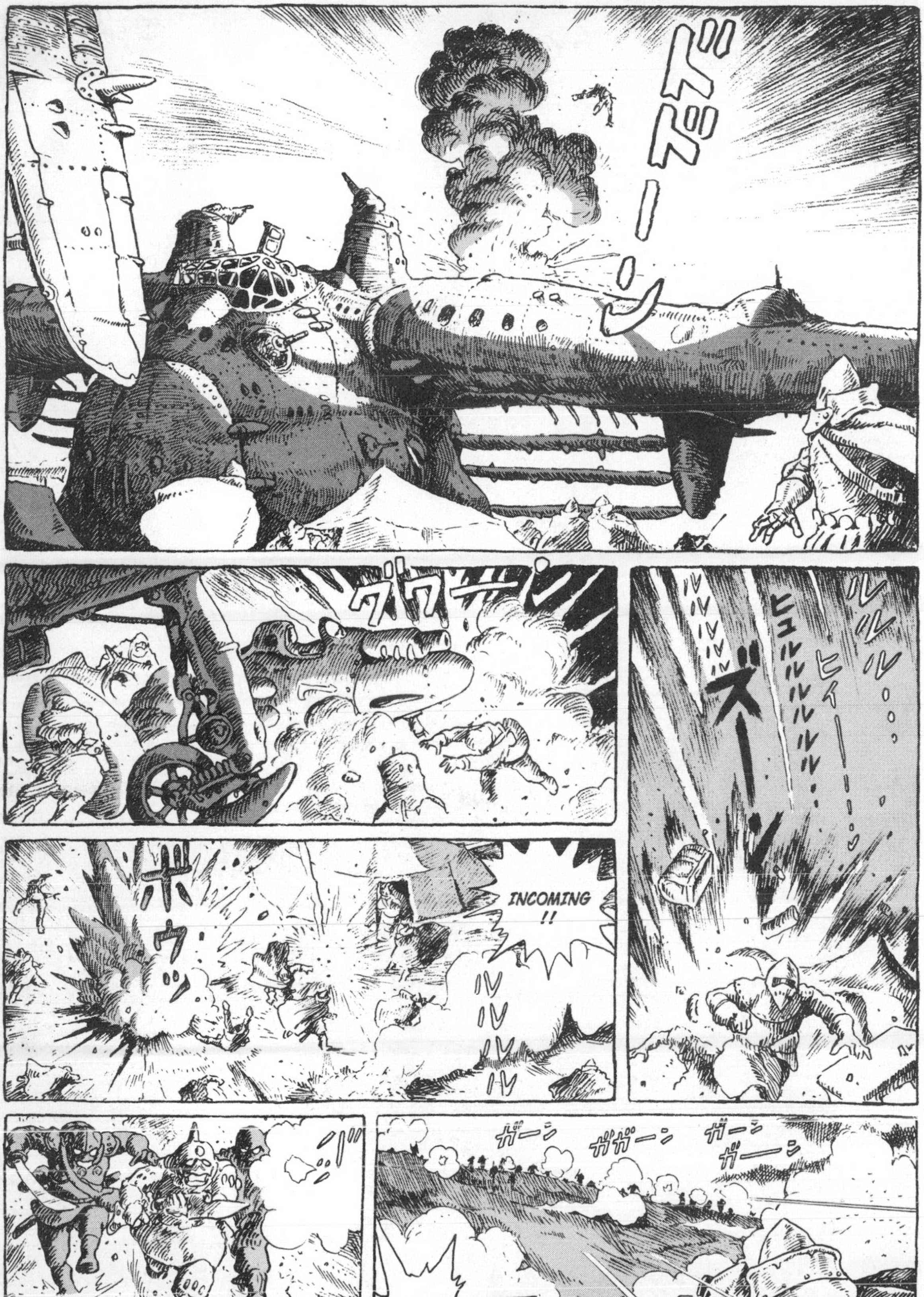
ズドーン
ルルル…
ヒュルルルルルル…
ヒィー…
ズーン
グワーン
INCOMING !!
ボウ
ルルルルル
ガーン
ガガーン
ガーン
ガーン
DOROKS !

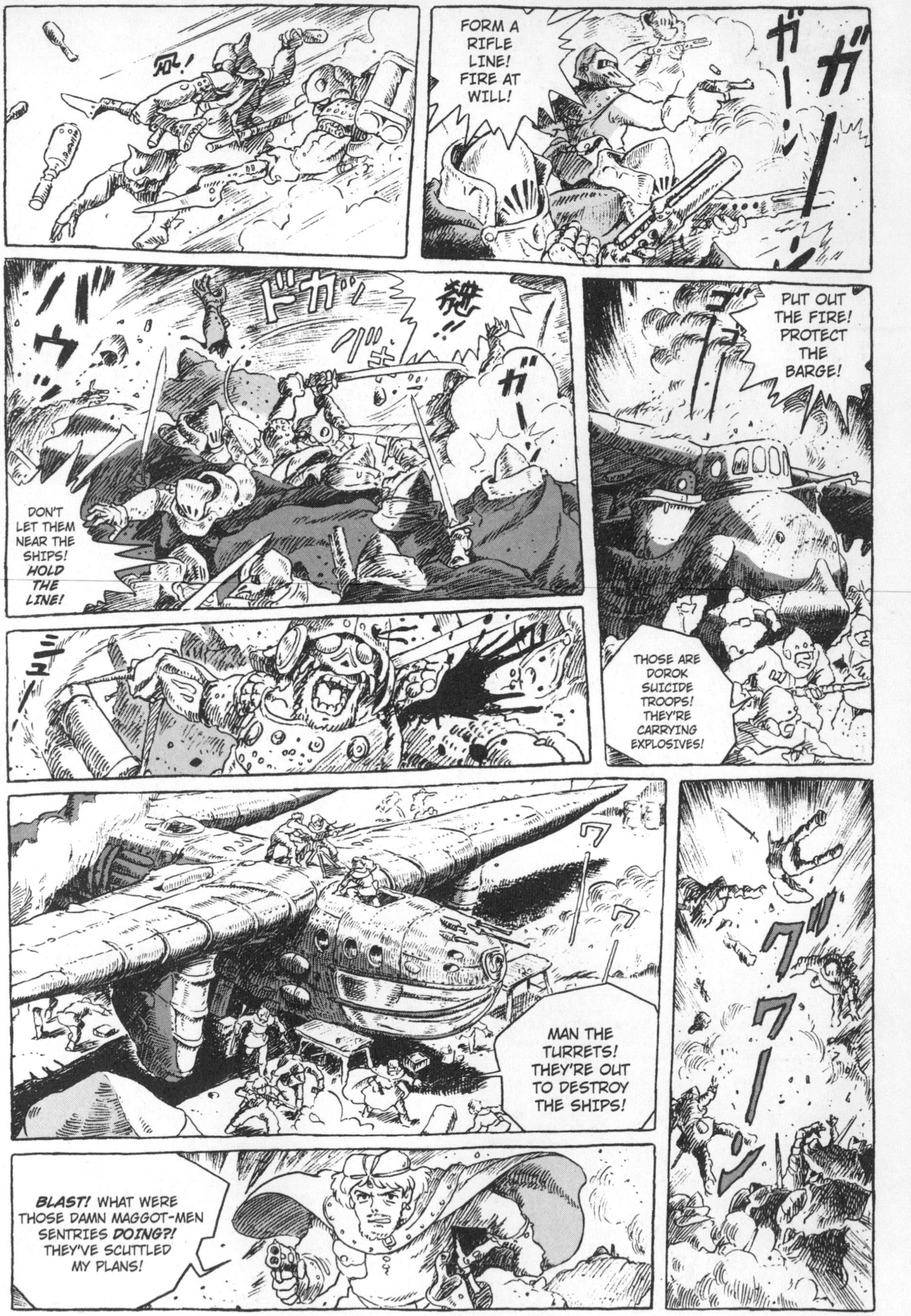
FORM A RIFLE LINE! FIRE AT WILL!
PUT OUT THE FIRE! PROTECT THE BARGE!
THOSE ARE DOROK SUICIDE TROOPS! THEY'RE CARRYING EXPLOSIVES!
DON'T LET THEM NEAR THE SHIPS! ***HOLD THE LINE!***
MAN THE TURRETS! THEY'RE OUT TO DESTROY THE SHIPS!
BLAST! WHAT WERE THOSE DAMN MAGGOT-MEN SENTRIES ***DOING?!*** THEY'VE SCUTTLED MY PLANS!

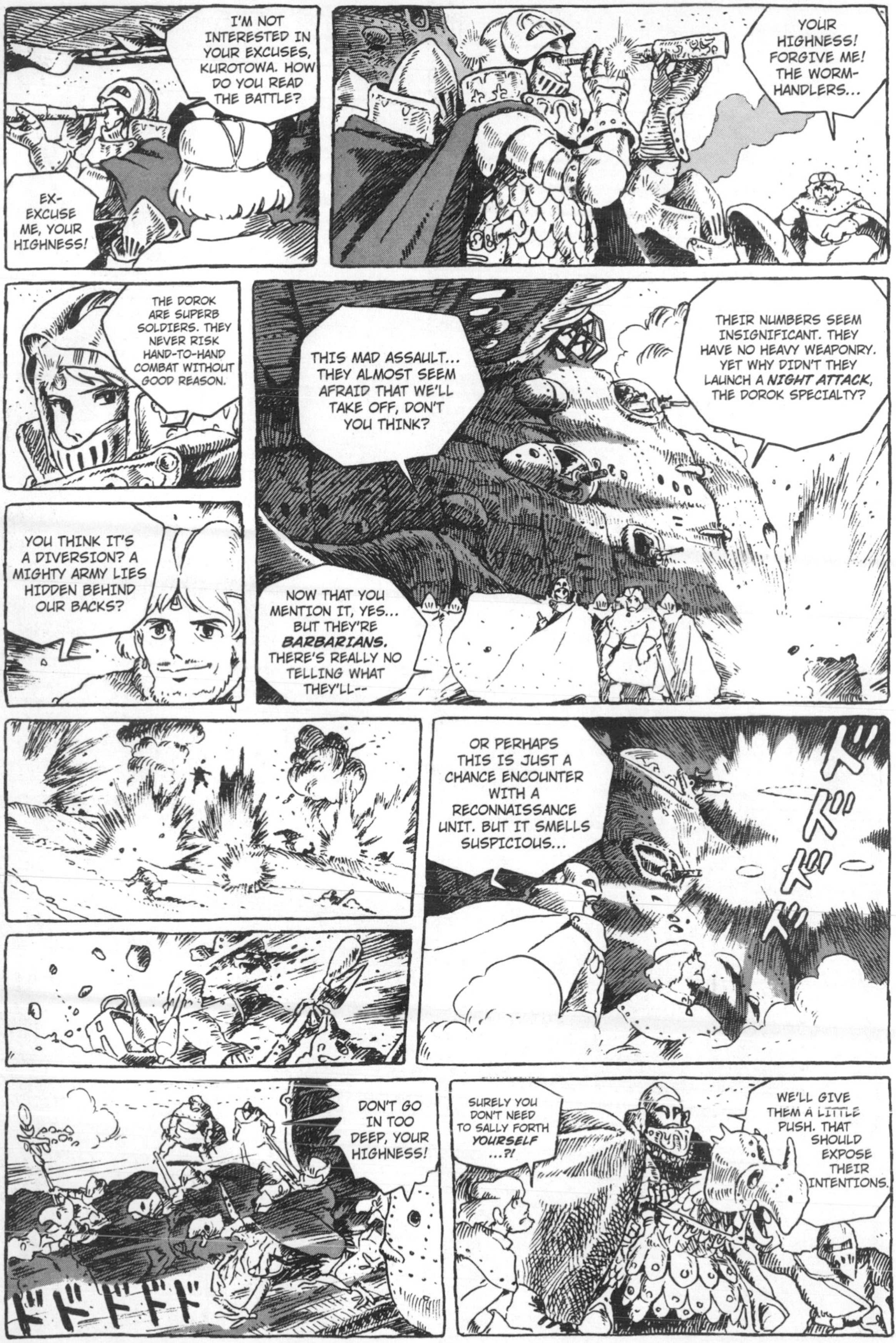
YOUR HIGHNESS! FORGIVE ME! THE WORM-HANDLERS...
I'M NOT INTERESTED IN YOUR EXCUSES, KUROTOWA. HOW DO YOU READ THE BATTLE?
EX-EXCUSE ME, YOUR HIGHNESS!
THEIR NUMBERS SEEM INSIGNIFICANT. THEY HAVE NO HEAVY WEAPONRY. YET WHY DIDN'T THEY LAUNCH A ***NIGHT ATTACK***, THE DOROK SPECIALTY?
THIS MAD ASSAULT... THEY ALMOST SEEM AFRAID THAT WE'LL TAKE OFF, DON'T YOU THINK?
NOW THAT YOU MENTION IT, YES... BUT THEY'RE ***BARBARIANS.*** THERE'S REALLY NO TELLING WHAT THEY'LL--
THE DOROK ARE SUPERB SOLDIERS. THEY NEVER RISK HAND-TO-HAND COMBAT WITHOUT GOOD REASON.
YOU THINK IT'S A DIVERSION? A MIGHTY ARMY LIES HIDDEN BEHIND OUR BACKS?
OR PERHAPS THIS IS JUST A CHANCE ENCOUNTER WITH A RECONNAISSANCE UNIT. BUT IT SMELLS SUSPICIOUS...
WE'LL GIVE THEM A LITTLE PUSH. THAT SHOULD EXPOSE THEIR INTENTIONS.
SURELY YOU DON'T NEED TO SALLY FORTH ***YOURSELF***...?!
DON'T GO IN TOO DEEP, YOUR HIGHNESS!
ドドドドド

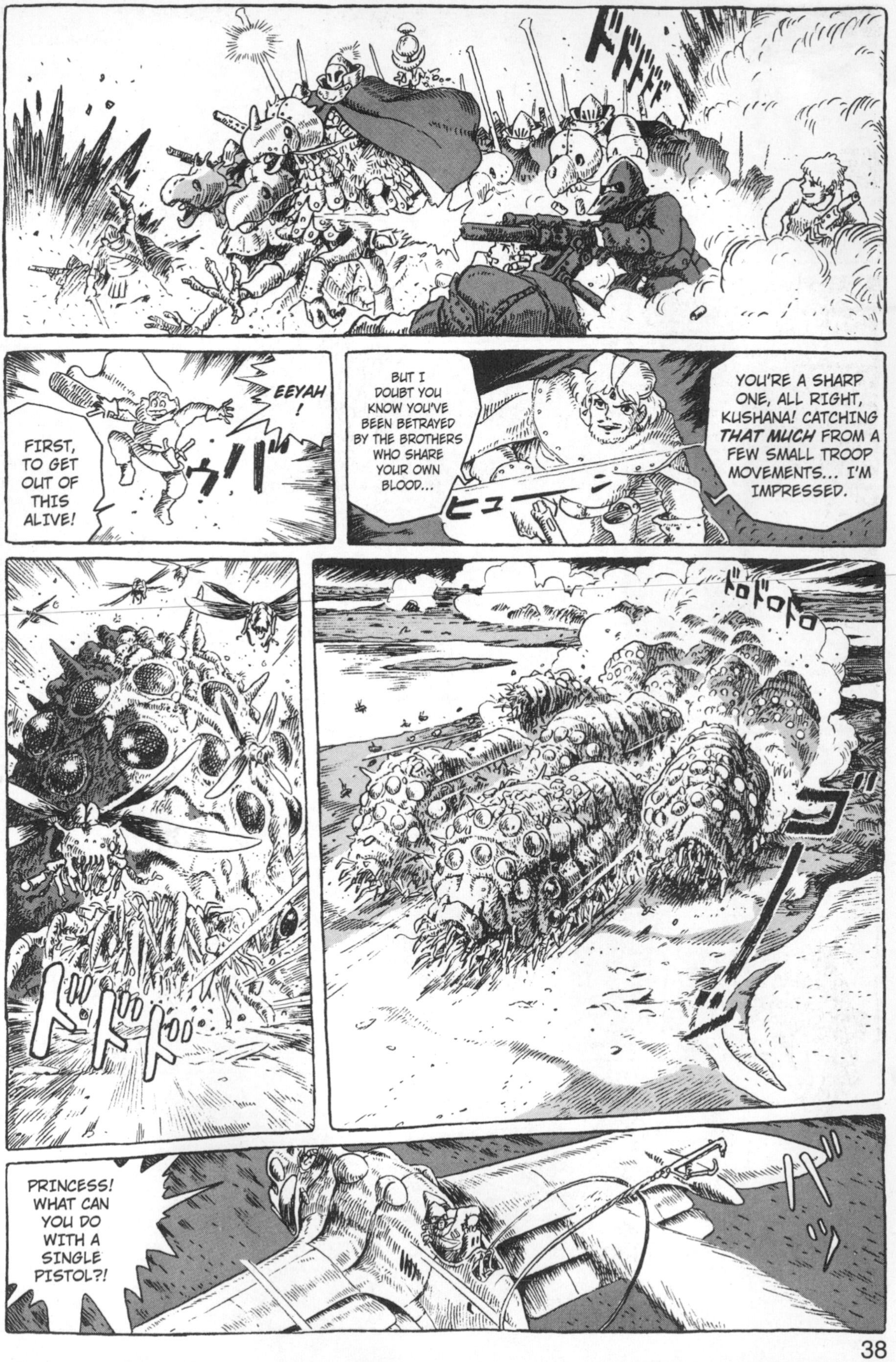
YOU'RE A SHARP ONE, ALL RIGHT, KUSHANA! CATCHING *THAT MUCH* FROM A FEW SMALL TROOP MOVEMENTS... I'M IMPRESSED.
BUT I DOUBT YOU KNOW YOU'VE BEEN BETRAYED BY THE BROTHERS WHO SHARE YOUR OWN BLOOD...
EEYAH!
FIRST, TO GET OUT OF THIS ALIVE!
PRINCESS! WHAT CAN YOU DO WITH A SINGLE PISTOL?!

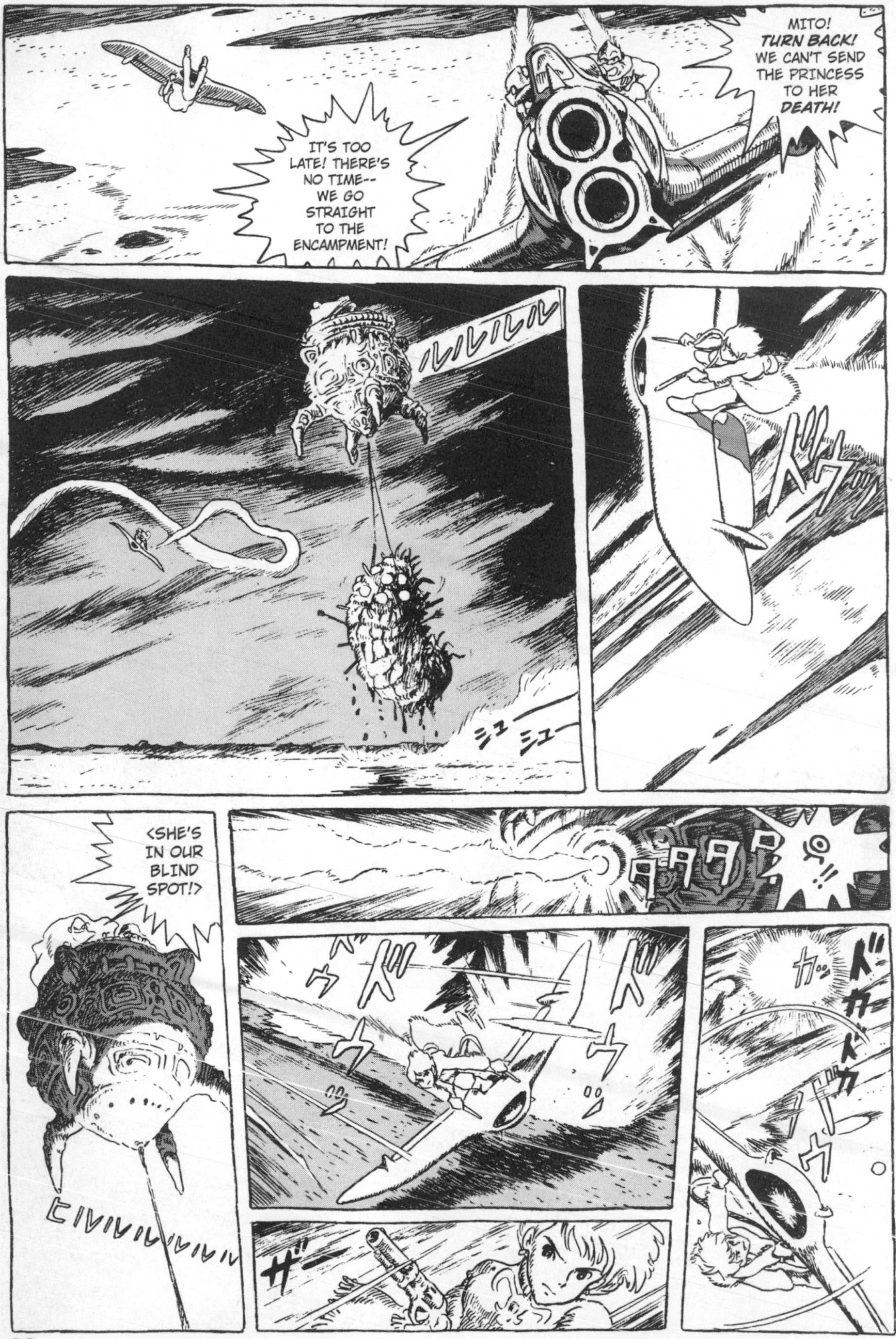
MITO! **TURN BACK!** WE CAN'T SEND THE PRINCESS TO HER **DEATH!**
IT'S TOO LATE! THERE'S NO TIME-- WE GO STRAIGHT TO THE ENCAMPMENT!
ルルルルル
シュ シュ
ザー
<SHE'S IN OUR BLIND SPOT!>

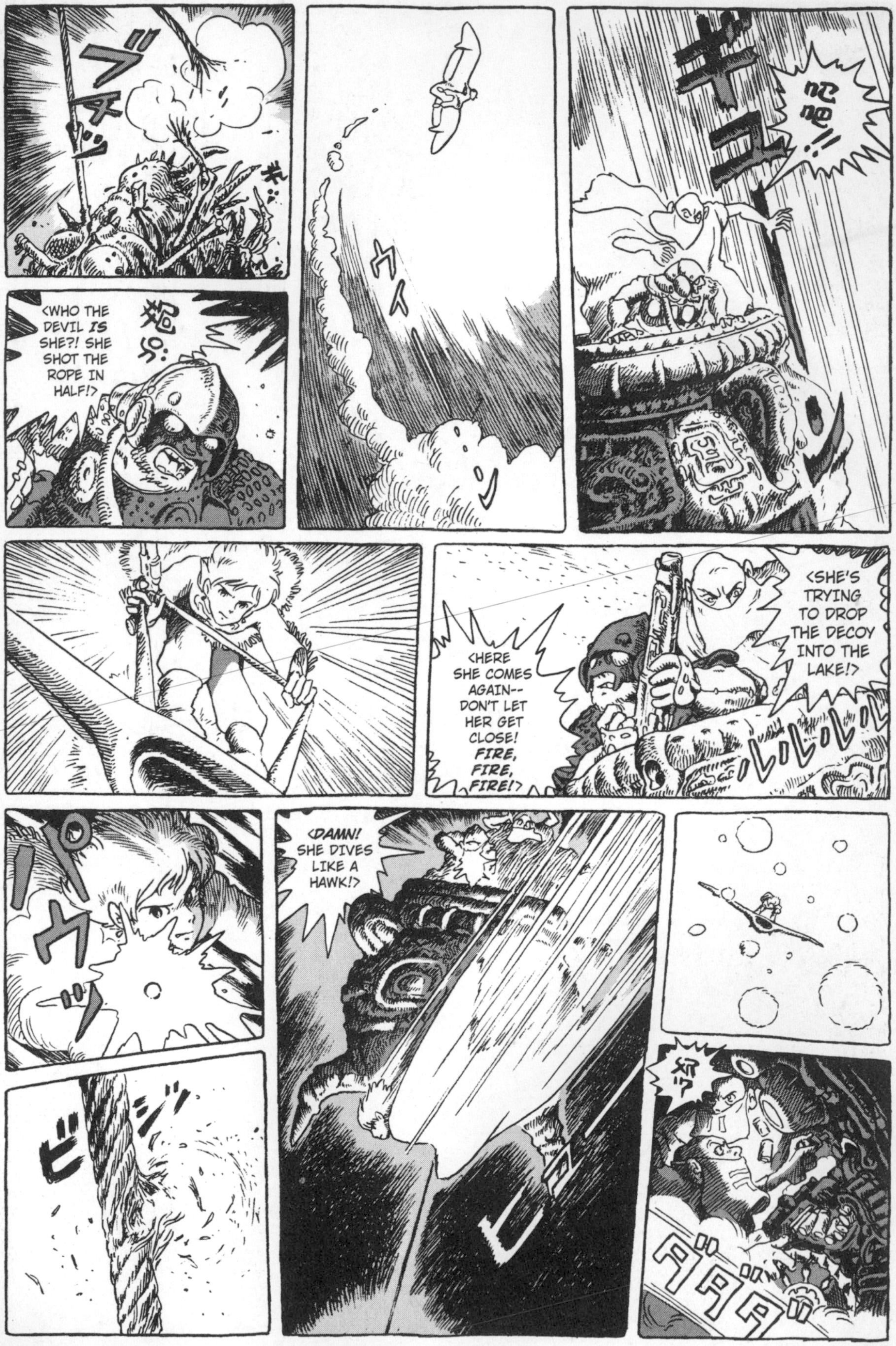
<WHO THE DEVIL *IS* SHE?! SHE SHOT THE ROPE IN HALF!>
<SHE'S TRYING TO DROP THE DECOY INTO THE LAKE!>
<HERE SHE COMES AGAIN-- DON'T LET HER GET CLOSE! *FIRE, FIRE, FIRE!*>
<*DAMN!* SHE DIVES LIKE A HAWK!>

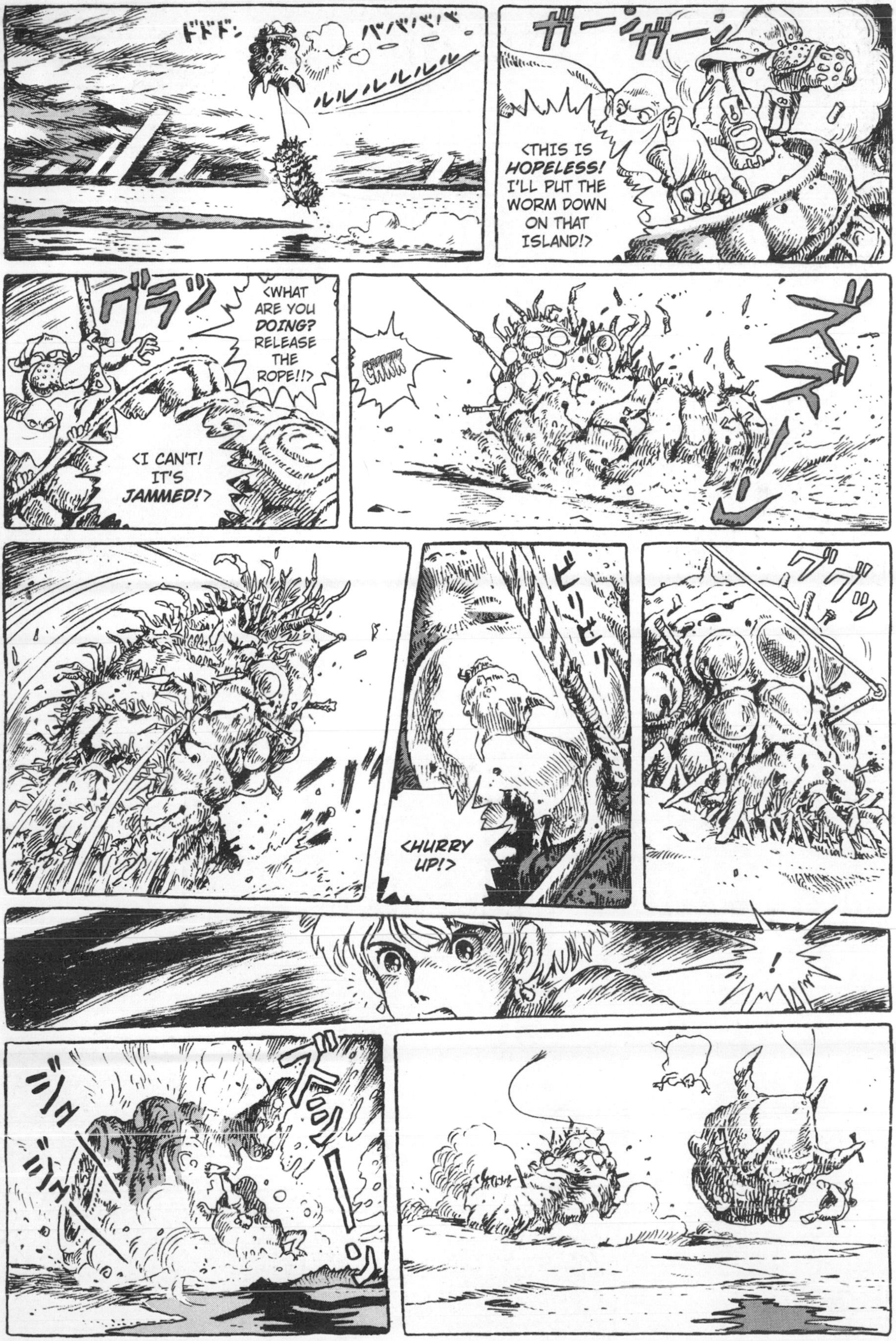
<THIS IS HOPELESS! I'LL PUT THE WORM DOWN ON THAT ISLAND!>
<WHAT ARE YOU DOING? RELEASE THE ROPE!!>
<I CAN'T! IT'S JAMMED!>
<HURRY UP!>
!

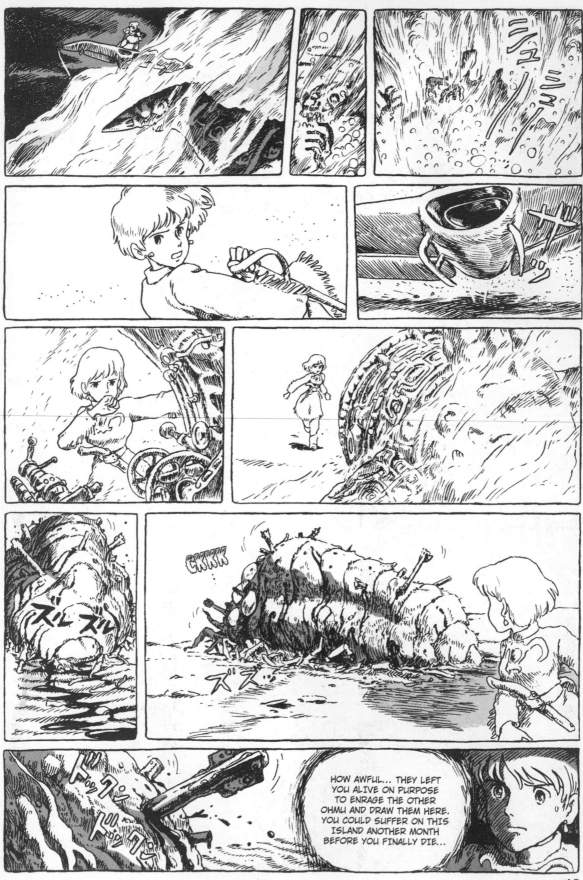

HOW AWFUL... THEY LEFT YOU ALIVE ON PURPOSE TO ENRAGE THE OTHER OHMU AND DRAW THEM HERE. YOU COULD SUFFER ON THIS ISLAND ANOTHER MONTH BEFORE YOU FINALLY DIE...

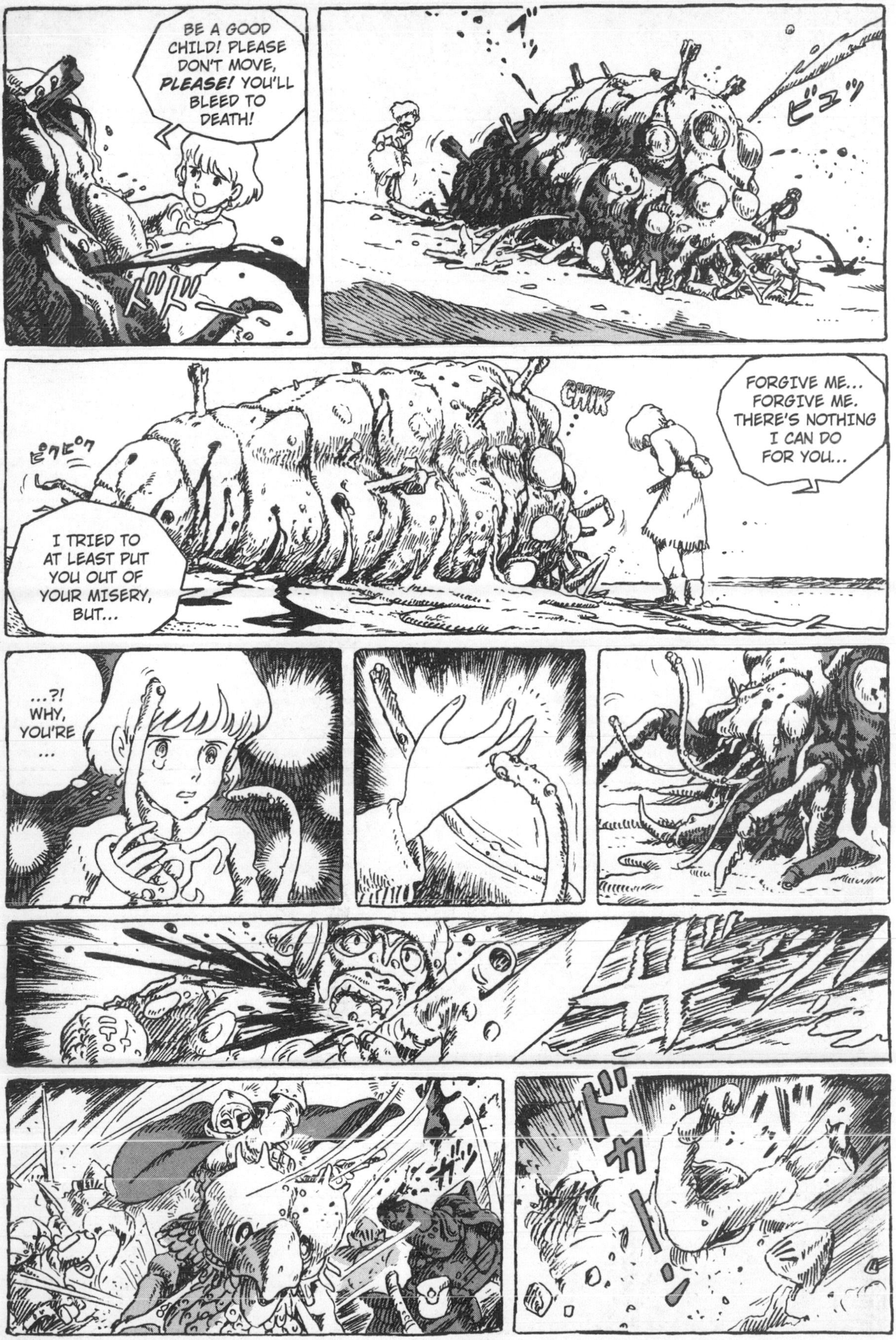
BE A GOOD CHILD! PLEASE DON'T MOVE, ***PLEASE!*** YOU'LL BLEED TO DEATH!
FORGIVE ME... FORGIVE ME. THERE'S NOTHING I CAN DO FOR YOU...
CHIK
I TRIED TO AT LEAST PUT YOU OUT OF YOUR MISERY, BUT...
...?! WHY, YOU'RE ...

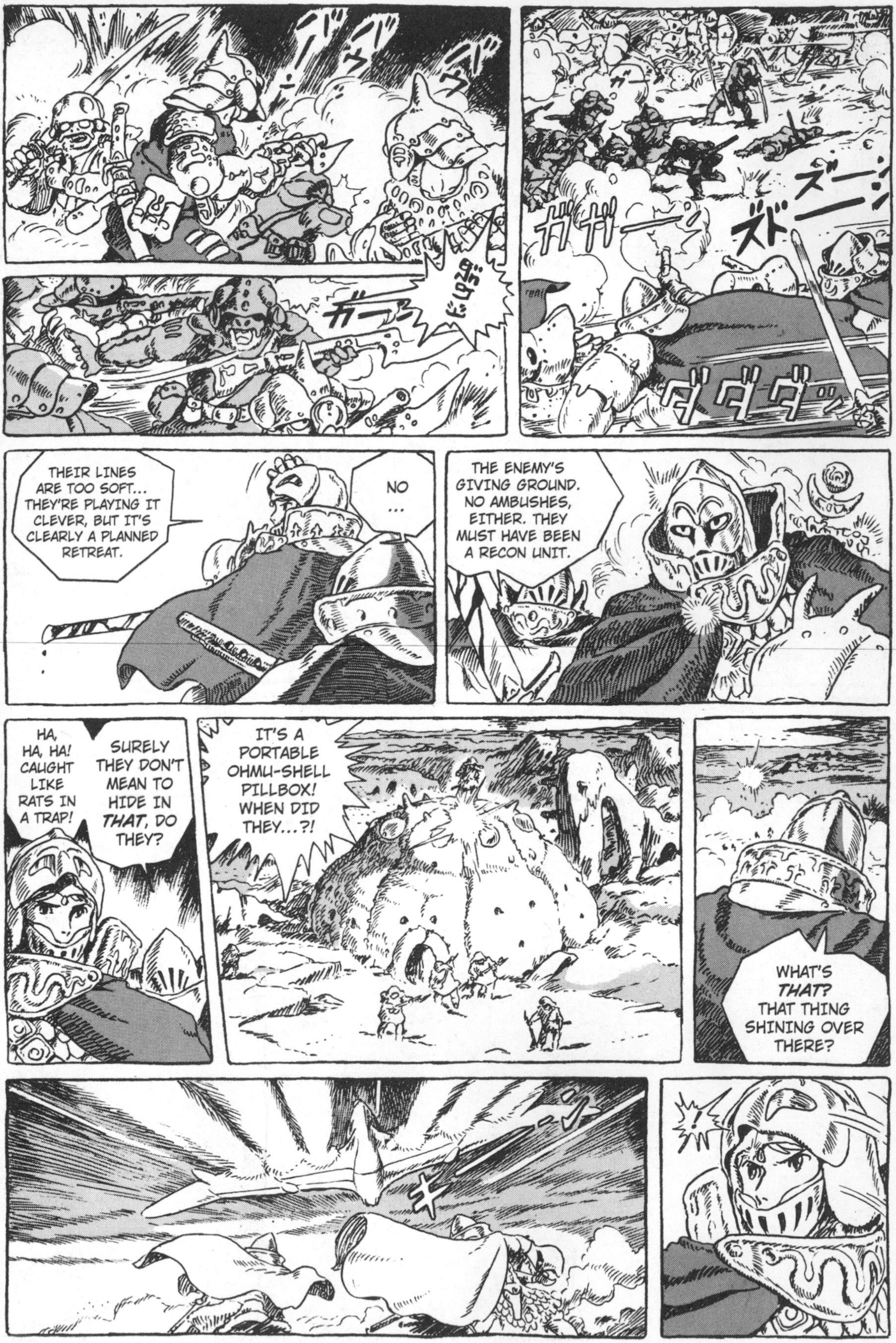
THE ENEMY'S GIVING GROUND. NO AMBUSHES, EITHER. THEY MUST HAVE BEEN A RECON UNIT.
NO ...
THEIR LINES ARE TOO SOFT... THEY'RE PLAYING IT CLEVER, BUT IT'S CLEARLY A PLANNED RETREAT.
WHAT'S *THAT?* THAT THING SHINING OVER THERE?
IT'S A PORTABLE OHMU-SHELL PILLBOX! WHEN DID THEY...?!
SURELY THEY DON'T MEAN TO HIDE IN *THAT*, DO THEY?
HA, HA, HA! CAUGHT LIKE RATS IN A TRAP!

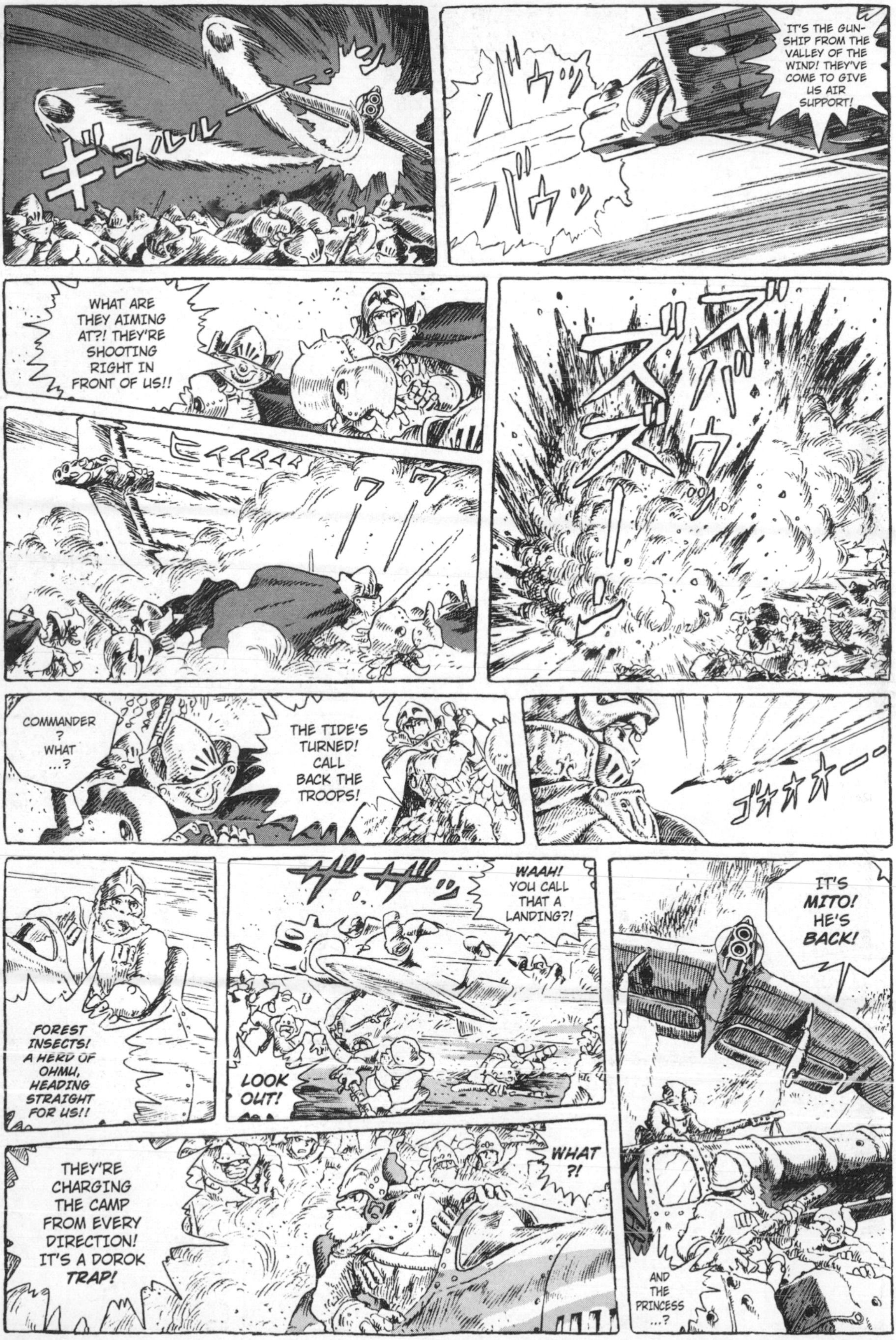
IT'S THE GUN-SHIP FROM THE VALLEY OF THE WIND! THEY'VE COME TO GIVE US AIR SUPPORT!
WHAT ARE THEY AIMING AT?! THEY'RE SHOOTING RIGHT IN FRONT OF US!!
THE TIDE'S TURNED! CALL BACK THE TROOPS!
COMMANDER? WHAT...?
IT'S MITO! HE'S BACK!
AND THE PRINCESS...?
WAAH! YOU CALL THAT A LANDING?!
LOOK OUT!
FOREST INSECTS! A HERD OF OHMU, HEADING STRAIGHT FOR US!!
WHAT?!
THEY'RE CHARGING THE CAMP FROM EVERY DIRECTION! IT'S A DOROK TRAP!

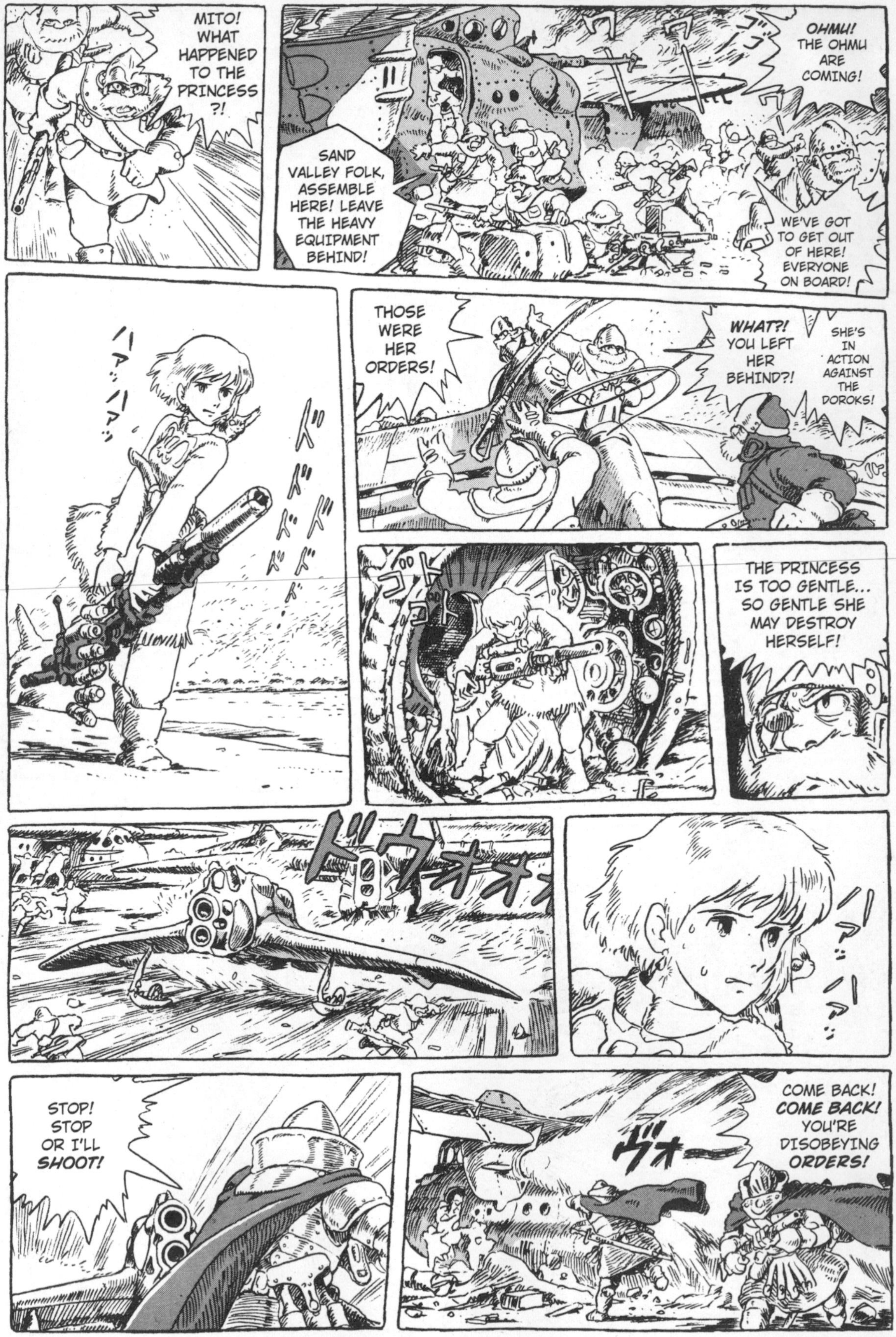

OHMU! THE OHMU ARE COMING!
WE'VE GOT TO GET OUT OF HERE! EVERYONE ON BOARD!
SAND VALLEY FOLK, ASSEMBLE HERE! LEAVE THE HEAVY EQUIPMENT BEHIND!
MITO! WHAT HAPPENED TO THE PRINCESS?!
SHE'S IN ACTION AGAINST THE DOROKS!
WHAT?! YOU LEFT HER BEHIND?!
THOSE WERE HER ORDERS!
THE PRINCESS IS TOO GENTLE... SO GENTLE SHE MAY DESTROY HERSELF!
ハァッハァッ
ドウオオオ
COME BACK! COME BACK! YOU'RE DISOBEYING ORDERS!
ヴォー
STOP! STOP OR I'LL SHOOT!

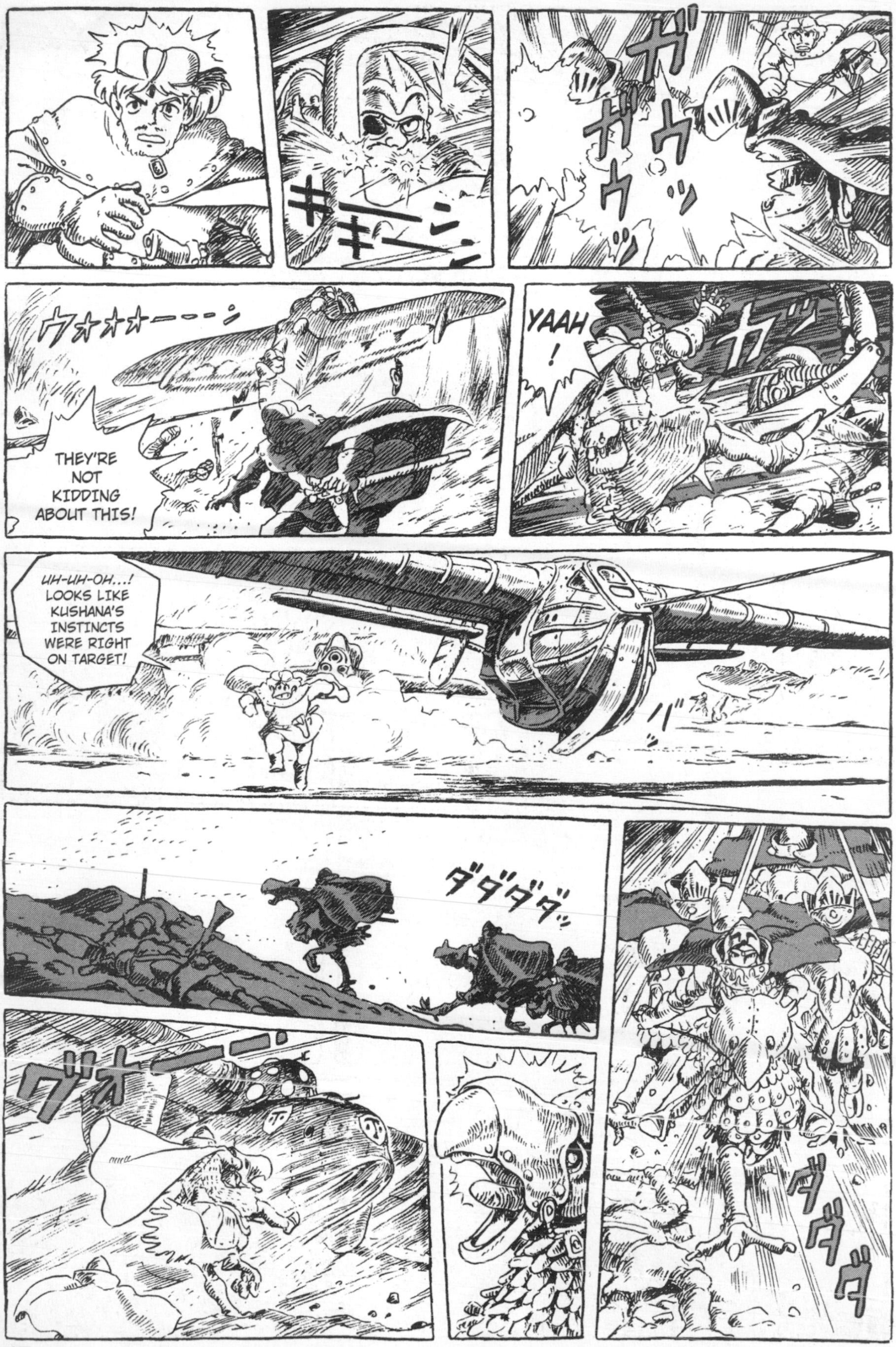
YAAH!
ウォォォーーーン
THEY'RE NOT KIDDING ABOUT THIS!
UH-UH-OH...! LOOKS LIKE KUSHANA'S INSTINCTS WERE RIGHT ON TARGET!
ダダダダッ

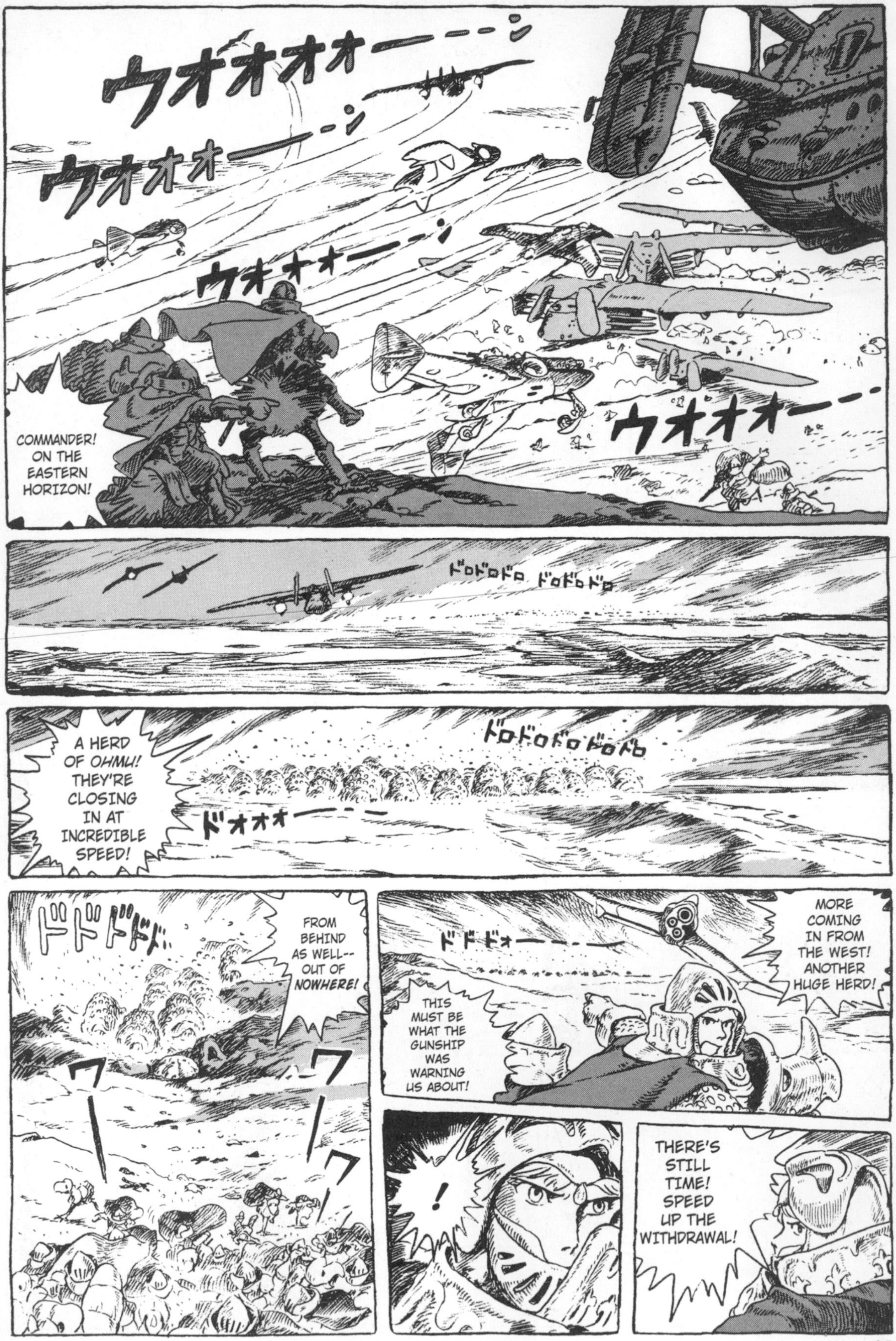

ウオオオオーーーン
ウオオオーーーン
ウオオオーーーン
ウオオオーーー
COMMANDER! ON THE EASTERN HORIZON!
ドドドドド ドドドドド
A HERD OF OHMU! THEY'RE CLOSING IN AT INCREDIBLE SPEED!
ドドドドドドドドド
ドオオオーーー
MORE COMING IN FROM THE WEST! ANOTHER HUGE HERD!
ドドドォーーー
THIS MUST BE WHAT THE GUNSHIP WAS WARNING US ABOUT!
THERE'S STILL TIME! SPEED UP THE WITHDRAWAL!
!
ドドドドド
FROM BEHIND AS WELL--OUT OF NOWHERE!
ワー
ワー
ワ

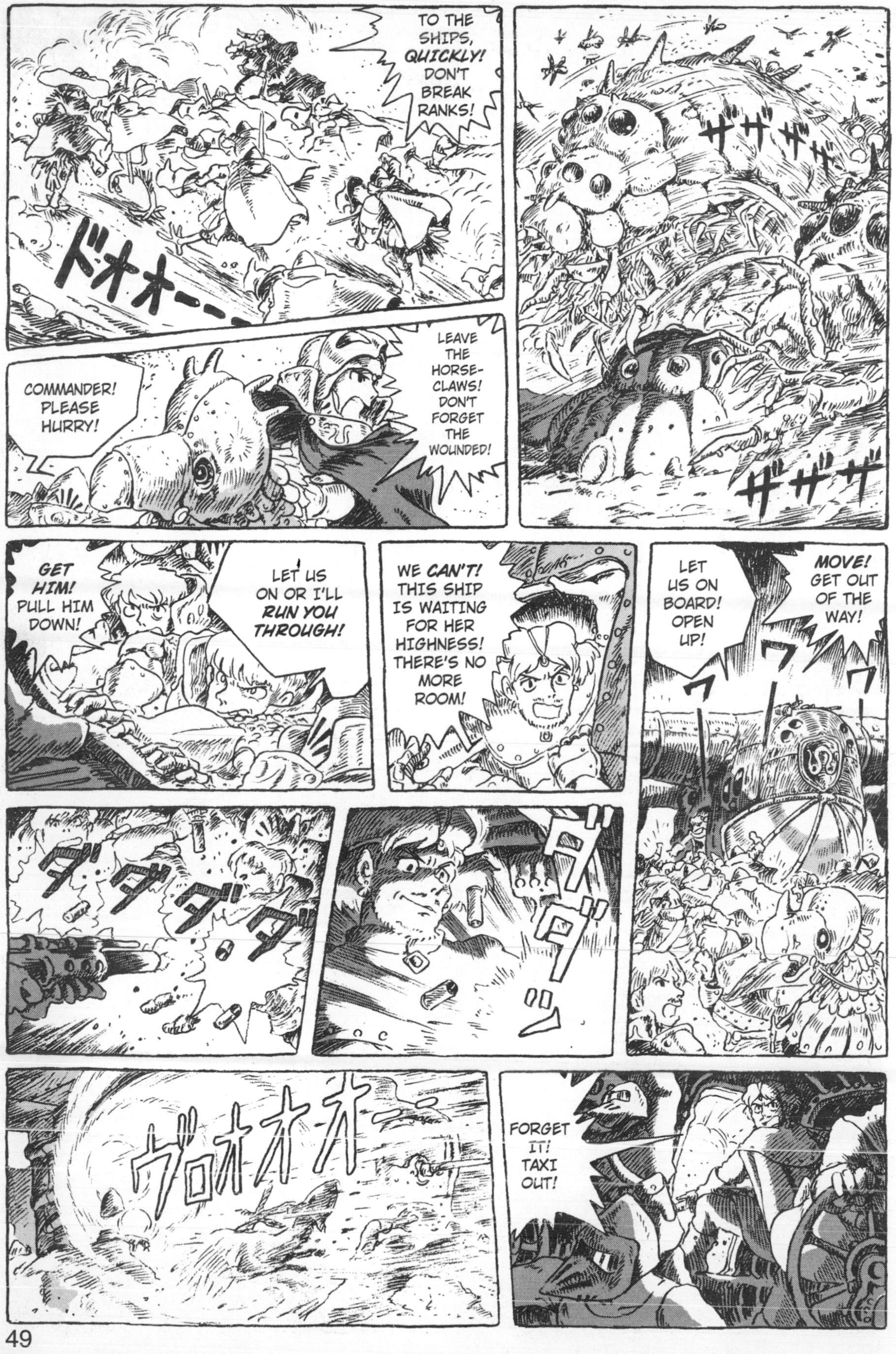
ザザザザ
ザザザ
TO THE SHIPS, *QUICKLY!* DON'T BREAK RANKS!
ドオオーーー
LEAVE THE HORSE-CLAWS! DON'T FORGET THE WOUNDED!
COMMANDER! PLEASE HURRY!
MOVE! GET OUT OF THE WAY!
LET US ON BOARD! OPEN UP!
ワ
ワ
ワ
WE *CAN'T!* THIS SHIP IS WAITING FOR HER HIGHNESS! THERE'S NO MORE ROOM!
LET US ON OR I'LL *RUN YOU THROUGH!*
GET HIM! PULL HIM DOWN!
ダダッ
ダダダダ
FORGET IT! TAXI OUT!
ヴロオオオーー

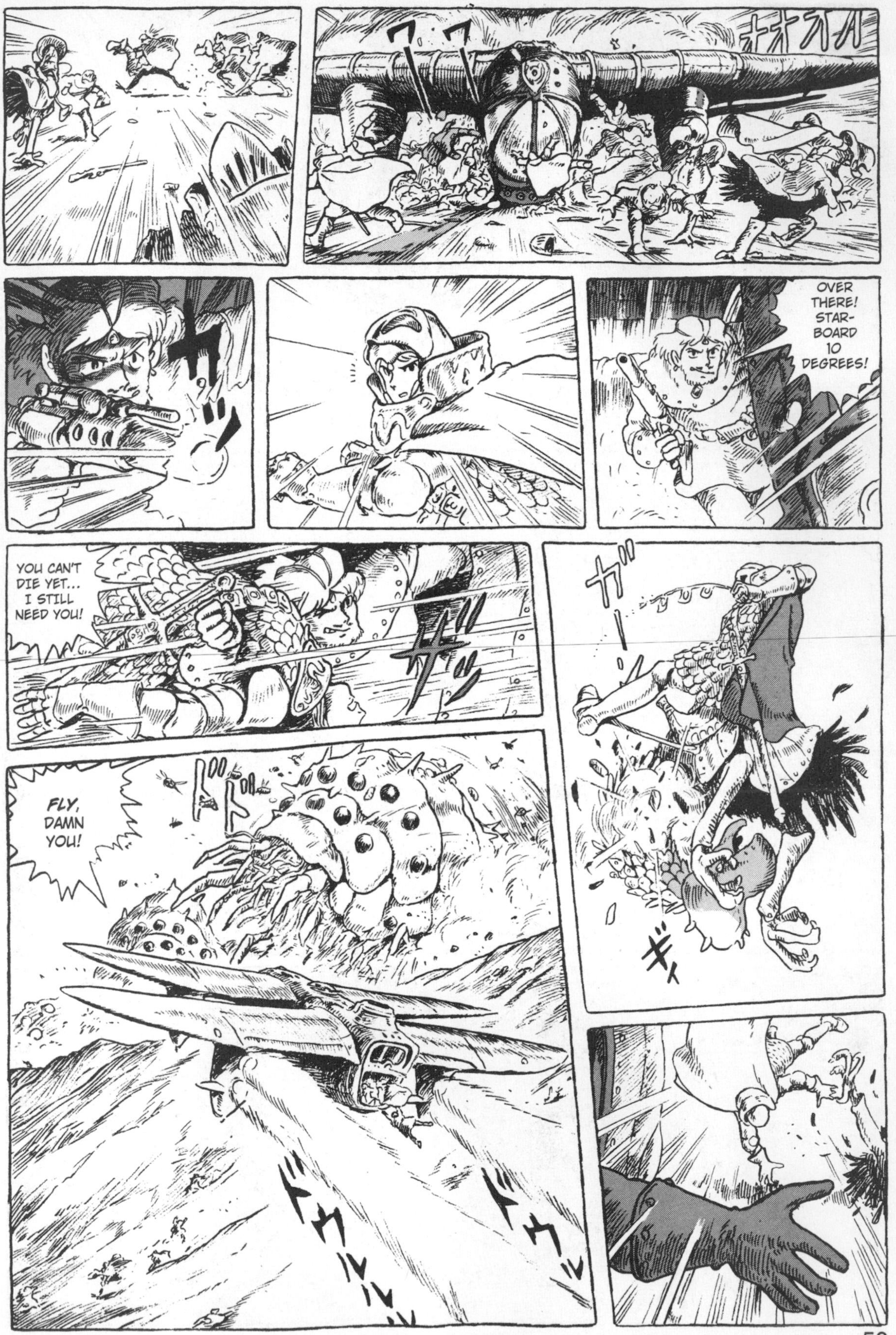
OVER THERE! STAR-BOARD 10 DEGREES!
YOU CAN'T DIE YET... I STILL NEED YOU!
FLY, DAMN YOU!

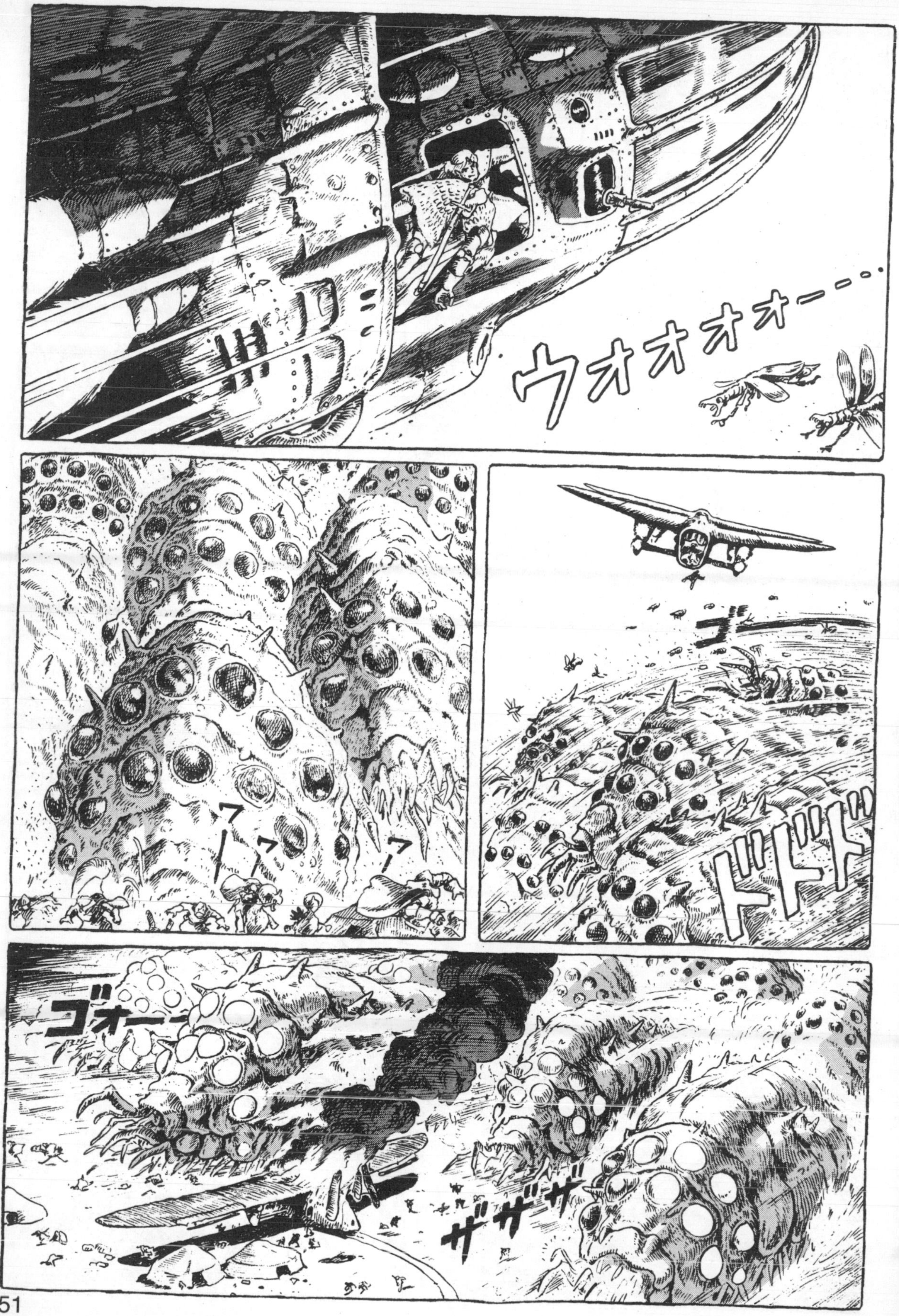
ウオオオオー・・・
ゴー
ドドド
ゴオー
ザザザ

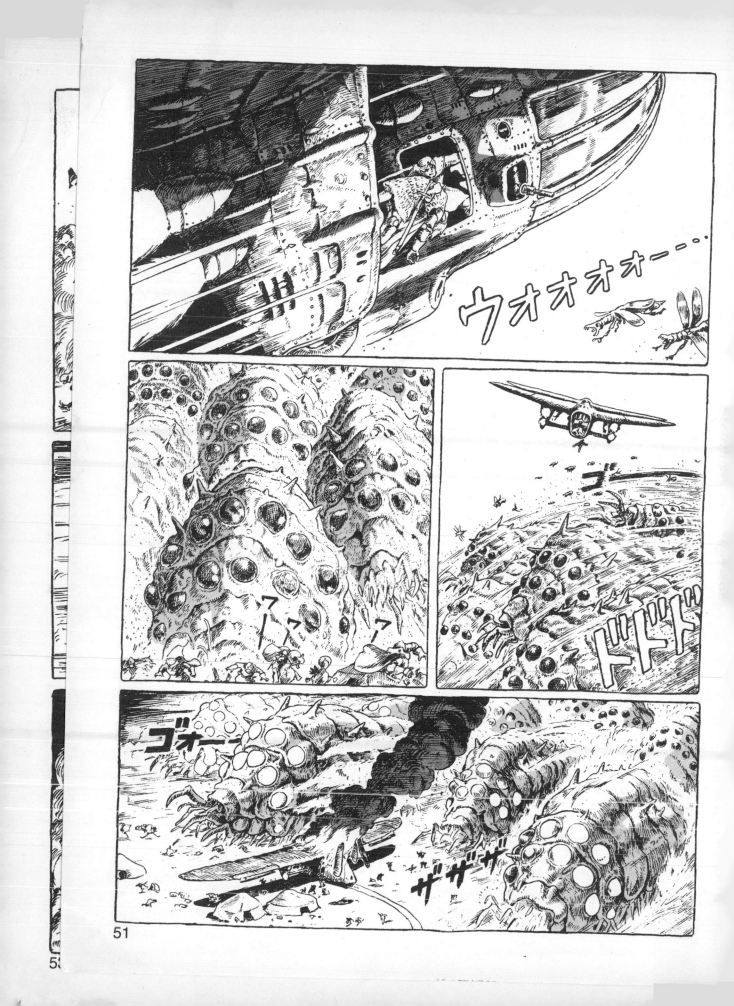

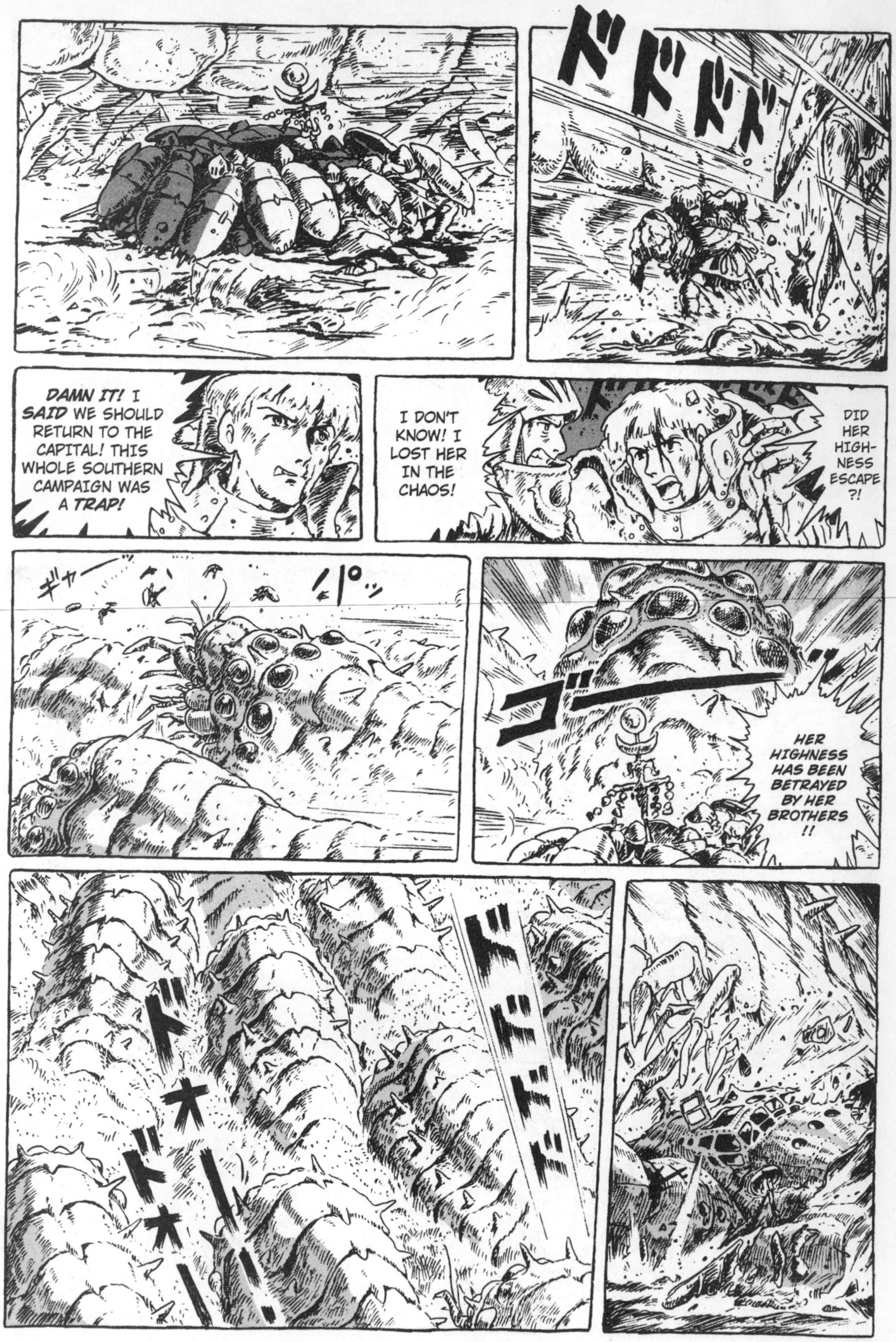
ドドドド
DID HER HIGHNESS ESCAPE?!
I DON'T KNOW! I LOST HER IN THE CHAOS!
DAMN IT! I SAID WE SHOULD RETURN TO THE CAPITAL! THIS WHOLE SOUTHERN CAMPAIGN WAS A TRAP!
ゴーッ
HER HIGHNESS HAS BEEN BETRAYED BY HER BROTHERS!!
ギャー
パッ
ドドド
ドオドオー
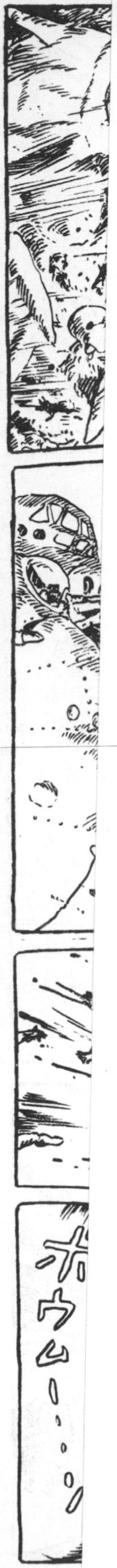

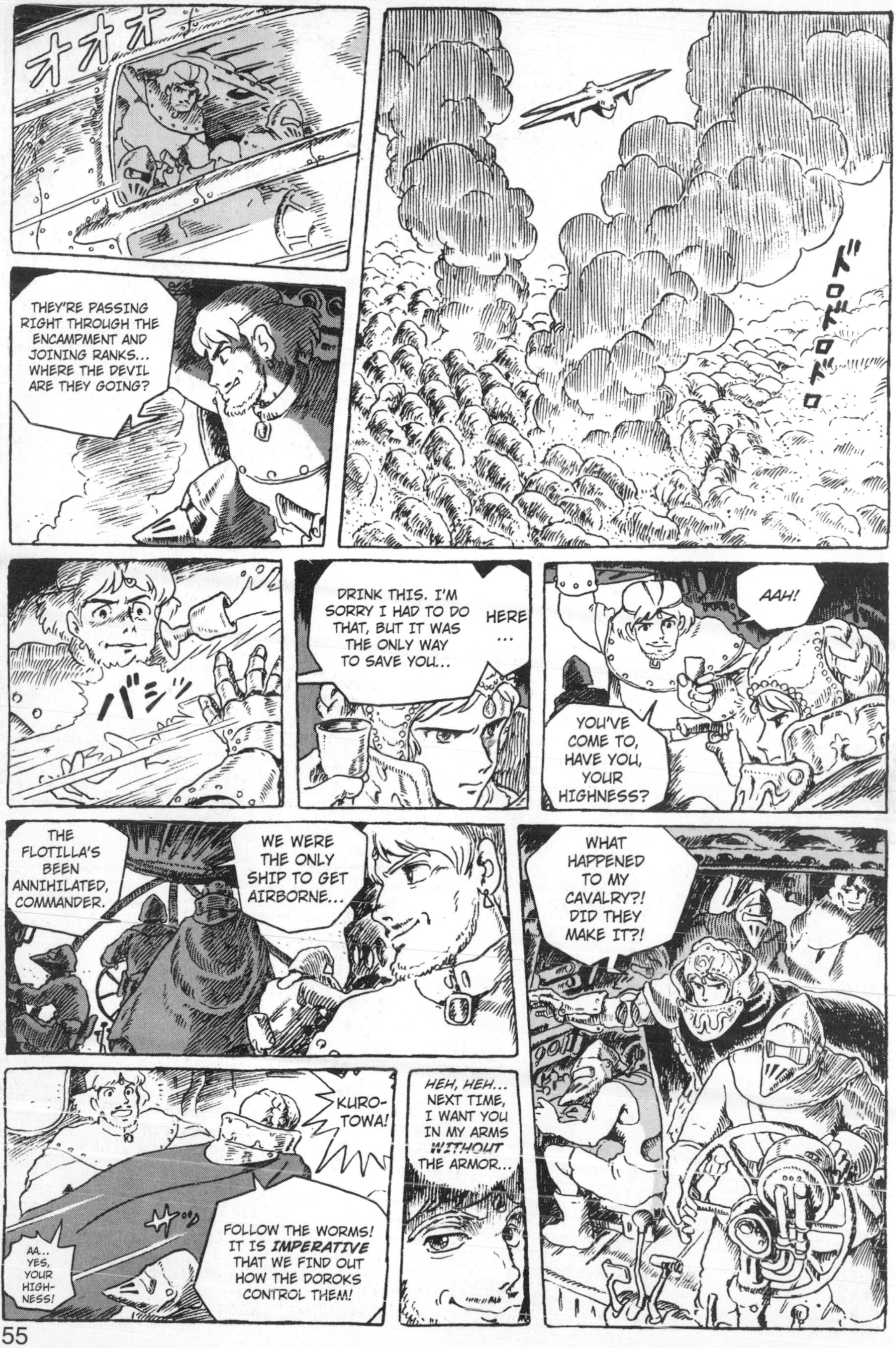
ドロドロドロ
オオオ
THEY'RE PASSING RIGHT THROUGH THE ENCAMPMENT AND JOINING RANKS... WHERE THE DEVIL ARE THEY GOING?
AAH!
YOU'VE COME TO, HAVE YOU, YOUR HIGHNESS?
DRINK THIS. I'M SORRY I HAD TO DO THAT, BUT IT WAS THE ONLY WAY TO SAVE YOU...
HERE...
バシッ
WHAT HAPPENED TO MY CAVALRY?! DID THEY MAKE IT?!
WE WERE THE ONLY SHIP TO GET AIRBORNE...
THE FLOTILLA'S BEEN ANNIHILATED, COMMANDER.
HEH, HEH... NEXT TIME, I WANT YOU IN MY ARMS ***WITHOUT*** THE ARMOR...
KURO-TOWA!
FOLLOW THE WORMS! IT IS ***IMPERATIVE*** THAT WE FIND OUT HOW THE DOROKS CONTROL THEM!
AA... YES, YOUR HIGH-NESS!

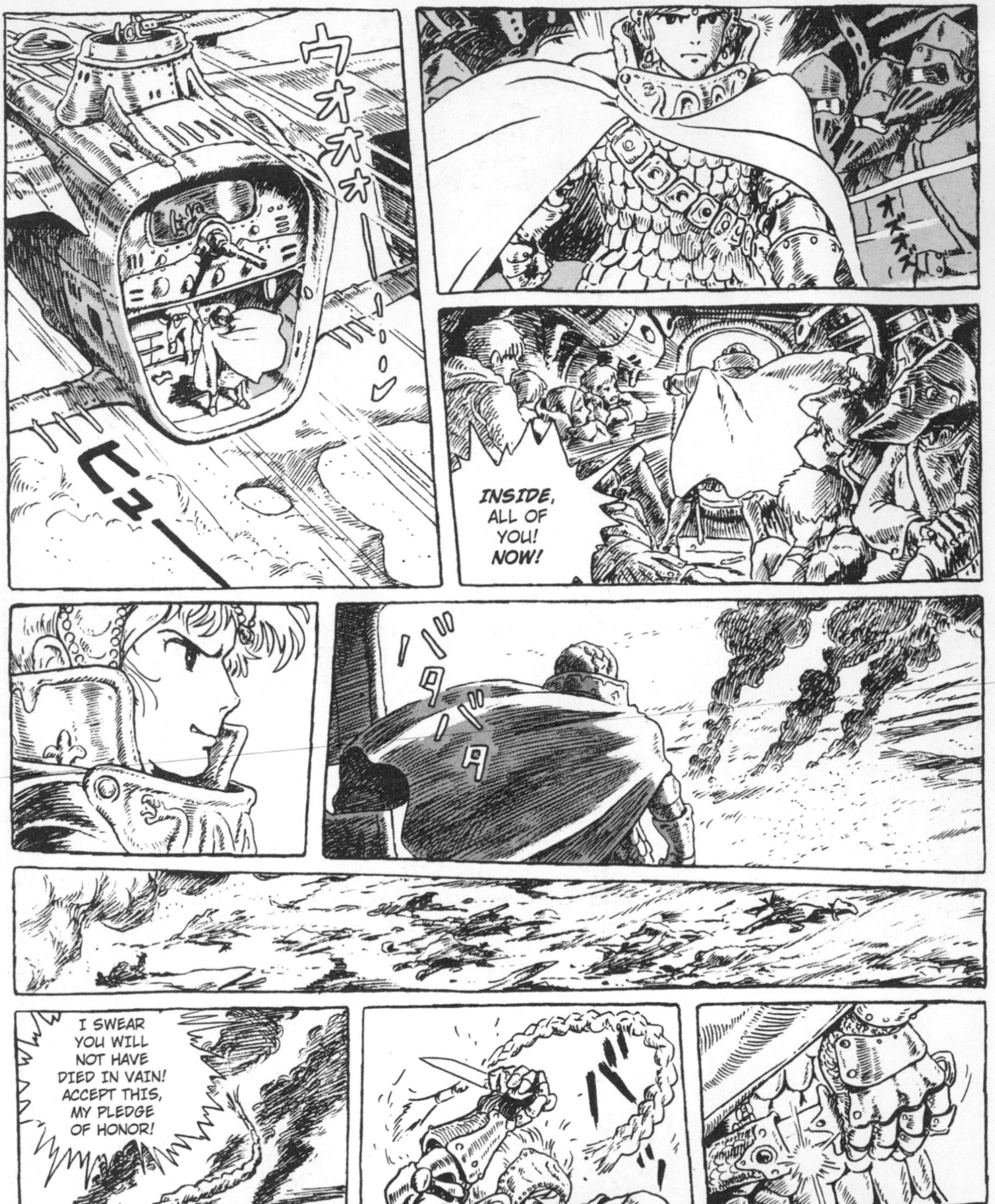
INSIDE, ALL OF YOU! NOW!
ウオオオー
ヒュー
バタバタ
I SWEAR YOU WILL NOT HAVE DIED IN VAIN! ACCEPT THIS, MY PLEDGE OF HONOR!

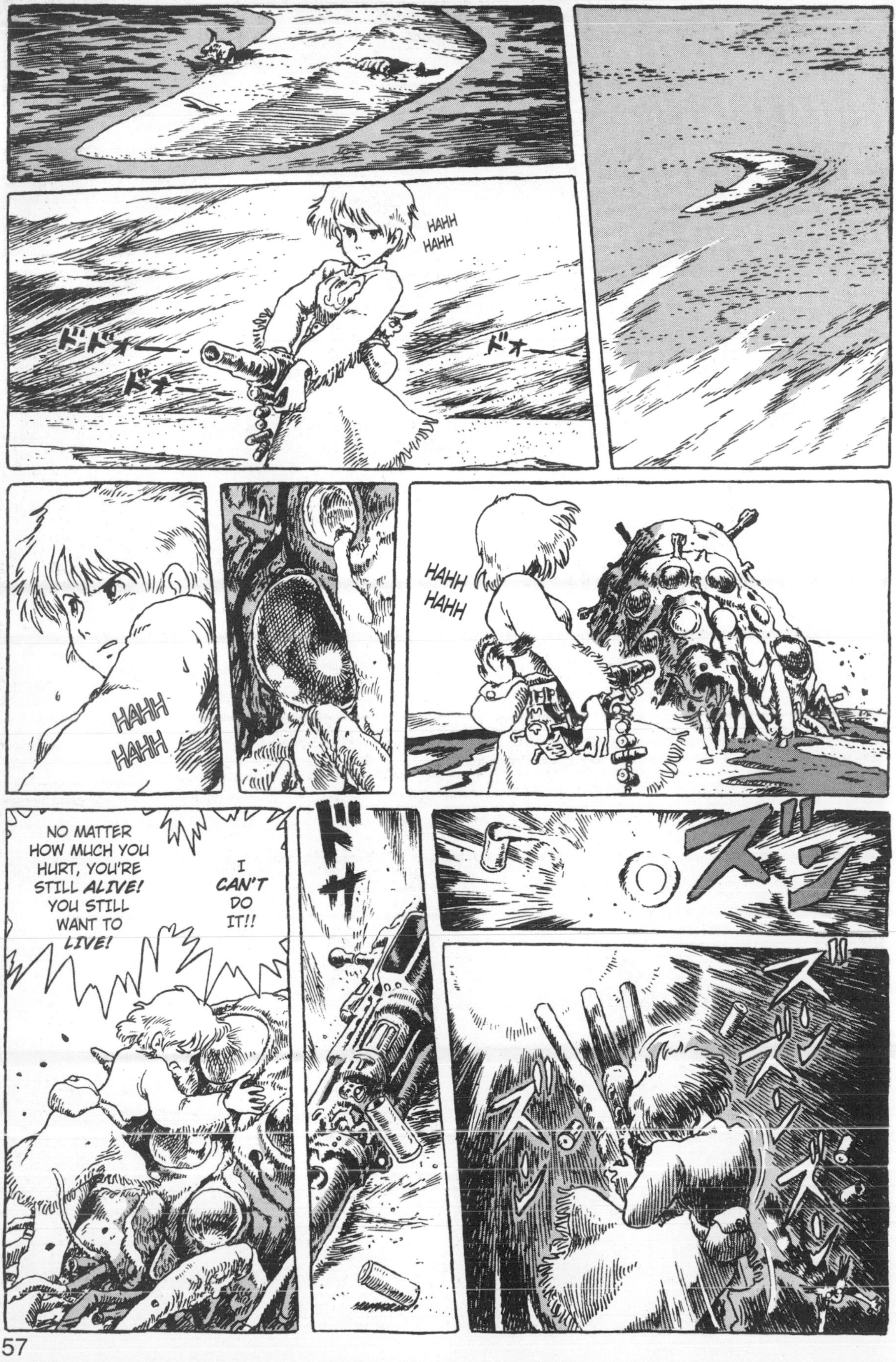
HAHH HAHH
HAHH HAHH
HAHH HAHH
I CAN'T DO IT!!
NO MATTER HOW MUCH YOU HURT, YOU'RE STILL ALIVE! YOU STILL WANT TO LIVE!

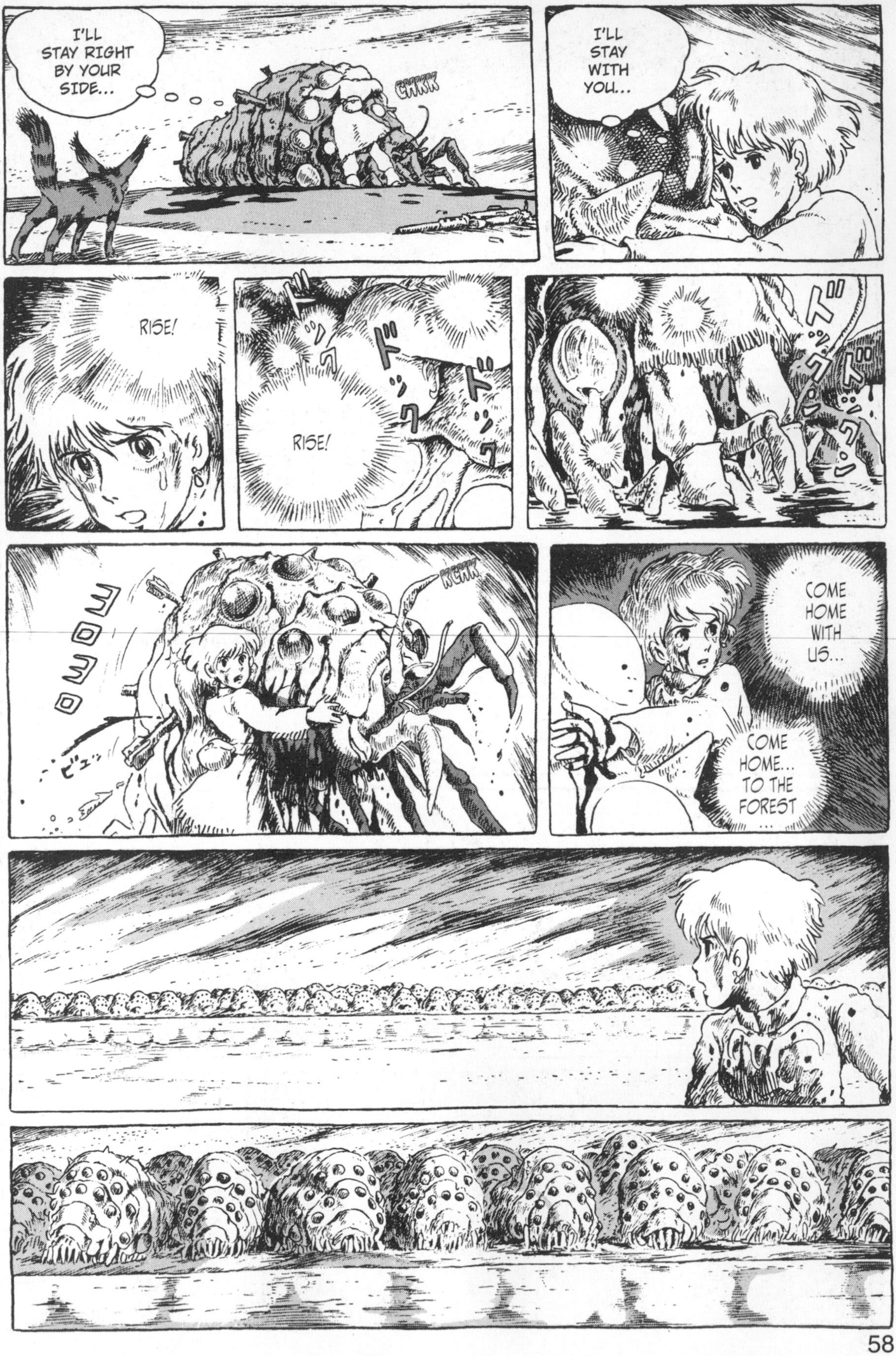
I'LL STAY WITH YOU...
I'LL STAY RIGHT BY YOUR SIDE...
RISE!
RISE!
COME HOME WITH US...
COME HOME... TO THE FOREST ...

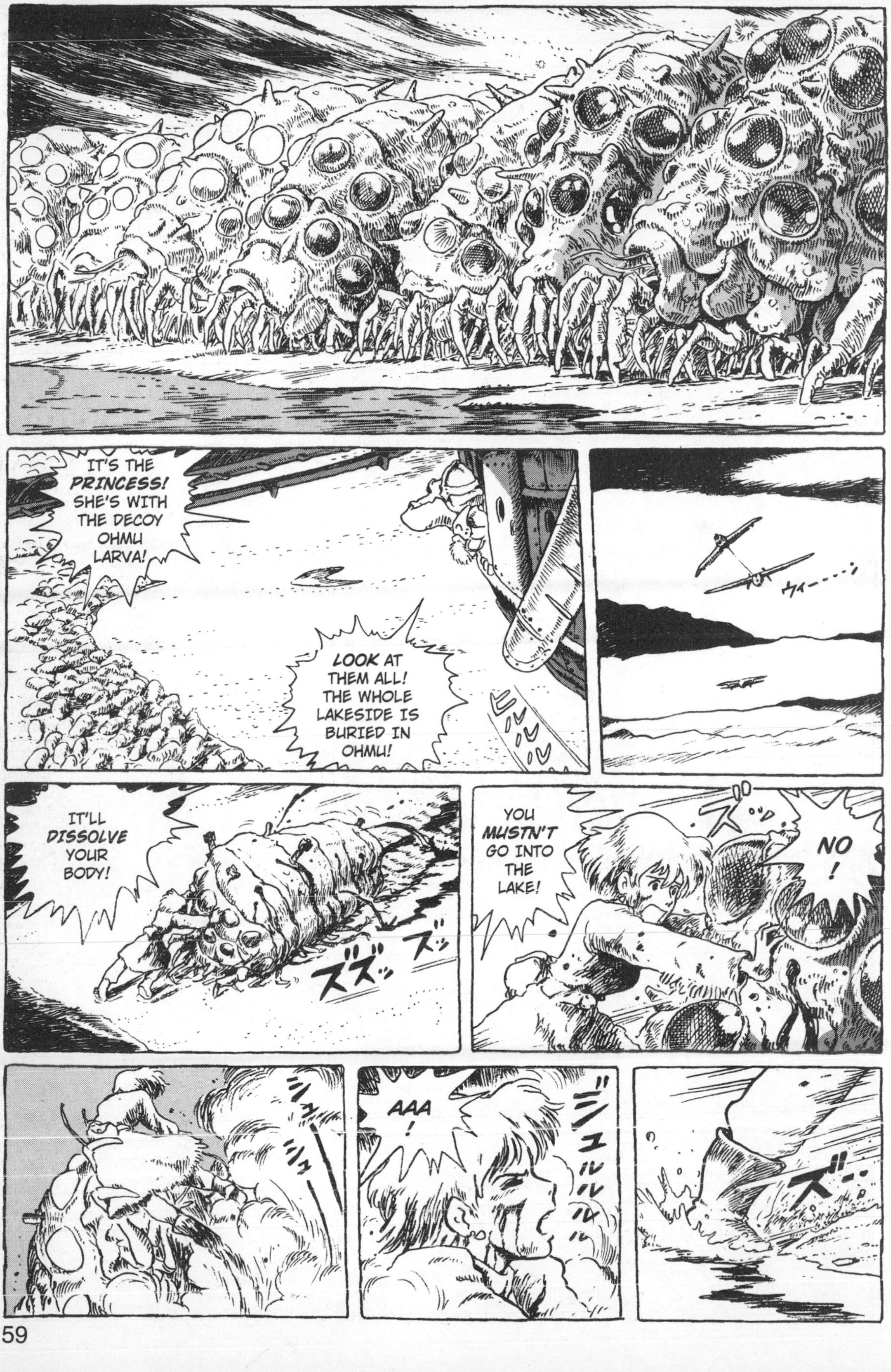

IT'S THE PRINCESS! SHE'S WITH THE DECOY OHMU LARVA!
LOOK AT THEM ALL! THE WHOLE LAKESIDE IS BURIED IN OHMU!
NO!
YOU MUSTN'T GO INTO THE LAKE!
IT'LL DISSOLVE YOUR BODY!
AAA!

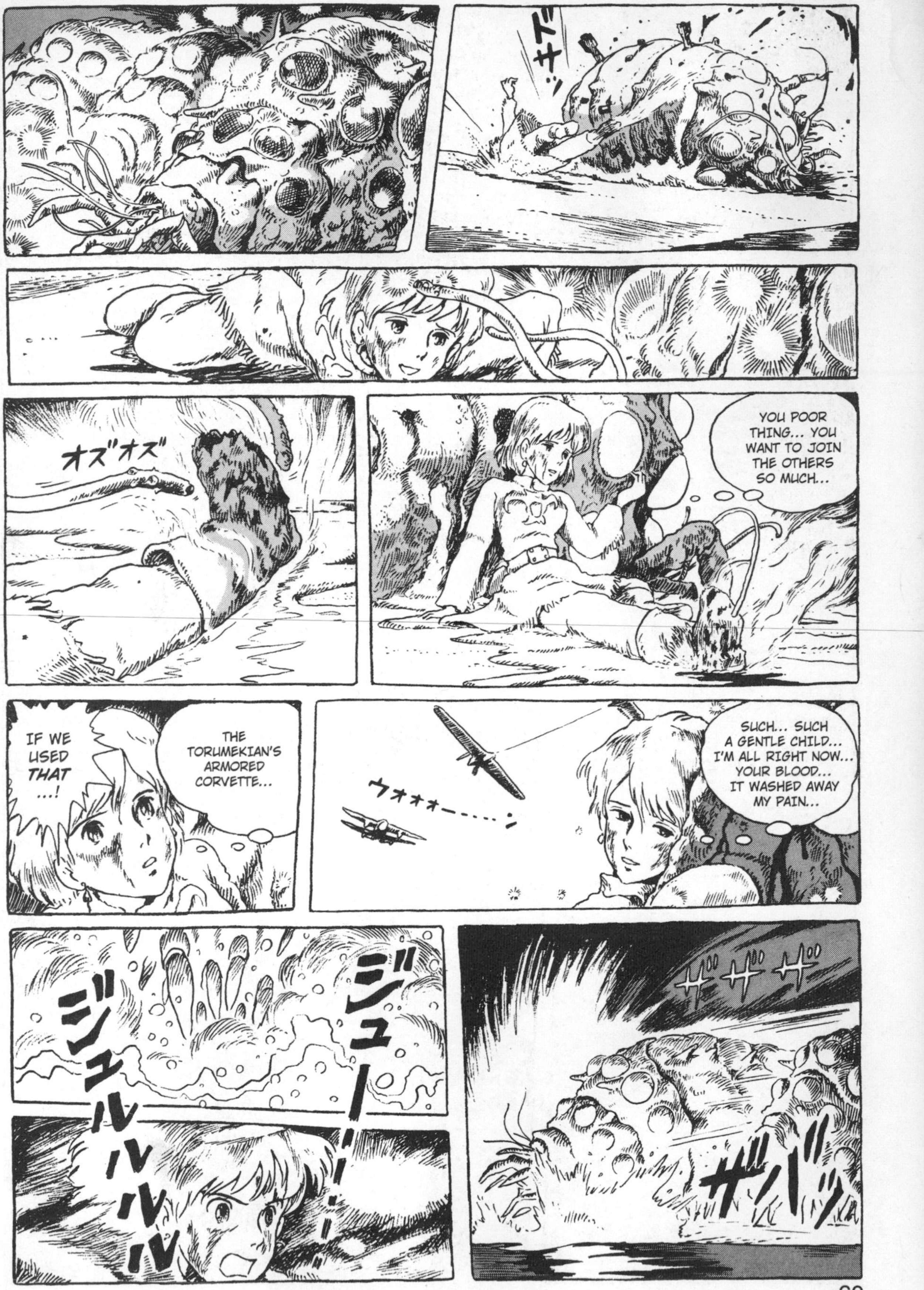
ドサッ
. . .
YOU POOR THING... YOU WANT TO JOIN THE OTHERS SO MUCH...
オズオズ
SUCH... SUCH A GENTLE CHILD... I'M ALL RIGHT NOW... YOUR BLOOD... IT WASHED AWAY MY PAIN...
ウォォォー・・・ン
THE TORUMEKIAN'S ARMORED CORVETTE...
IF WE USED ***THAT*** ...!
ザザザ
ザバッ
ジュー!!
ジュルルルル

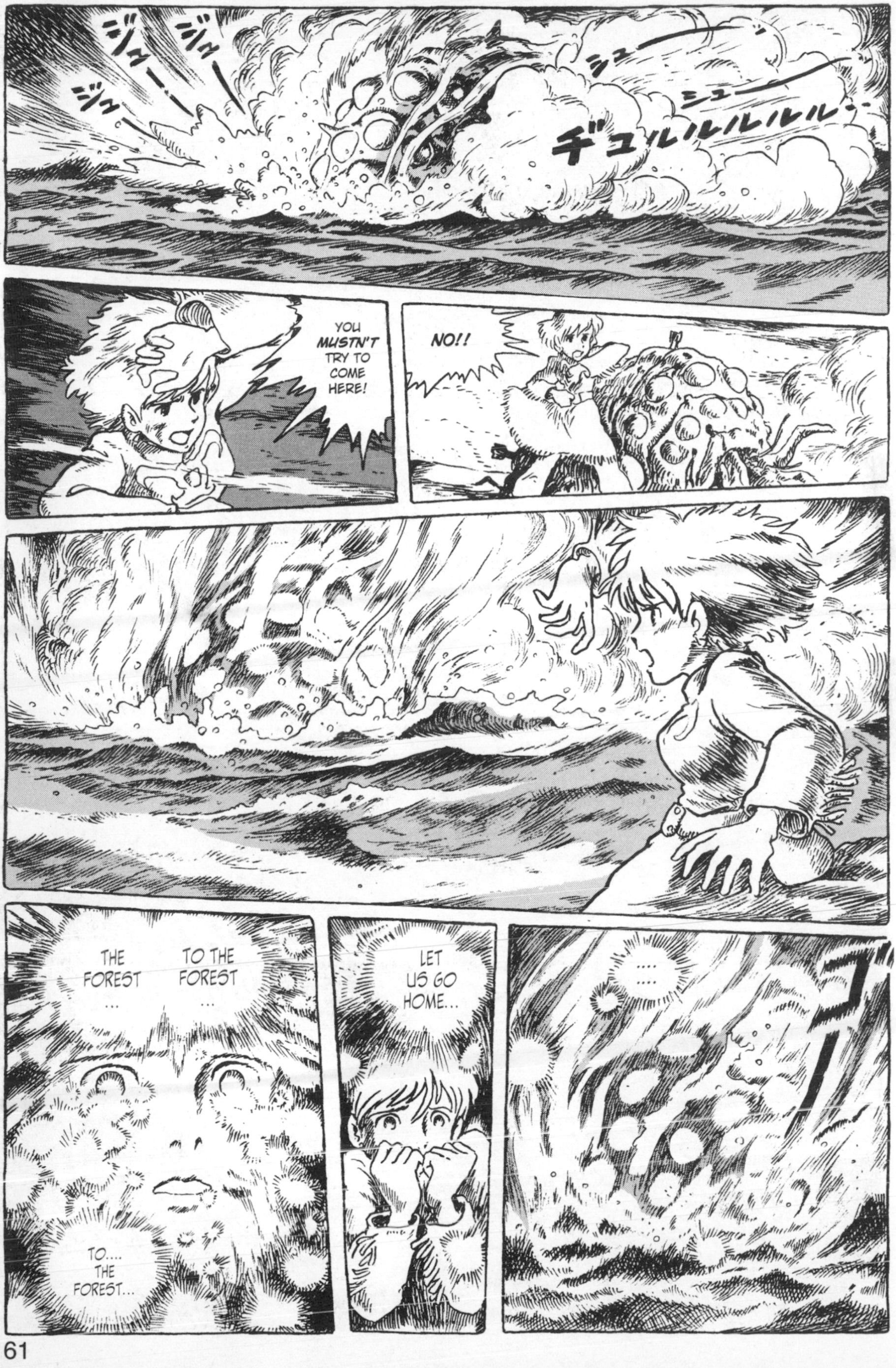
シュー
シュー
ギュルルルルル
ジュ
ジュー
ジュ
NO!!
YOU MUSTN'T TRY TO COME HERE!
ゴ
....
....
LET US GO HOME...
TO THE FOREST ...
THE FOREST ...
TO.... THE FOREST...

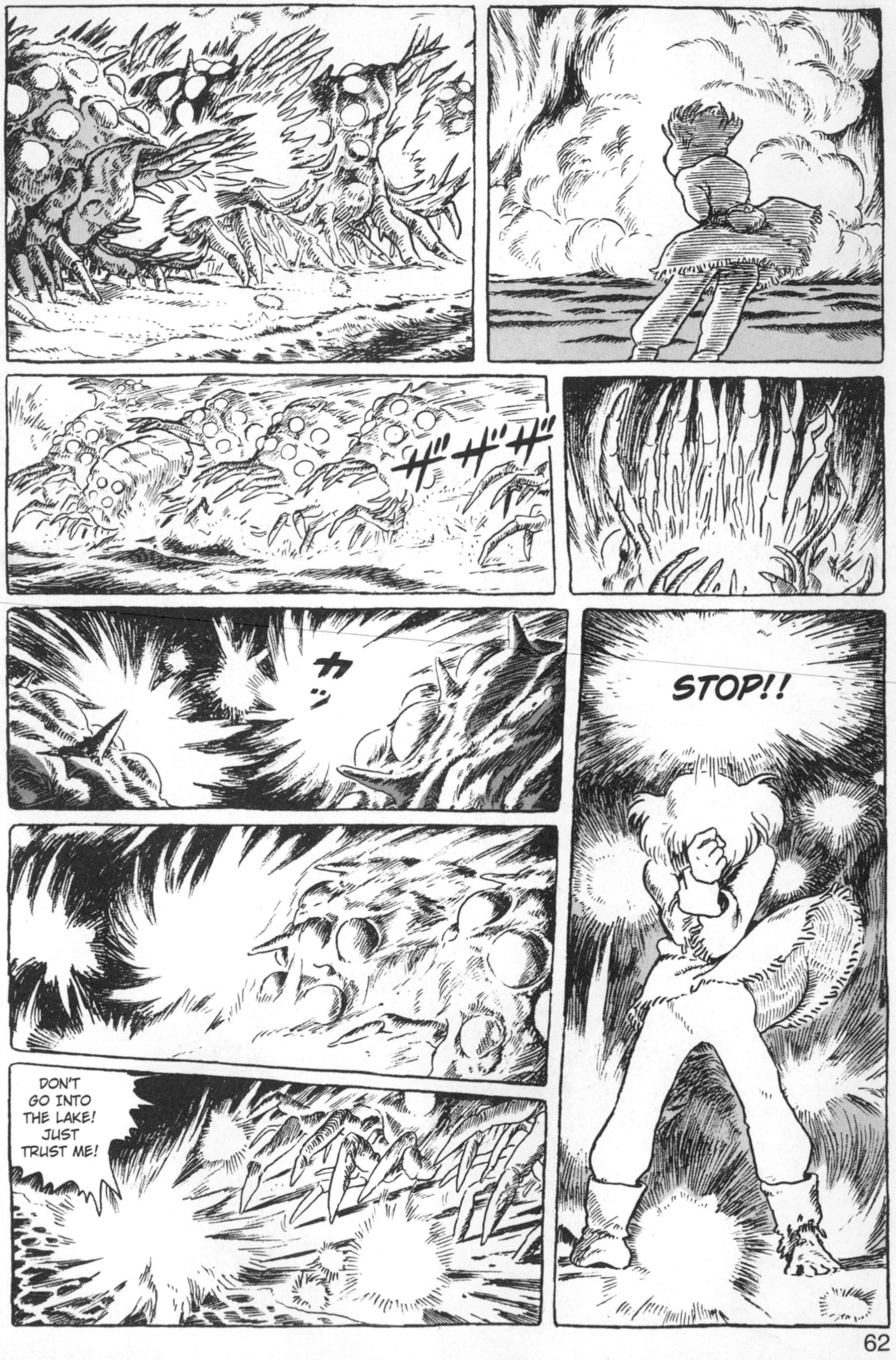
ザザザ
STOP!!
カッ
DON'T GO INTO THE LAKE! JUST TRUST ME!

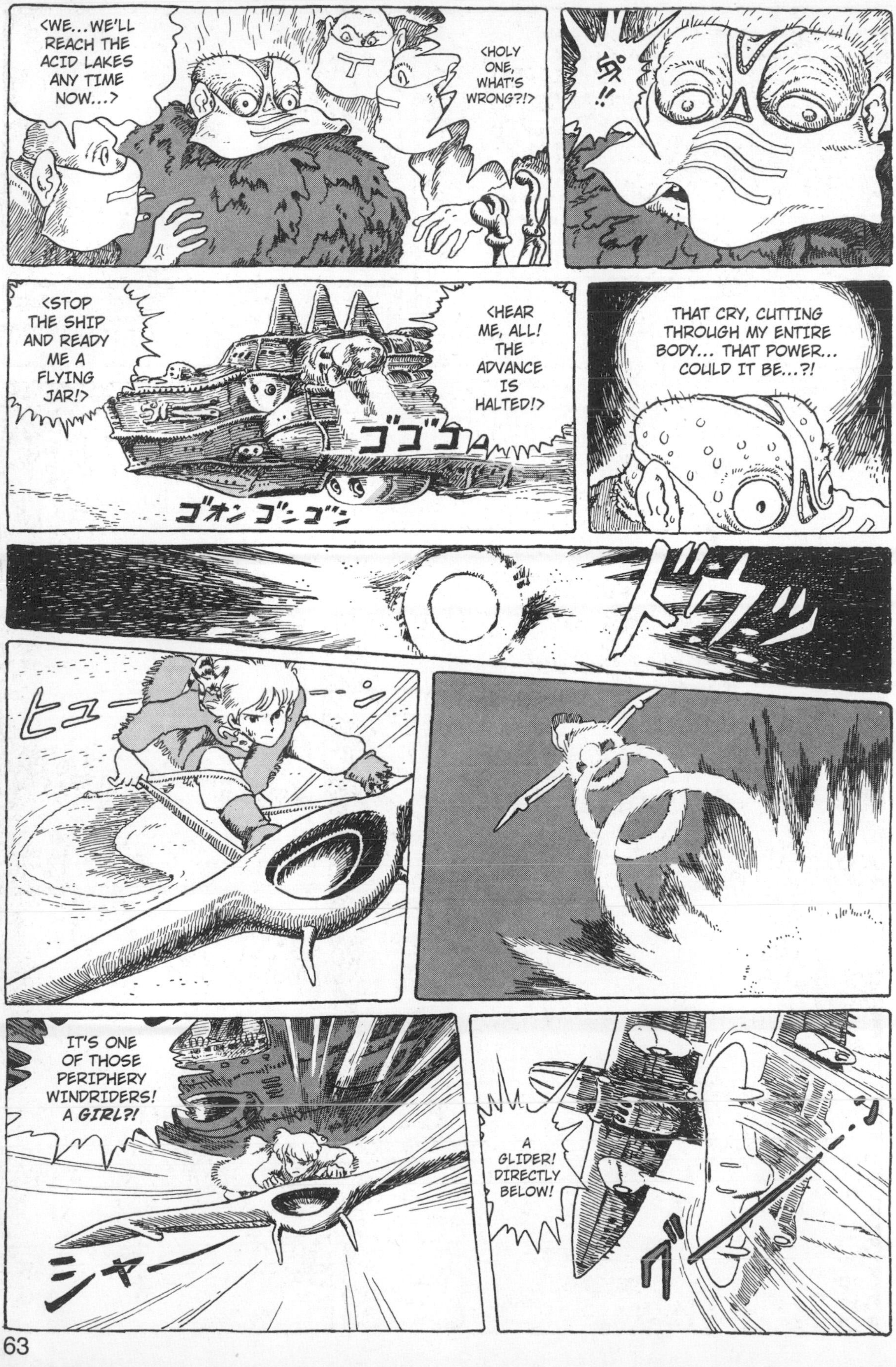
<HOLY ONE, WHAT'S WRONG?!>
<WE...WE'LL REACH THE ACID LAKES ANY TIME NOW...>
THAT CRY, CUTTING THROUGH MY ENTIRE BODY... THAT POWER... COULD IT BE...?!
<HEAR ME, ALL! THE ADVANCE IS HALTED!>
<STOP THE SHIP AND READY ME A FLYING JAR!>
ゴゴゴ
ドウッ
A GLIDER! DIRECTLY BELOW!
IT'S ONE OF THOSE PERIPHERY WINDRIDERS! A *GIRL*?!
シャー

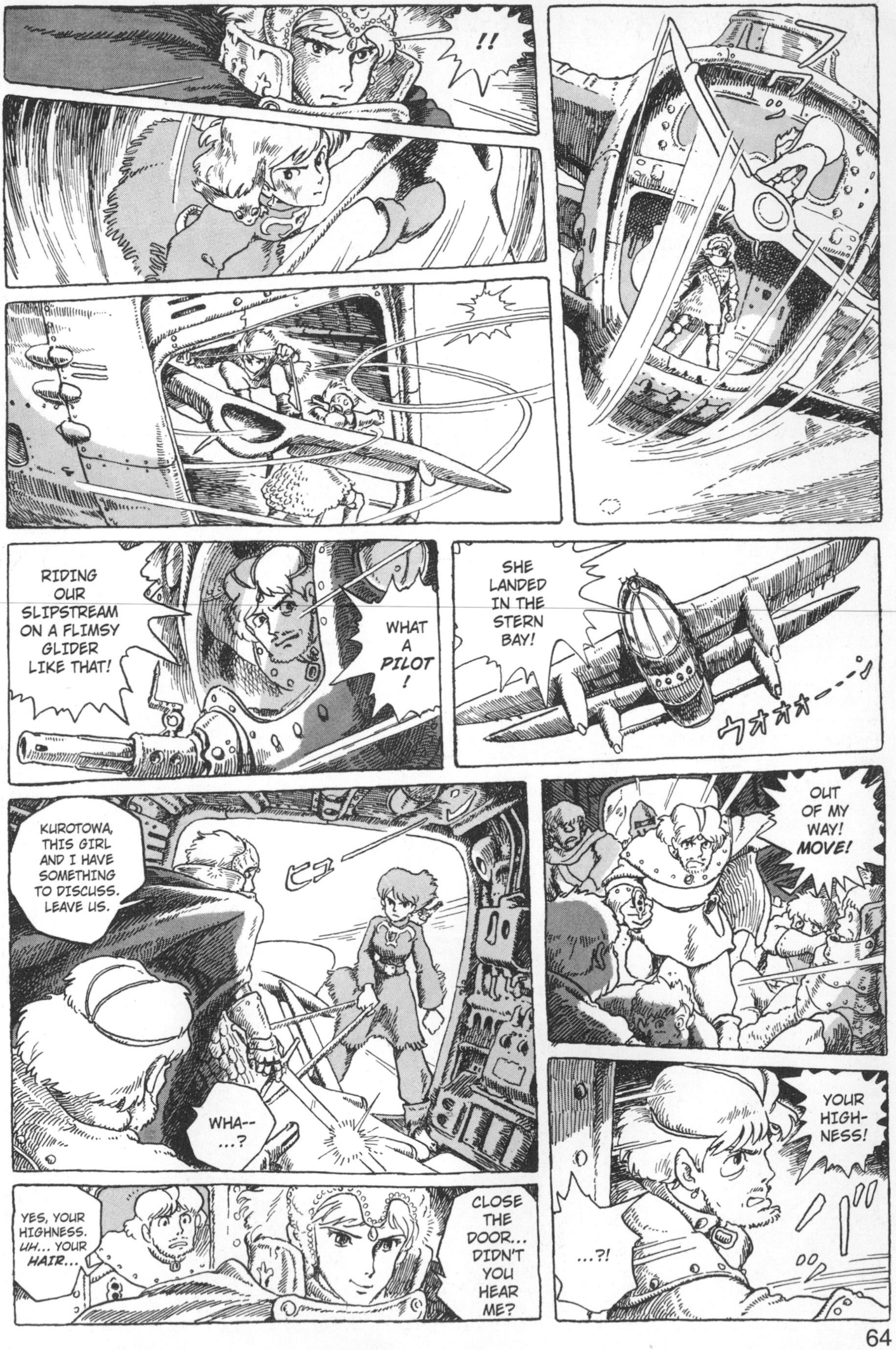
!!
SHE LANDED IN THE STERN BAY!
ウォオオー・・・ン
RIDING OUR SLIPSTREAM ON A FLIMSY GLIDER LIKE THAT!
WHAT A *PILOT*!
OUT OF MY WAY! *MOVE!*
YOUR HIGHNESS!
...?!
KUROTOWA, THIS GIRL AND I HAVE SOMETHING TO DISCUSS. LEAVE US.
ヒュ
WHA-- ...?
CLOSE THE DOOR... DIDN'T YOU HEAR ME?
YES, YOUR HIGHNESS. UH... YOUR *HAIR*...

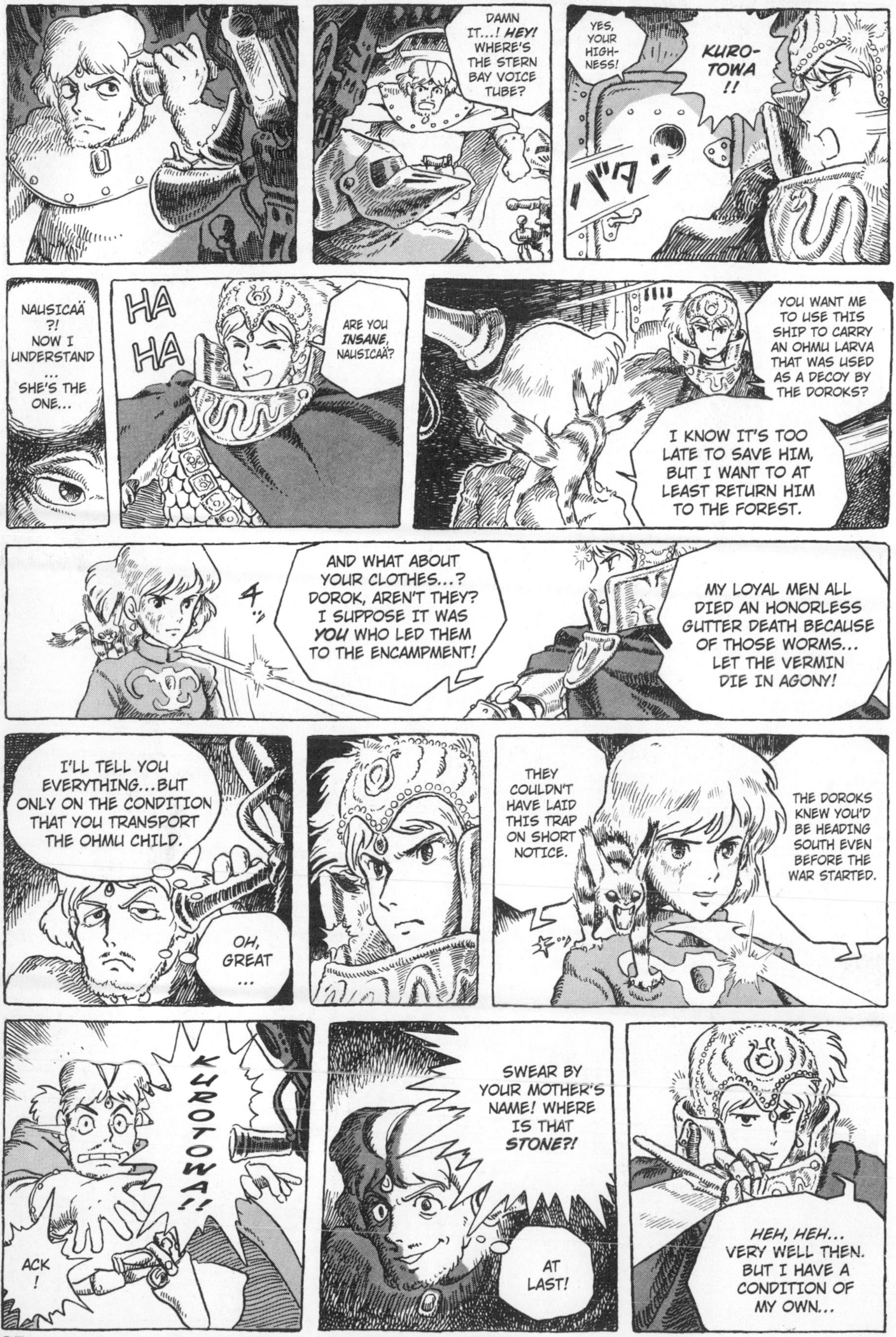
KURO-TOWA !!
YES, YOUR HIGH-NESS!
DAMN IT...! *HEY!* WHERE'S THE STERN BAY VOICE TUBE?
YOU WANT ME TO USE THIS SHIP TO CARRY AN OHMU LARVA THAT WAS USED AS A DECOY BY THE DOROKS?
I KNOW IT'S TOO LATE TO SAVE HIM, BUT I WANT TO AT LEAST RETURN HIM TO THE FOREST.
HA HA
ARE YOU *INSANE*, NAUSICAÄ?
NAUSICAÄ ?! NOW I UNDERSTAND ... SHE'S THE ONE...
MY LOYAL MEN ALL DIED AN HONORLESS GUTTER DEATH BECAUSE OF THOSE WORMS... LET THE VERMIN DIE IN AGONY!
AND WHAT ABOUT YOUR CLOTHES...? DOROK, AREN'T THEY? I SUPPOSE IT WAS *YOU* WHO LED THEM TO THE ENCAMPMENT!
THE DOROKS KNEW YOU'D BE HEADING SOUTH EVEN BEFORE THE WAR STARTED.
THEY COULDN'T HAVE LAID THIS TRAP ON SHORT NOTICE.
I'LL TELL YOU EVERYTHING...BUT ONLY ON THE CONDITION THAT YOU TRANSPORT THE OHMU CHILD.
OH, GREAT ...
HEH, HEH... VERY WELL THEN. BUT I HAVE A CONDITION OF MY OWN...
SWEAR BY YOUR MOTHER'S NAME! WHERE IS THAT *STONE?!*
AT LAST!
KUROTOWA!!
ACK !

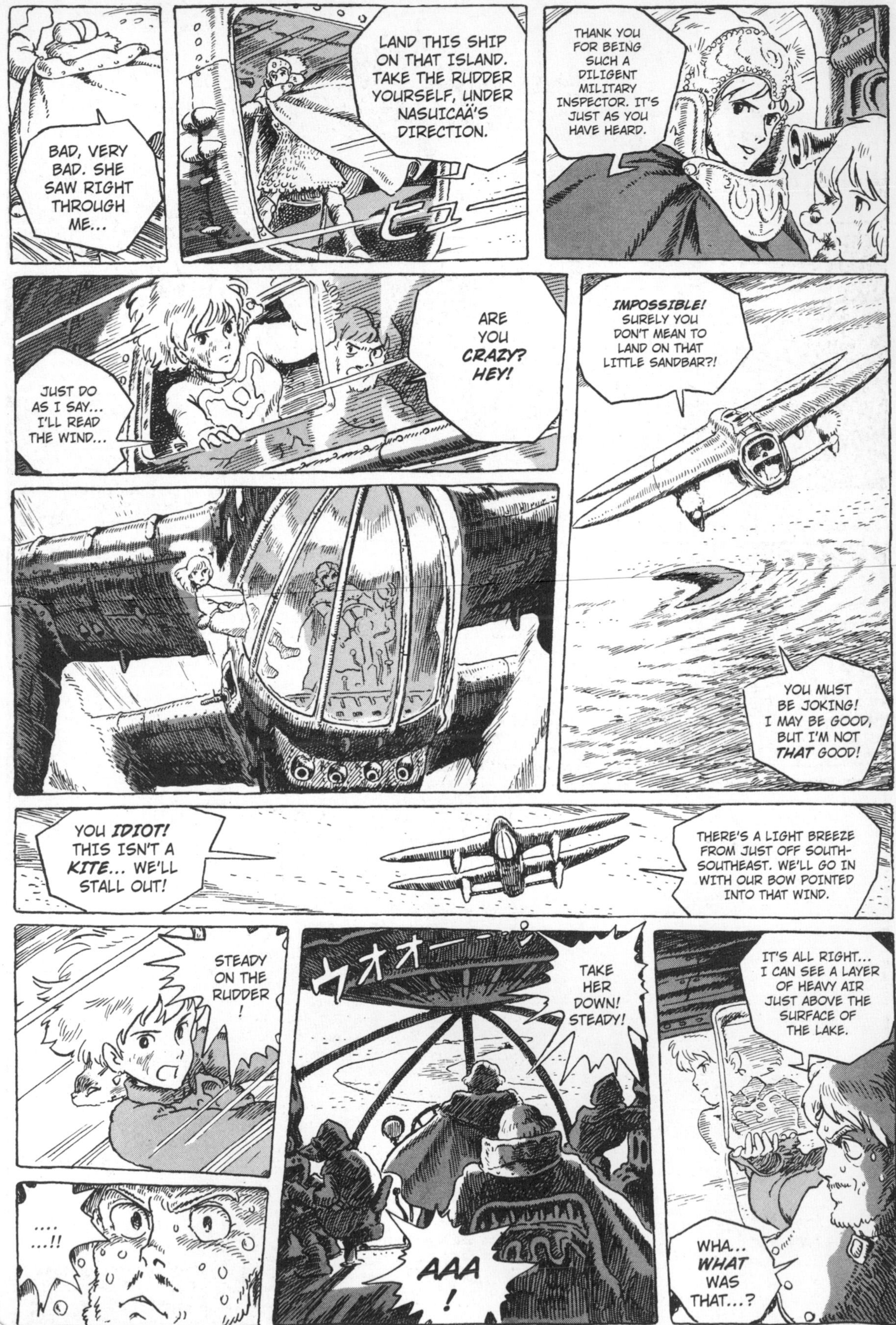
THANK YOU FOR BEING SUCH A DILIGENT MILITARY INSPECTOR. IT'S JUST AS YOU HAVE HEARD.
LAND THIS SHIP ON THAT ISLAND. TAKE THE RUDDER YOURSELF, UNDER NAUSICAÄ'S DIRECTION.
ヒュー
BAD, VERY BAD. SHE SAW RIGHT THROUGH ME...
IMPOSSIBLE! SURELY YOU DON'T MEAN TO LAND ON THAT LITTLE SANDBAR?!
YOU MUST BE JOKING! I MAY BE GOOD, BUT I'M NOT *THAT* GOOD!
ARE YOU *CRAZY? HEY!*
JUST DO AS I SAY... I'LL READ THE WIND...
THERE'S A LIGHT BREEZE FROM JUST OFF SOUTH-SOUTHEAST. WE'LL GO IN WITH OUR BOW POINTED INTO THAT WIND.
YOU *IDIOT!* THIS ISN'T A *KITE*... WE'LL STALL OUT!
IT'S ALL RIGHT... I CAN SEE A LAYER OF HEAVY AIR JUST ABOVE THE SURFACE OF THE LAKE.
WHA... *WHAT* WAS THAT...?
ウオオーー
TAKE HER DOWN! STEADY!
AAA!
STEADY ON THE RUDDER!
....!!

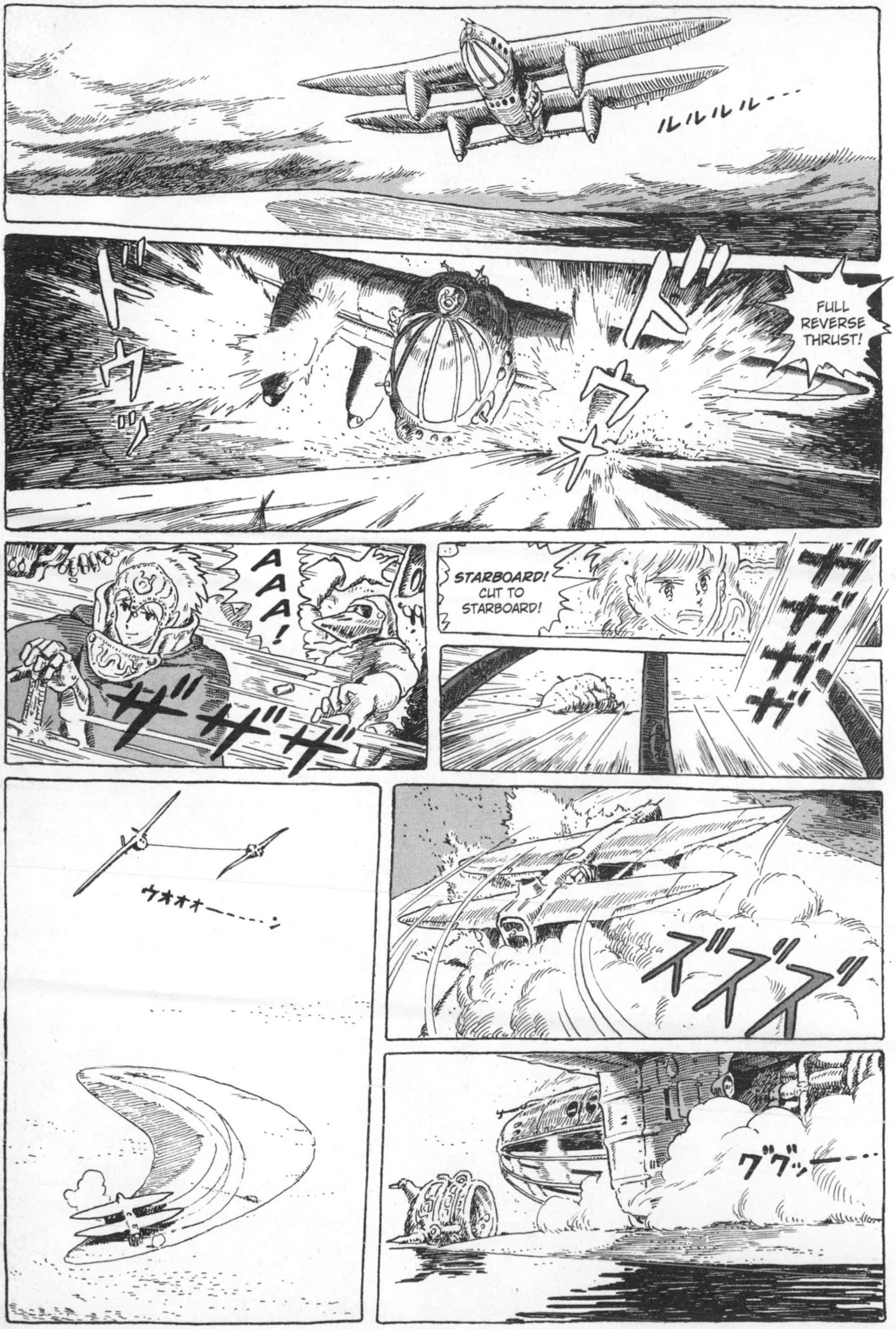
ルルルルー・・・
FULL REVERSE THRUST!
STARBOARD! CUT TO STARBOARD!
ガガガガ
AAAA!
ザザザ
ズズズ
グヴッー・・・
ウオオオー・・・ン

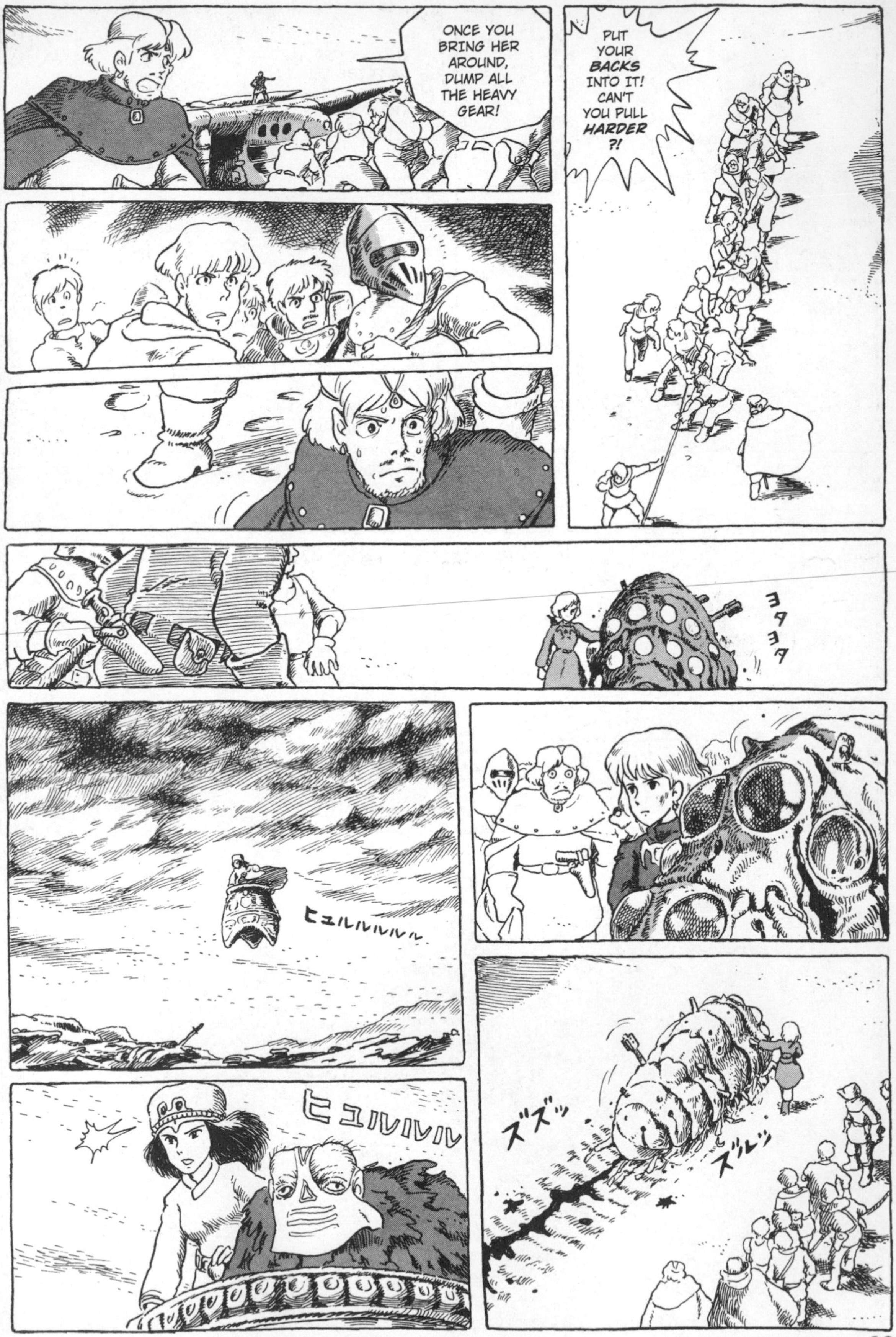
PUT YOUR **BACKS** INTO IT! CAN'T YOU PULL **HARDER** ?!
ONCE YOU BRING HER AROUND, DUMP ALL THE HEAVY GEAR!
ヨタヨタ
ズズッ
ズルッ
ヒュルルルルルル
ヒュルルルル

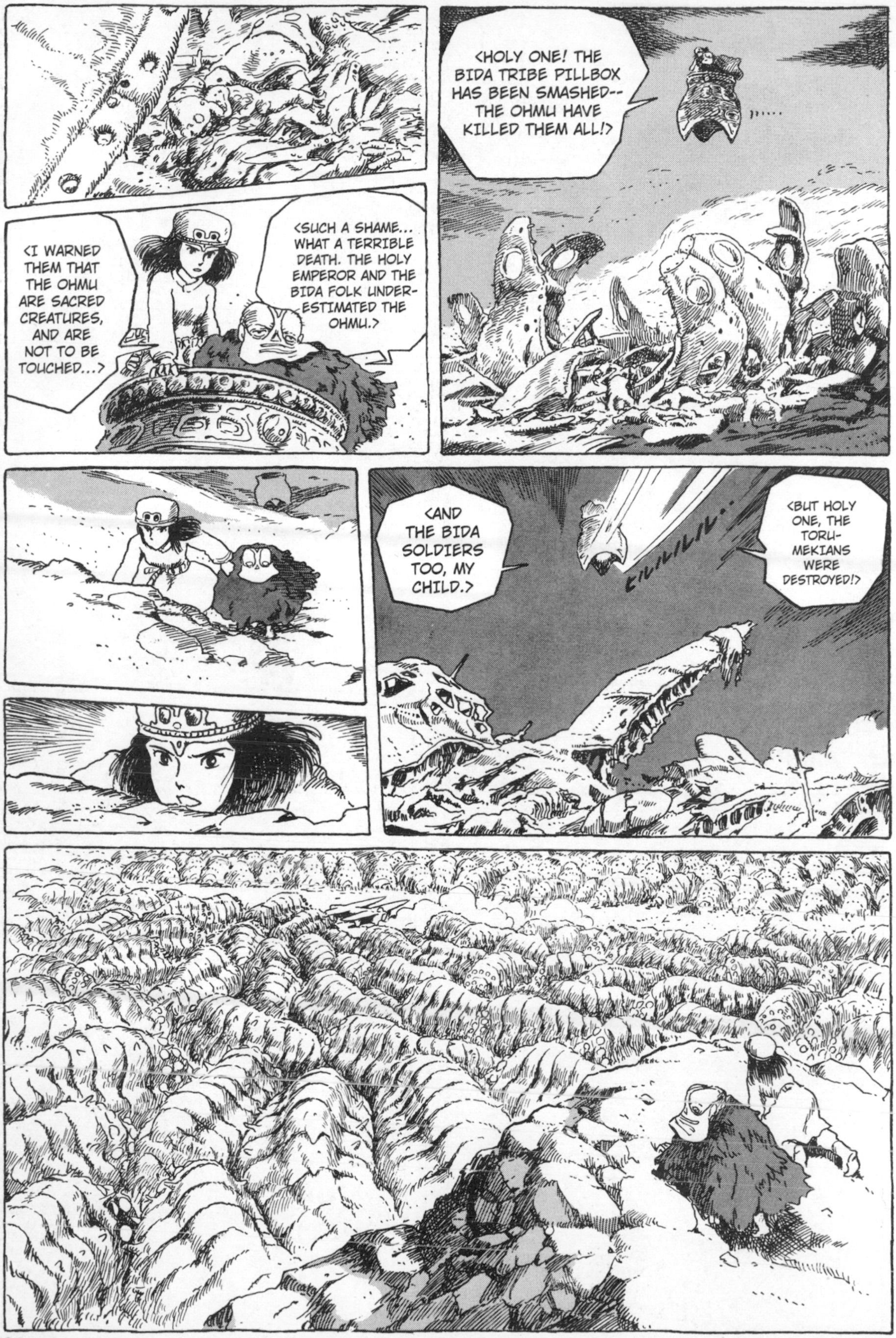
<HOLY ONE! THE BIDA TRIBE PILLBOX HAS BEEN SMASHED-- THE OHMU HAVE KILLED THEM ALL!>
......
<SUCH A SHAME... WHAT A TERRIBLE DEATH. THE HOLY EMPEROR AND THE BIDA FOLK UNDER-ESTIMATED THE OHMU.>
<I WARNED THEM THAT THE OHMU ARE SACRED CREATURES, AND ARE NOT TO BE TOUCHED...>
<BUT HOLY ONE, THE TORU-MEKIANS WERE DESTROYED!>
<AND THE BIDA SOLDIERS TOO, MY CHILD.>

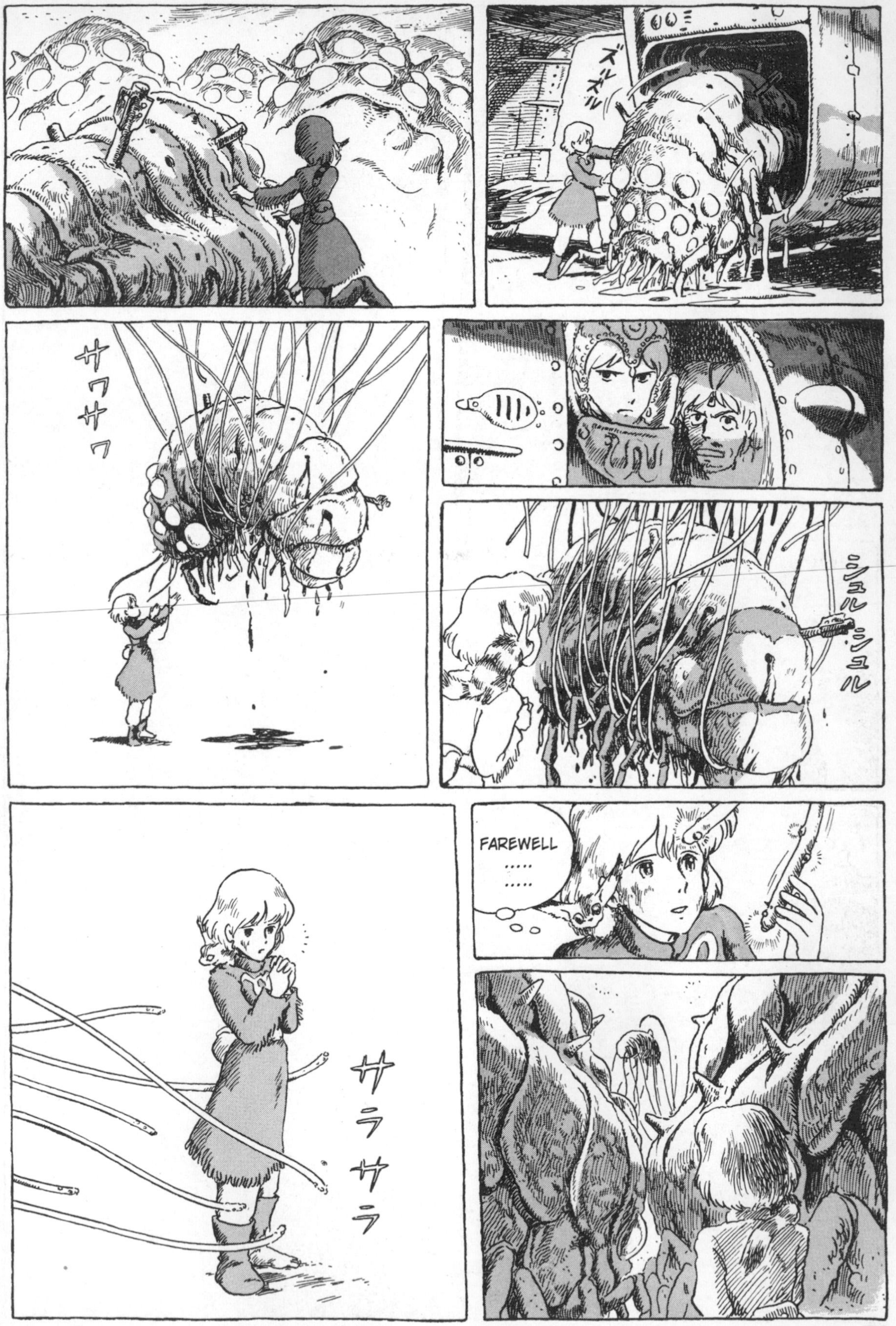
ズルズル
シュル シュル
サワサワ
FAREWELL ....
サラサラ

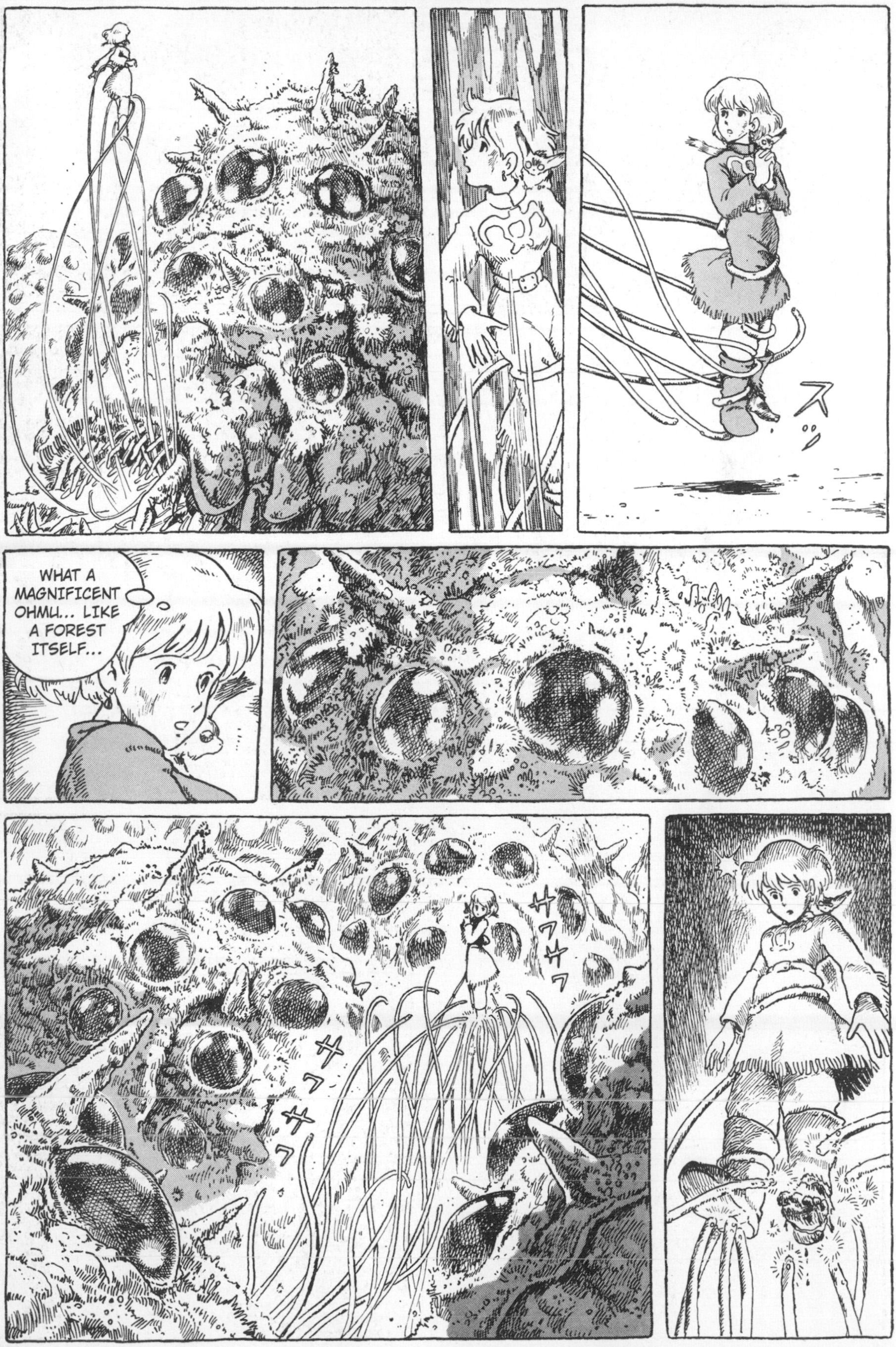
ス
WHAT A MAGNIFICENT OHMU... LIKE A FOREST ITSELF...
サワサワ
サワサワ

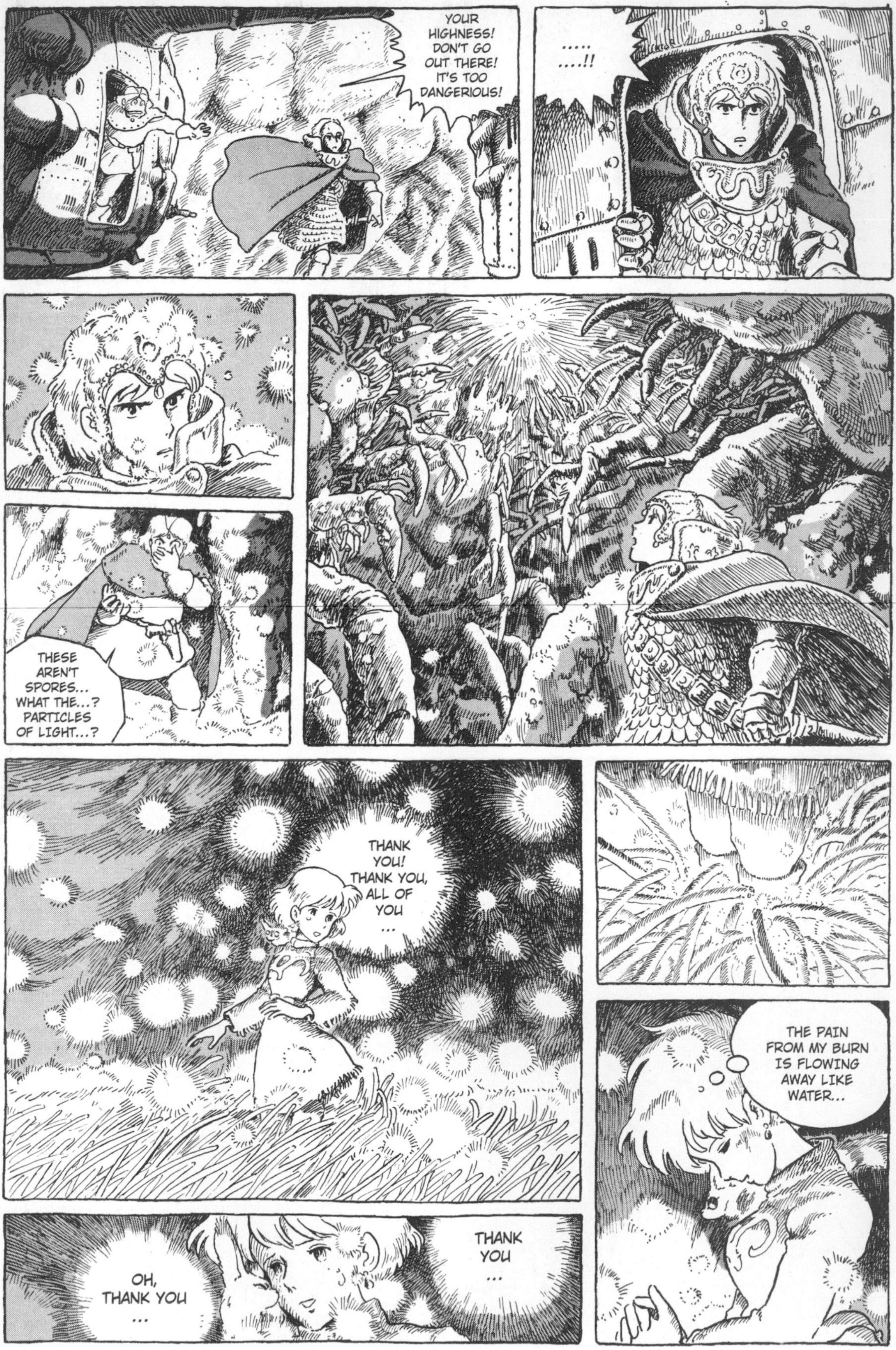
.....
....!!
YOUR HIGHNESS! DON'T GO OUT THERE! IT'S TOO DANGERIOUS!
THESE AREN'T SPORES... WHAT THE...? PARTICLES OF LIGHT...?
THANK YOU! THANK YOU, ALL OF YOU ...
THE PAIN FROM MY BURN IS FLOWING AWAY LIKE WATER...
THANK YOU ...
OH, THANK YOU ...

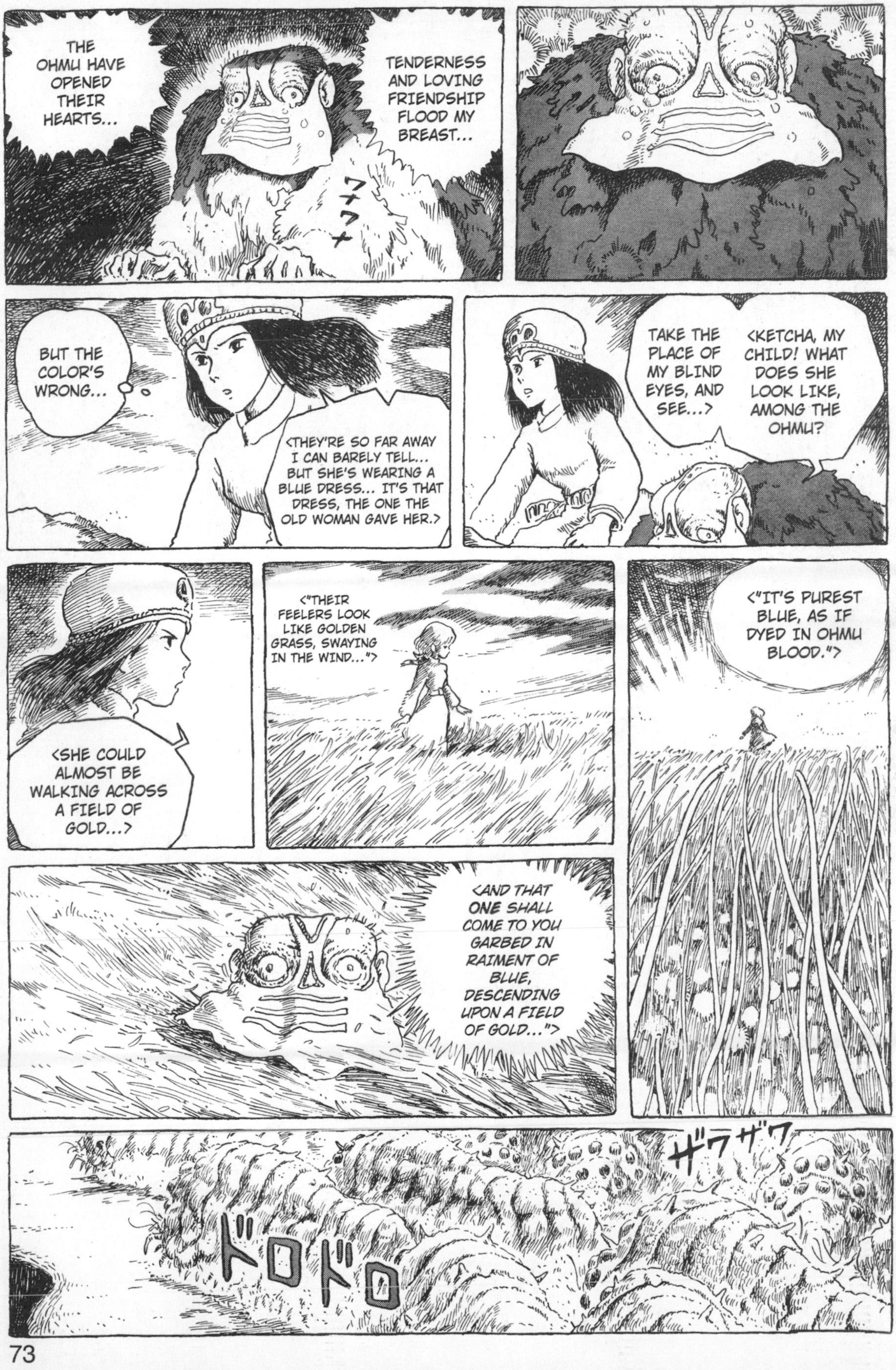
THE OHMU HAVE OPENED THEIR HEARTS...
TENDERNESS AND LOVING FRIENDSHIP FLOOD MY BREAST...
ワナワナ
<KETCHA, MY CHILD! WHAT DOES SHE LOOK LIKE, AMONG THE OHMU?
TAKE THE PLACE OF MY BLIND EYES, AND SEE...>
<THEY'RE SO FAR AWAY I CAN BARELY TELL... BUT SHE'S WEARING A BLUE DRESS... IT'S THAT DRESS, THE ONE THE OLD WOMAN GAVE HER.>
BUT THE COLOR'S WRONG...
<"IT'S PUREST BLUE, AS IF DYED IN OHMU BLOOD.">
<"THEIR FEELERS LOOK LIKE GOLDEN GRASS, SWAYING IN THE WIND...">
<SHE COULD ALMOST BE WALKING ACROSS A FIELD OF GOLD...>
<AND THAT ONE SHALL COME TO YOU GARBED IN RAIMENT OF BLUE, DESCENDING UPON A FIELD OF GOLD...">
ザワザワ
ドロドロ

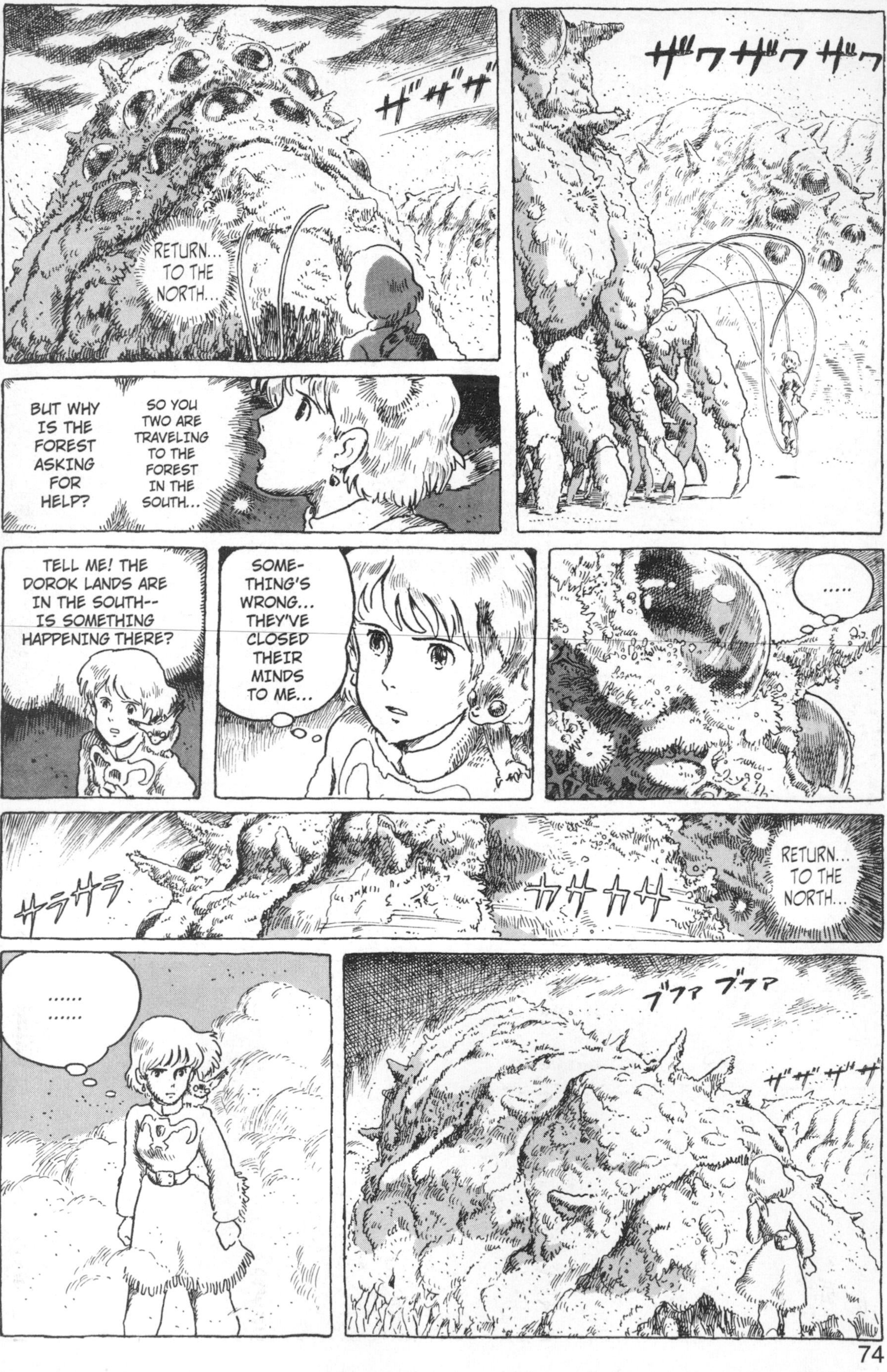
ザワザワザワ
ザザザ
RETURN... TO THE NORTH...
SO YOU TWO ARE TRAVELING TO THE FOREST IN THE SOUTH...
BUT WHY IS THE FOREST ASKING FOR HELP?
.....
SOMETHING'S WRONG... THEY'VE CLOSED THEIR MINDS TO ME...
TELL ME! THE DOROK LANDS ARE IN THE SOUTH-- IS SOMETHING HAPPENING THERE?
RETURN... TO THE NORTH...
カサカサ
サラサラ
ブファ ブファ
ザザザザ
....

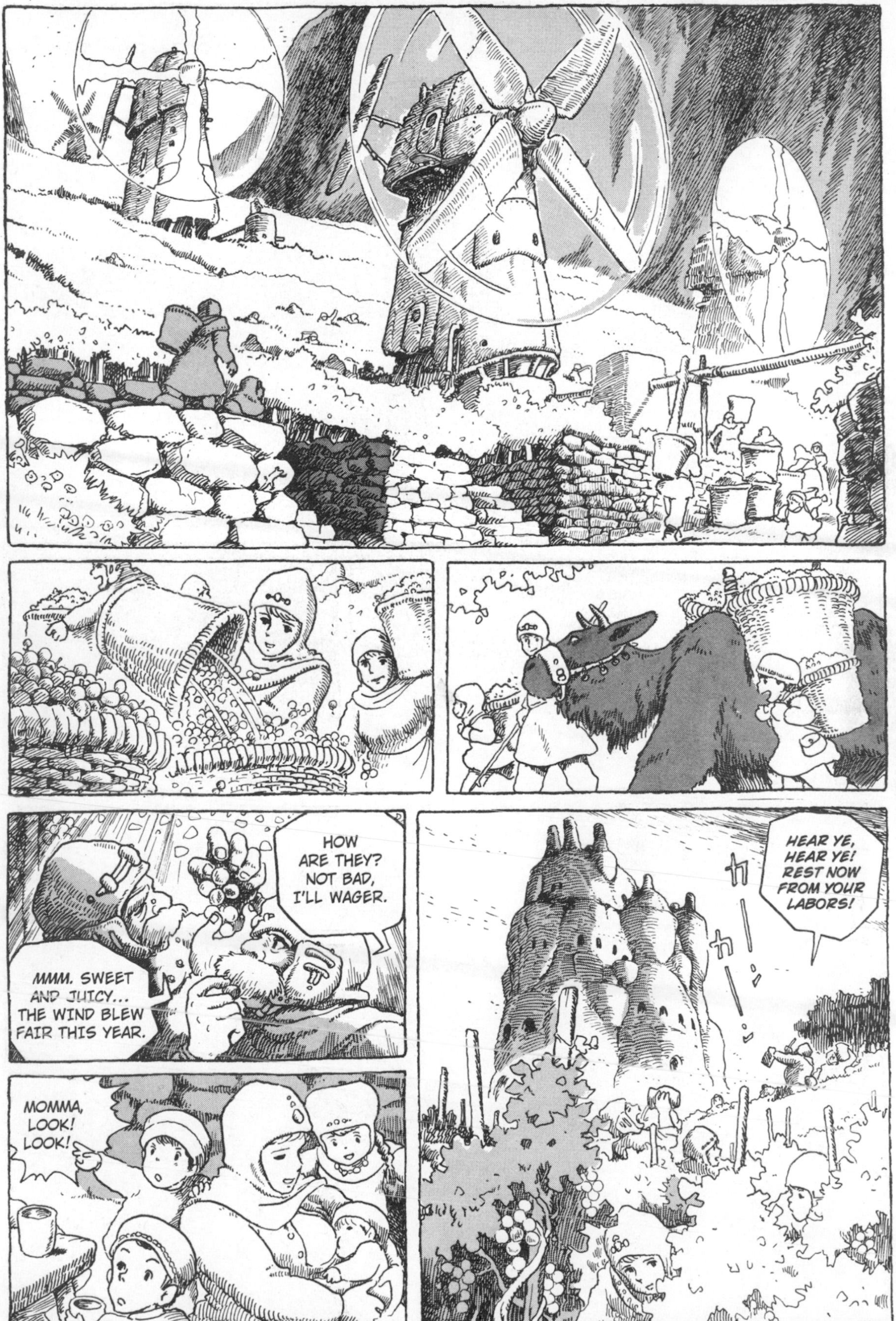
HEAR YE, HEAR YE! REST NOW FROM YOUR LABORS!
HOW ARE THEY? NOT BAD, I'LL WAGER.
MMM. SWEET AND JUICY... THE WIND BLEW FAIR THIS YEAR.
MOMMA, LOOK! LOOK!

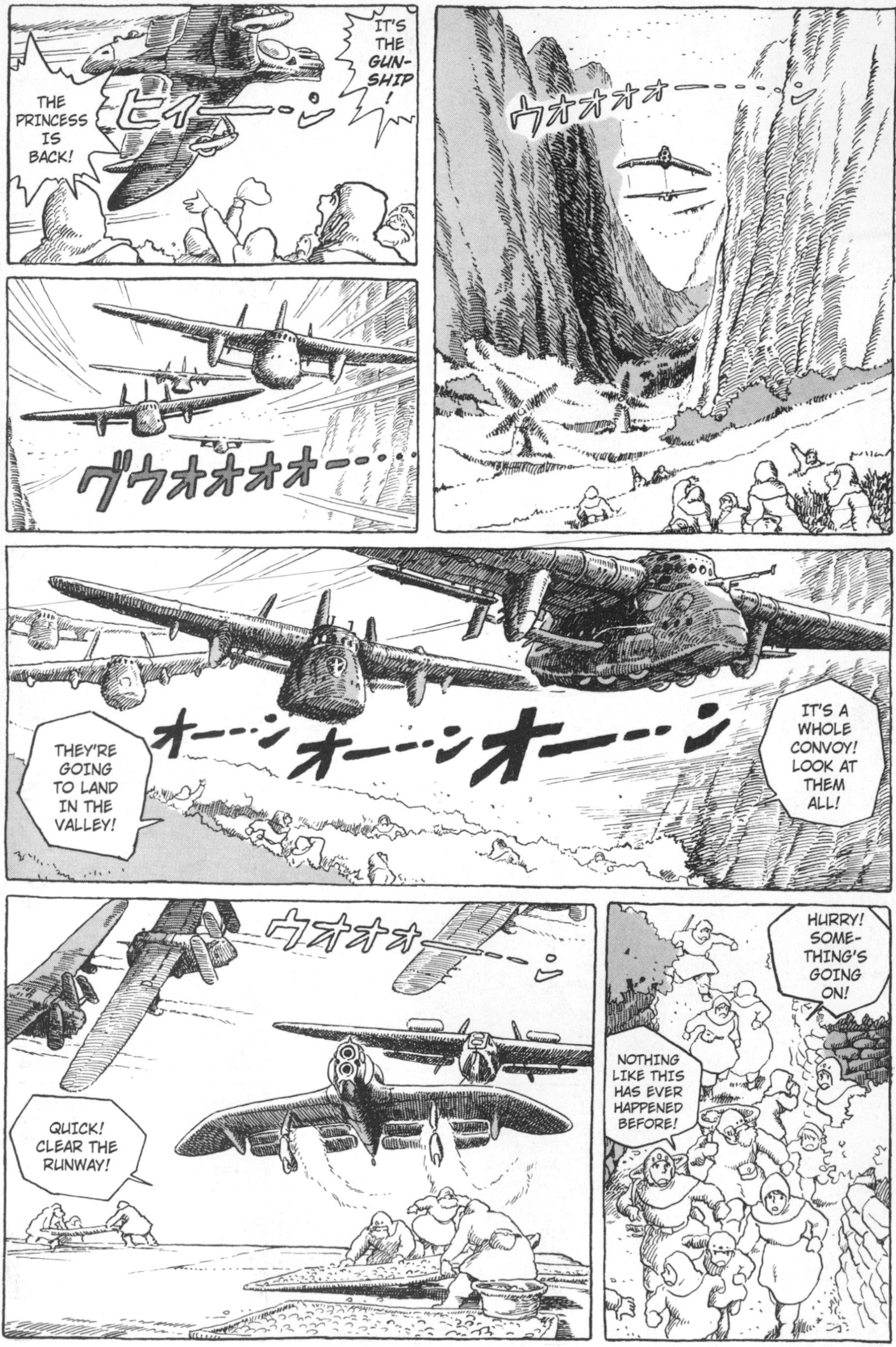
ウオオオオー・・・ン
IT'S THE GUNSHIP!
ヒィー・・ン
THE PRINCESS IS BACK!
グウオオオオー・・・
IT'S A WHOLE CONVOY! LOOK AT THEM ALL!
オー・・ンオー・・ンオー・・ン
THEY'RE GOING TO LAND IN THE VALLEY!
HURRY! SOMETHING'S GOING ON!
NOTHING LIKE THIS HAS EVER HAPPENED BEFORE!
ウオオオオー・・ン
QUICK! CLEAR THE RUNWAY!

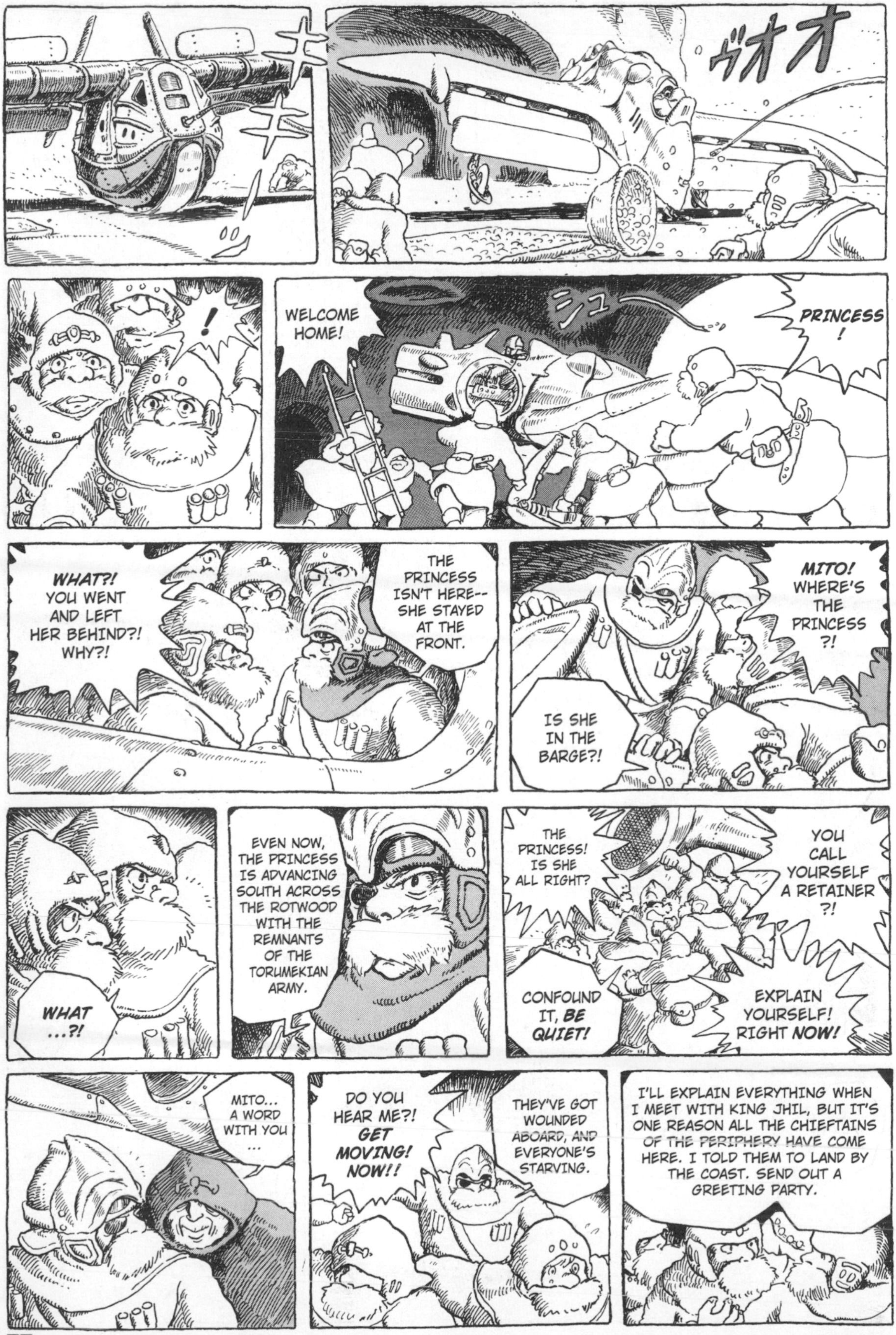
ヴオオ
ギギギ
シュー
PRINCESS !
WELCOME HOME!
!
MITO! WHERE'S THE PRINCESS ?!
IS SHE IN THE BARGE?!
THE PRINCESS ISN'T HERE-- SHE STAYED AT THE FRONT.
WHAT?! YOU WENT AND LEFT HER BEHIND?! WHY?!
YOU CALL YOURSELF A RETAINER ?!
THE PRINCESS! IS SHE ALL RIGHT?
EXPLAIN YOURSELF! RIGHT NOW!
CONFOUND IT, BE QUIET!
EVEN NOW, THE PRINCESS IS ADVANCING SOUTH ACROSS THE ROTWOOD WITH THE REMNANTS OF THE TORUMEKIAN ARMY.
WHAT ...?!
I'LL EXPLAIN EVERYTHING WHEN I MEET WITH KING JHIL, BUT IT'S ONE REASON ALL THE CHIEFTAINS OF THE PERIPHERY HAVE COME HERE. I TOLD THEM TO LAND BY THE COAST. SEND OUT A GREETING PARTY.
THEY'VE GOT WOUNDED ABOARD, AND EVERYONE'S STARVING.
DO YOU HEAR ME?! GET MOVING! NOW!!
MITO... A WORD WITH YOU ...

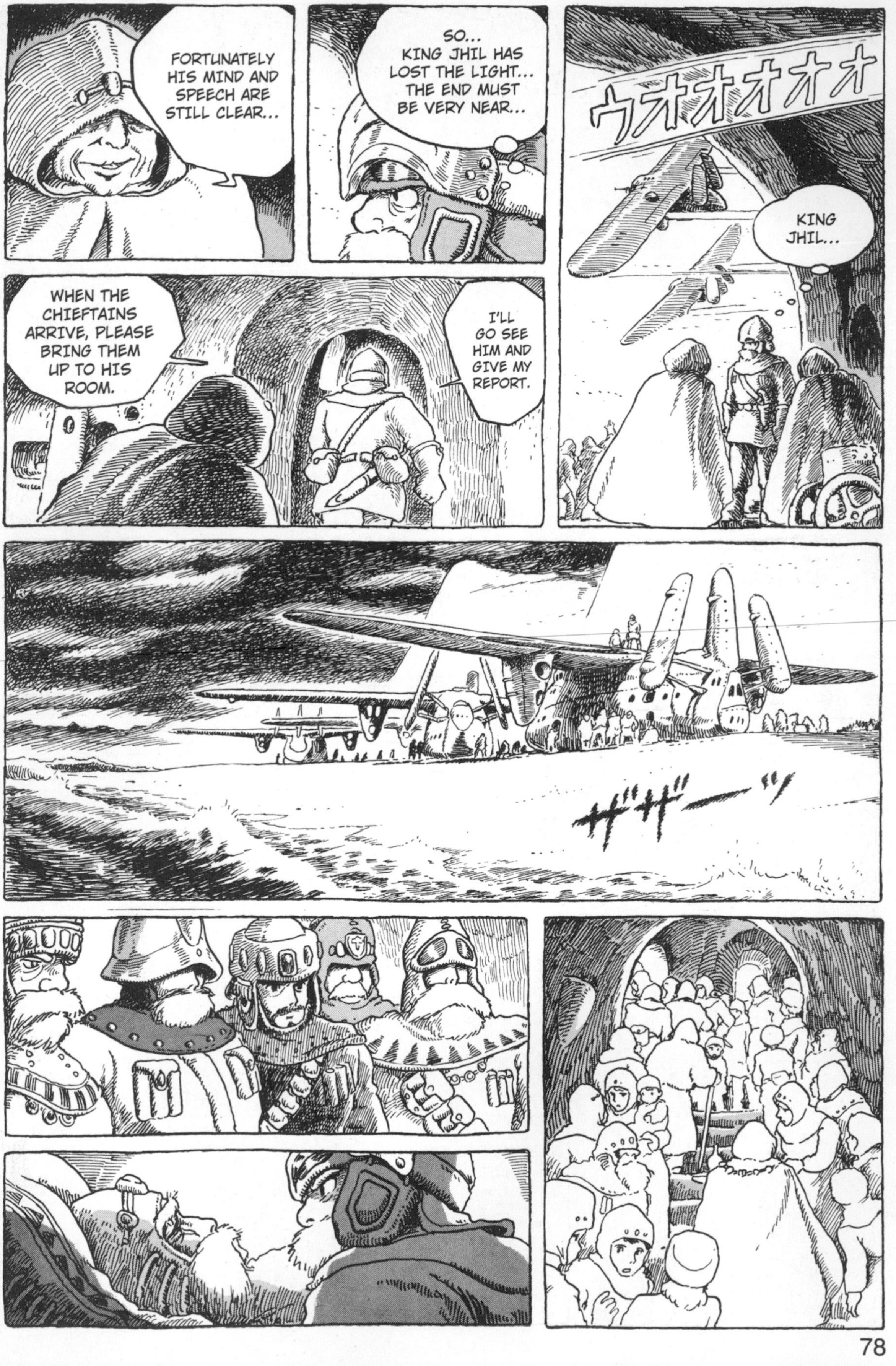
ウオオオオオ
KING JHIL...
SO... KING JHIL HAS LOST THE LIGHT... THE END MUST BE VERY NEAR...
FORTUNATELY HIS MIND AND SPEECH ARE STILL CLEAR...
I'LL GO SEE HIM AND GIVE MY REPORT.
WHEN THE CHIEFTAINS ARRIVE, PLEASE BRING THEM UP TO HIS ROOM.
ザザーッ

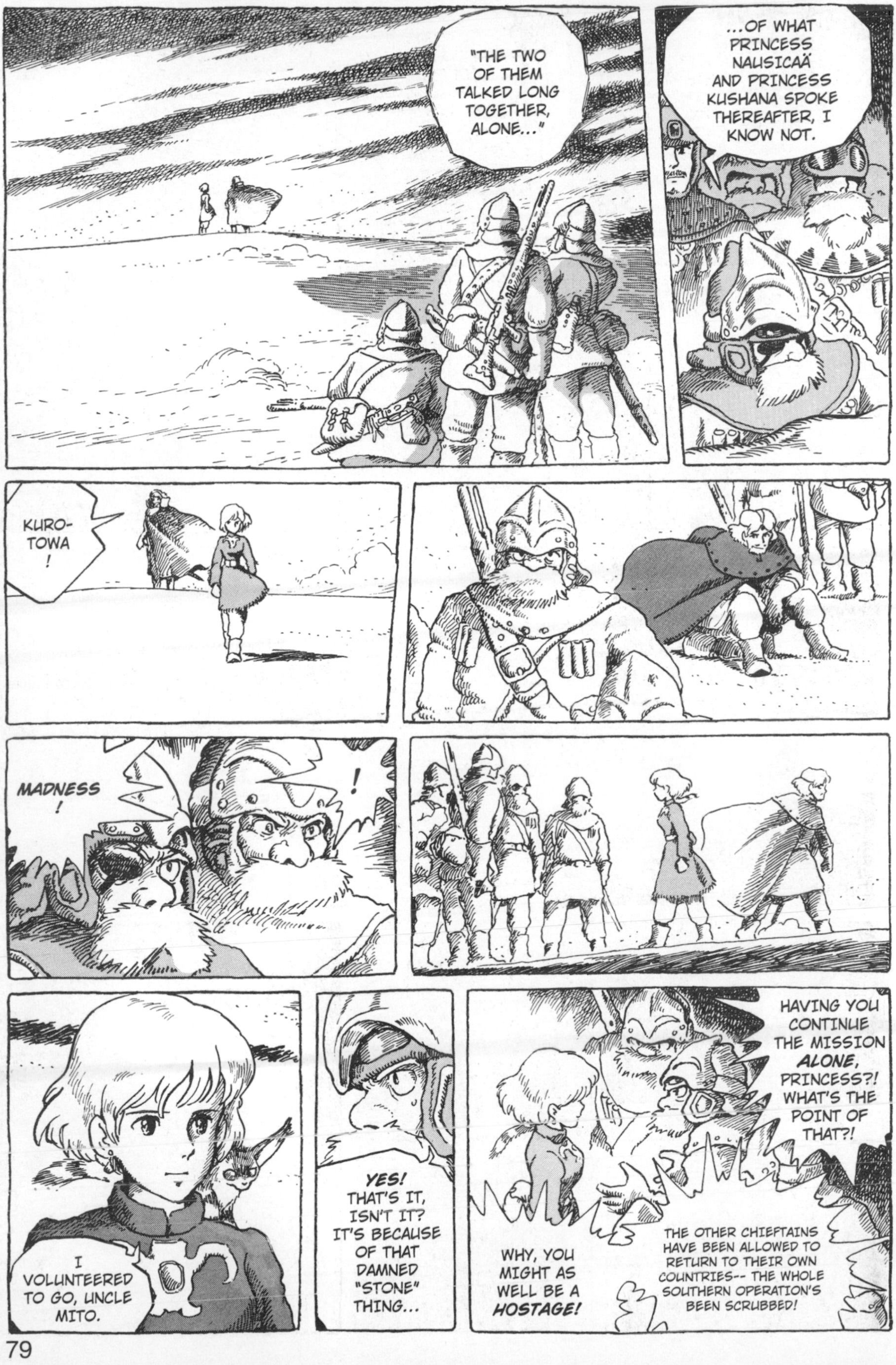
"THE TWO OF THEM TALKED LONG TOGETHER, ALONE..."
...OF WHAT PRINCESS NAUSICAÄ AND PRINCESS KUSHANA SPOKE THEREAFTER, I KNOW NOT.
KURO-TOWA!
MADNESS!
!
I VOLUNTEERED TO GO, UNCLE MITO.
YES! THAT'S IT, ISN'T IT? IT'S BECAUSE OF THAT DAMNED "STONE" THING...
HAVING YOU CONTINUE THE MISSION ALONE, PRINCESS?! WHAT'S THE POINT OF THAT?!
WHY, YOU MIGHT AS WELL BE A HOSTAGE!
THE OTHER CHIEFTAINS HAVE BEEN ALLOWED TO RETURN TO THEIR OWN COUNTRIES-- THE WHOLE SOUTHERN OPERATION'S BEEN SCRUBBED!

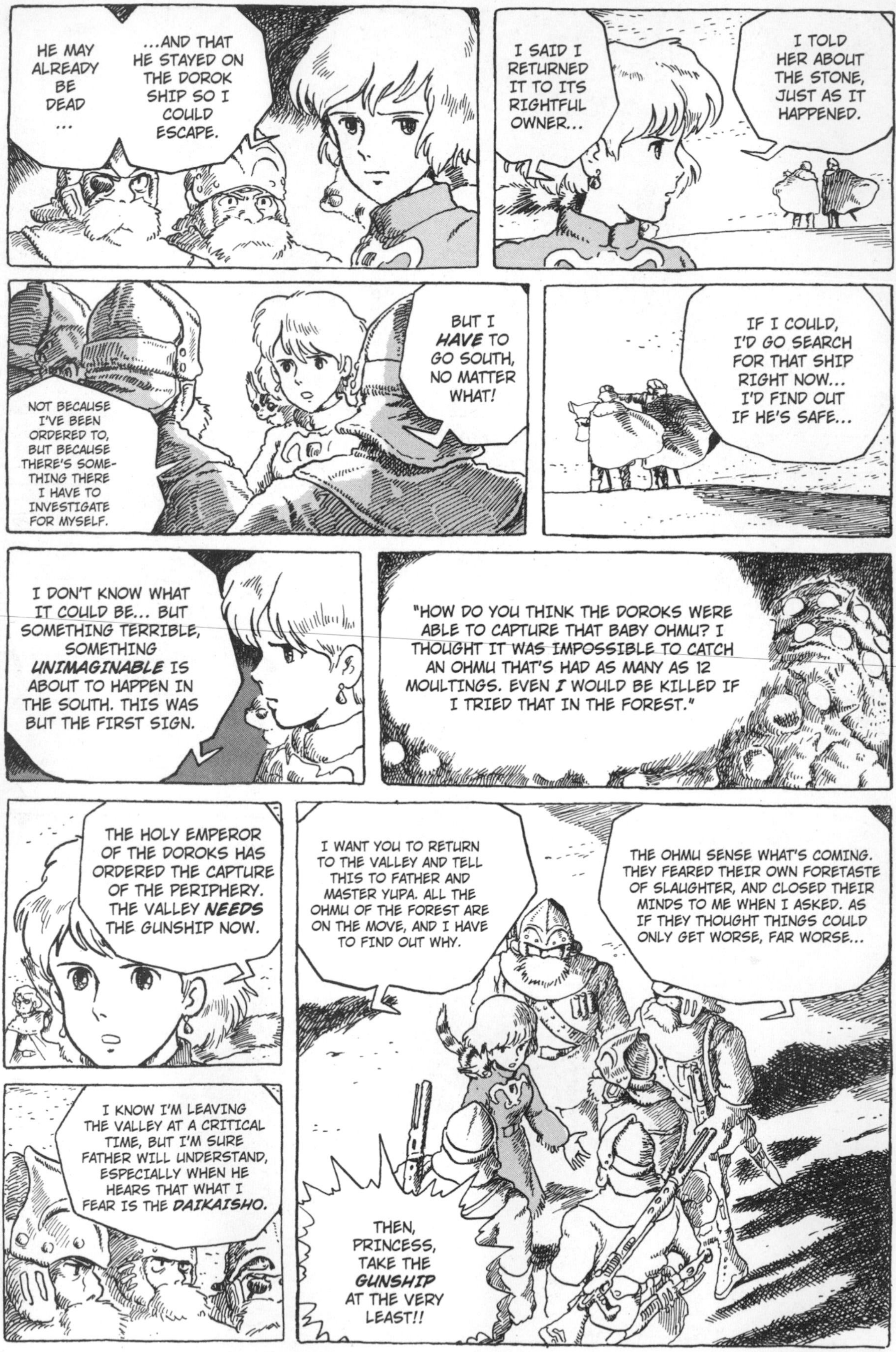
I TOLD HER ABOUT THE STONE, JUST AS IT HAPPENED.
I SAID I RETURNED IT TO ITS RIGHTFUL OWNER...
...AND THAT HE STAYED ON THE DOROK SHIP SO I COULD ESCAPE.
HE MAY ALREADY BE DEAD ...
IF I COULD, I'D GO SEARCH FOR THAT SHIP RIGHT NOW... I'D FIND OUT IF HE'S SAFE...
BUT I ***HAVE*** TO GO SOUTH, NO MATTER WHAT!
NOT BECAUSE I'VE BEEN ORDERED TO, BUT BECAUSE THERE'S SOMETHING THERE I HAVE TO INVESTIGATE FOR MYSELF.
"HOW DO YOU THINK THE DOROKS WERE ABLE TO CAPTURE THAT BABY OHMU? I THOUGHT IT WAS IMPOSSIBLE TO CATCH AN OHMU THAT'S HAD AS MANY AS 12 MOULTINGS. EVEN ***I*** WOULD BE KILLED IF I TRIED THAT IN THE FOREST."
I DON'T KNOW WHAT IT COULD BE... BUT SOMETHING TERRIBLE, SOMETHING ***UNIMAGINABLE*** IS ABOUT TO HAPPEN IN THE SOUTH. THIS WAS BUT THE FIRST SIGN.
THE OHMU SENSE WHAT'S COMING. THEY FEARED THEIR OWN FORETASTE OF SLAUGHTER, AND CLOSED THEIR MINDS TO ME WHEN I ASKED. AS IF THEY THOUGHT THINGS COULD ONLY GET WORSE, FAR WORSE...
I WANT YOU TO RETURN TO THE VALLEY AND TELL THIS TO FATHER AND MASTER YUPA. ALL THE OHMU OF THE FOREST ARE ON THE MOVE, AND I HAVE TO FIND OUT WHY.
THEN, PRINCESS, TAKE THE ***GUNSHIP*** AT THE VERY LEAST!!
THE HOLY EMPEROR OF THE DOROKS HAS ORDERED THE CAPTURE OF THE PERIPHERY. THE VALLEY ***NEEDS*** THE GUNSHIP NOW.
I KNOW I'M LEAVING THE VALLEY AT A CRITICAL TIME, BUT I'M SURE FATHER WILL UNDERSTAND, ESPECIALLY WHEN HE HEARS THAT WHAT I FEAR IS THE ***DAIKAISHO.***

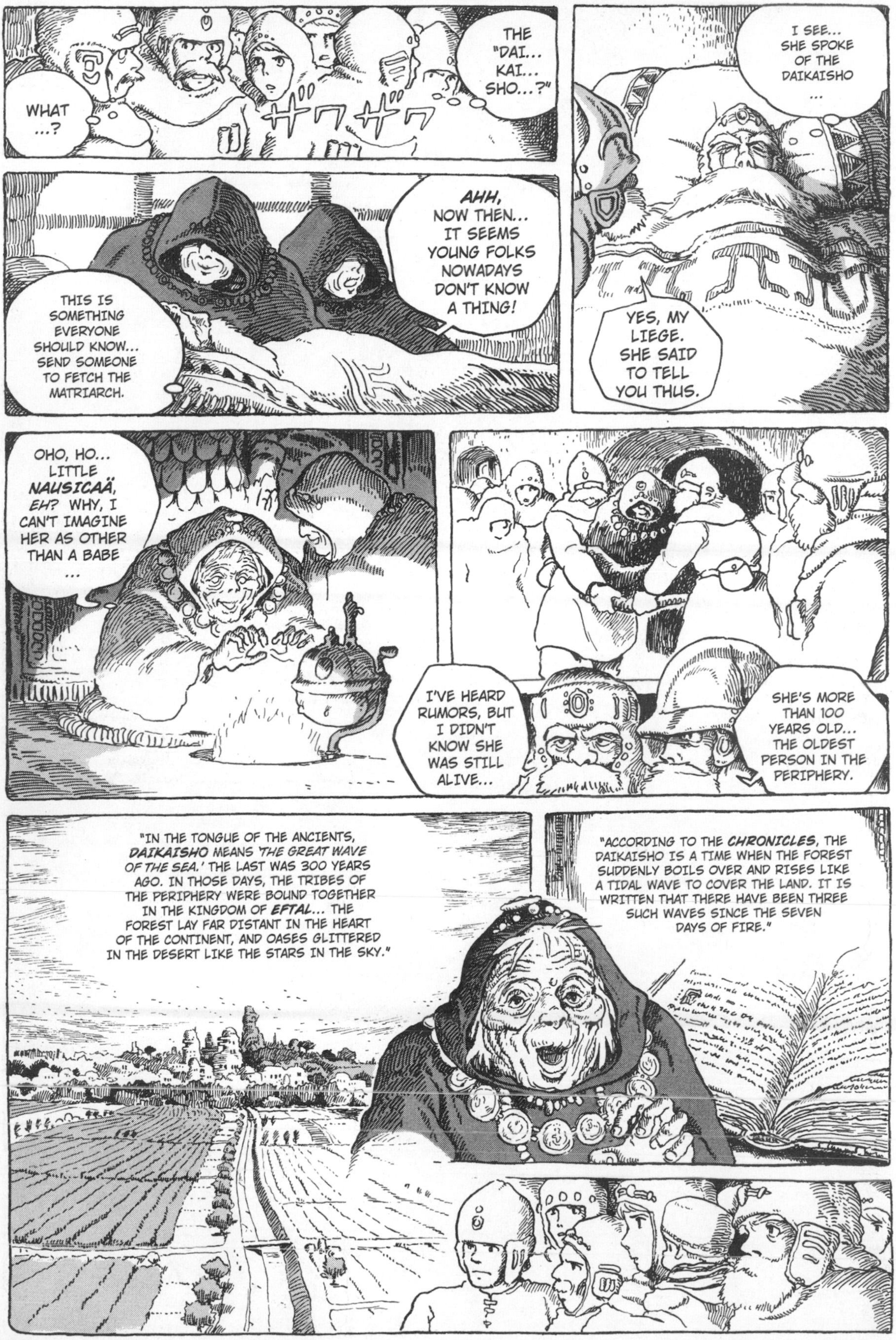
WHAT ...?
THE "DAI... KAI... SHO...?"
ザワザワ
I SEE... SHE SPOKE OF THE DAIKAISHO ...
AHH, NOW THEN... IT SEEMS YOUNG FOLKS NOWADAYS DON'T KNOW A THING!
THIS IS SOMETHING EVERYONE SHOULD KNOW... SEND SOMEONE TO FETCH THE MATRIARCH.
YES, MY LIEGE. SHE SAID TO TELL YOU THUS.
OHO, HO... LITTLE NAUSICAÄ, EH? WHY, I CAN'T IMAGINE HER AS OTHER THAN A BABE ...
I'VE HEARD RUMORS, BUT I DIDN'T KNOW SHE WAS STILL ALIVE...
SHE'S MORE THAN 100 YEARS OLD... THE OLDEST PERSON IN THE PERIPHERY.
"IN THE TONGUE OF THE ANCIENTS, DAIKAISHO MEANS 'THE GREAT WAVE OF THE SEA.' THE LAST WAS 300 YEARS AGO. IN THOSE DAYS, THE TRIBES OF THE PERIPHERY WERE BOUND TOGETHER IN THE KINGDOM OF EFTAL... THE FOREST LAY FAR DISTANT IN THE HEART OF THE CONTINENT, AND OASES GLITTERED IN THE DESERT LIKE THE STARS IN THE SKY."
"ACCORDING TO THE CHRONICLES, THE DAIKAISHO IS A TIME WHEN THE FOREST SUDDENLY BOILS OVER AND RISES LIKE A TIDAL WAVE TO COVER THE LAND. IT IS WRITTEN THAT THERE HAVE BEEN THREE SUCH WAVES SINCE THE SEVEN DAYS OF FIRE."

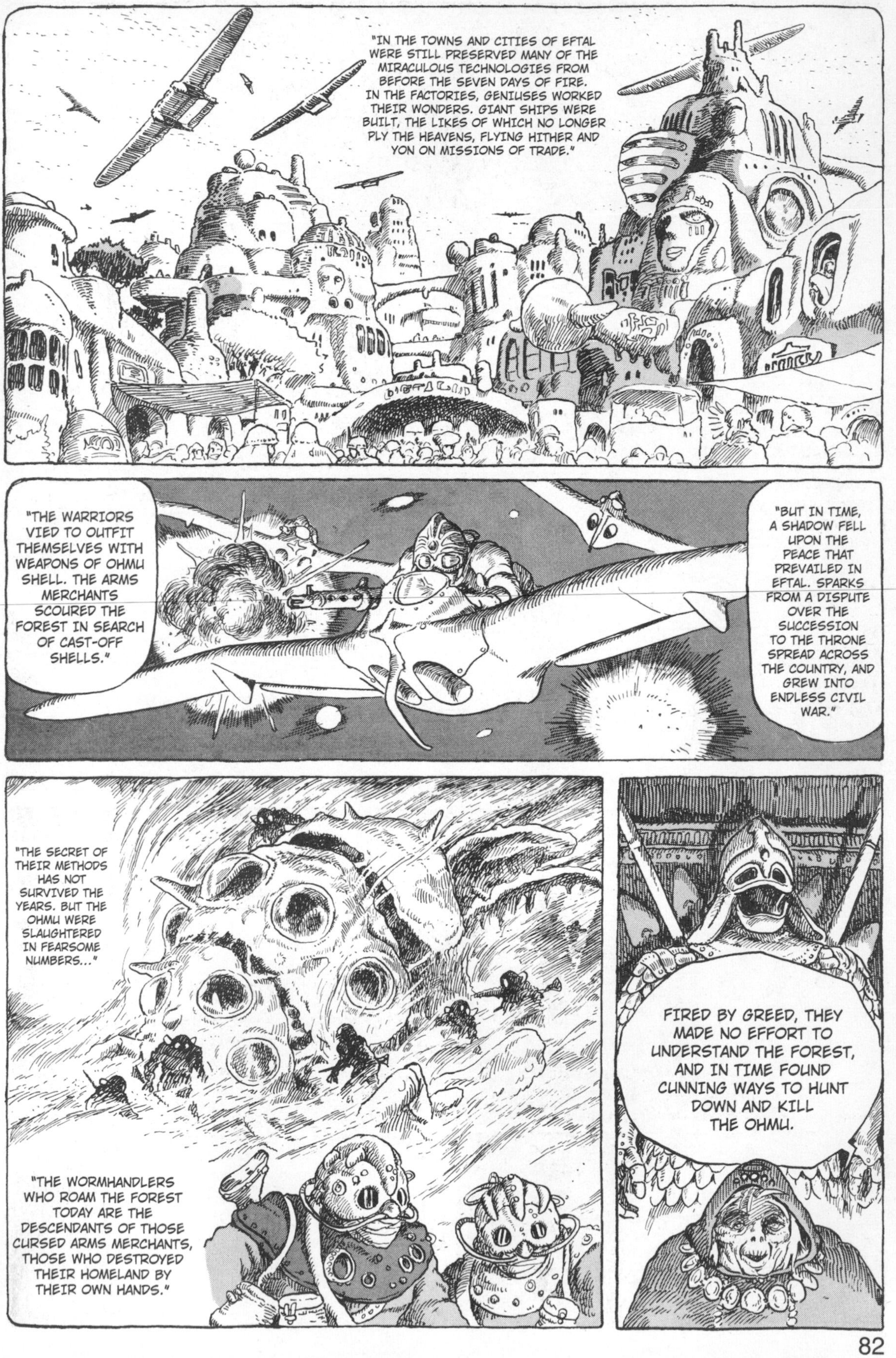
"IN THE TOWNS AND CITIES OF EFTAL WERE STILL PRESERVED MANY OF THE MIRACULOUS TECHNOLOGIES FROM BEFORE THE SEVEN DAYS OF FIRE. IN THE FACTORIES, GENIUSES WORKED THEIR WONDERS. GIANT SHIPS WERE BUILT, THE LIKES OF WHICH NO LONGER PLY THE HEAVENS, FLYING HITHER AND YON ON MISSIONS OF TRADE."
"BUT IN TIME, A SHADOW FELL UPON THE PEACE THAT PREVAILED IN EFTAL. SPARKS FROM A DISPUTE OVER THE SUCCESSION TO THE THRONE SPREAD ACROSS THE COUNTRY, AND GREW INTO ENDLESS CIVIL WAR."
"THE WARRIORS VIED TO OUTFIT THEMSELVES WITH WEAPONS OF OHMU SHELL. THE ARMS MERCHANTS SCOURED THE FOREST IN SEARCH OF CAST-OFF SHELLS."
FIRED BY GREED, THEY MADE NO EFFORT TO UNDERSTAND THE FOREST, AND IN TIME FOUND CUNNING WAYS TO HUNT DOWN AND KILL THE OHMU.
"THE SECRET OF THEIR METHODS HAS NOT SURVIVED THE YEARS. BUT THE OHMU WERE SLAUGHTERED IN FEARSOME NUMBERS..."
"THE WORMHANDLERS WHO ROAM THE FOREST TODAY ARE THE DESCENDANTS OF THOSE CURSED ARMS MERCHANTS, THOSE WHO DESTROYED THEIR HOMELAND BY THEIR OWN HANDS."

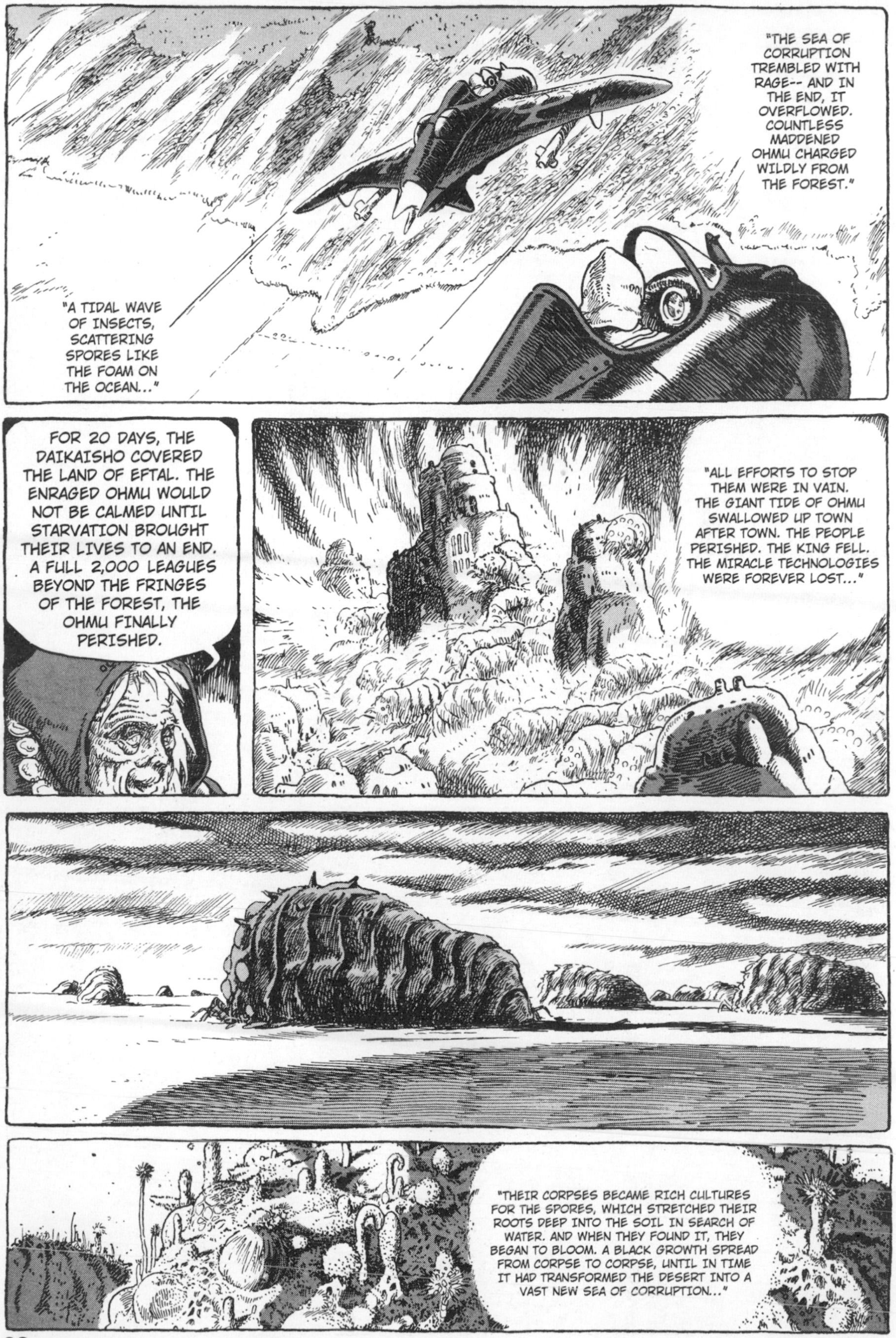
"THE SEA OF CORRUPTION TREMBLED WITH RAGE-- AND IN THE END, IT OVERFLOWED. COUNTLESS MADDENED OHMU CHARGED WILDLY FROM THE FOREST."
"A TIDAL WAVE OF INSECTS, SCATTERING SPORES LIKE THE FOAM ON THE OCEAN..."
"ALL EFFORTS TO STOP THEM WERE IN VAIN. THE GIANT TIDE OF OHMU SWALLOWED UP TOWN AFTER TOWN. THE PEOPLE PERISHED. THE KING FELL. THE MIRACLE TECHNOLOGIES WERE FOREVER LOST..."
FOR 20 DAYS, THE DAIKAISHO COVERED THE LAND OF EFTAL. THE ENRAGED OHMU WOULD NOT BE CALMED UNTIL STARVATION BROUGHT THEIR LIVES TO AN END. A FULL 2,000 LEAGUES BEYOND THE FRINGES OF THE FOREST, THE OHMU FINALLY PERISHED.
"THEIR CORPSES BECAME RICH CULTURES FOR THE SPORES, WHICH STRETCHED THEIR ROOTS DEEP INTO THE SOIL IN SEARCH OF WATER. AND WHEN THEY FOUND IT, THEY BEGAN TO BLOOM. A BLACK GROWTH SPREAD FROM CORPSE TO CORPSE, UNTIL IN TIME IT HAD TRANSFORMED THE DESERT INTO A VAST NEW SEA OF CORRUPTION..."

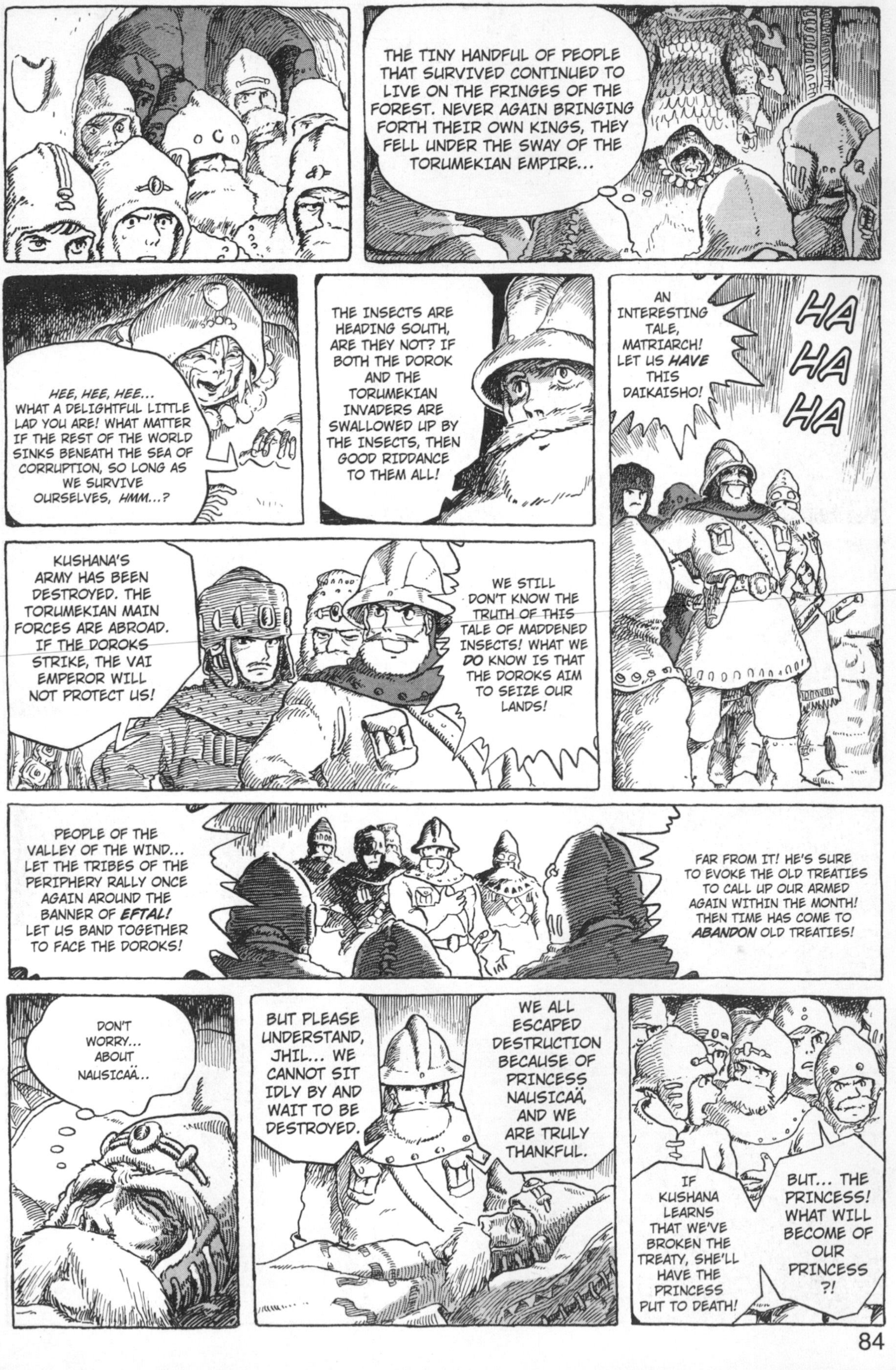
THE TINY HANDFUL OF PEOPLE THAT SURVIVED CONTINUED TO LIVE ON THE FRINGES OF THE FOREST. NEVER AGAIN BRINGING FORTH THEIR OWN KINGS, THEY FELL UNDER THE SWAY OF THE TORUMEKIAN EMPIRE...
HA HA HA
AN INTERESTING TALE, MATRIARCH! LET US *HAVE* THIS DAIKAISHO!
THE INSECTS ARE HEADING SOUTH, ARE THEY NOT? IF BOTH THE DOROK AND THE TORUMEKIAN INVADERS ARE SWALLOWED UP BY THE INSECTS, THEN GOOD RIDDANCE TO THEM ALL!
HEE, HEE, HEE... WHAT A DELIGHTFUL LITTLE LAD YOU ARE! WHAT MATTER IF THE REST OF THE WORLD SINKS BENEATH THE SEA OF CORRUPTION, SO LONG AS WE SURVIVE OURSELVES, *HMM...?*
WE STILL DON'T KNOW THE TRUTH OF THIS TALE OF MADDENED INSECTS! WHAT WE *DO* KNOW IS THAT THE DOROKS AIM TO SEIZE OUR LANDS!
KUSHANA'S ARMY HAS BEEN DESTROYED. THE TORUMEKIAN MAIN FORCES ARE ABROAD. IF THE DOROKS STRIKE, THE VAI EMPEROR WILL NOT PROTECT US!
FAR FROM IT! HE'S SURE TO EVOKE THE OLD TREATIES TO CALL UP OUR ARMED AGAIN WITHIN THE MONTH! THEN TIME HAS COME TO *ABANDON* OLD TREATIES!
PEOPLE OF THE VALLEY OF THE WIND... LET THE TRIBES OF THE PERIPHERY RALLY ONCE AGAIN AROUND THE BANNER OF *EFTAL!* LET US BAND TOGETHER TO FACE THE DOROKS!
BUT... THE PRINCESS! WHAT WILL BECOME OF OUR PRINCESS ?!
IF KUSHANA LEARNS THAT WE'VE BROKEN THE TREATY, SHE'LL HAVE THE PRINCESS PUT TO DEATH!
WE ALL ESCAPED DESTRUCTION BECAUSE OF PRINCESS NAUSICAÄ, AND WE ARE TRULY THANKFUL.
BUT PLEASE UNDERSTAND, JHIL... WE CANNOT SIT IDLY BY AND WAIT TO BE DESTROYED.
DON'T WORRY... ABOUT NAUSICAÄ...

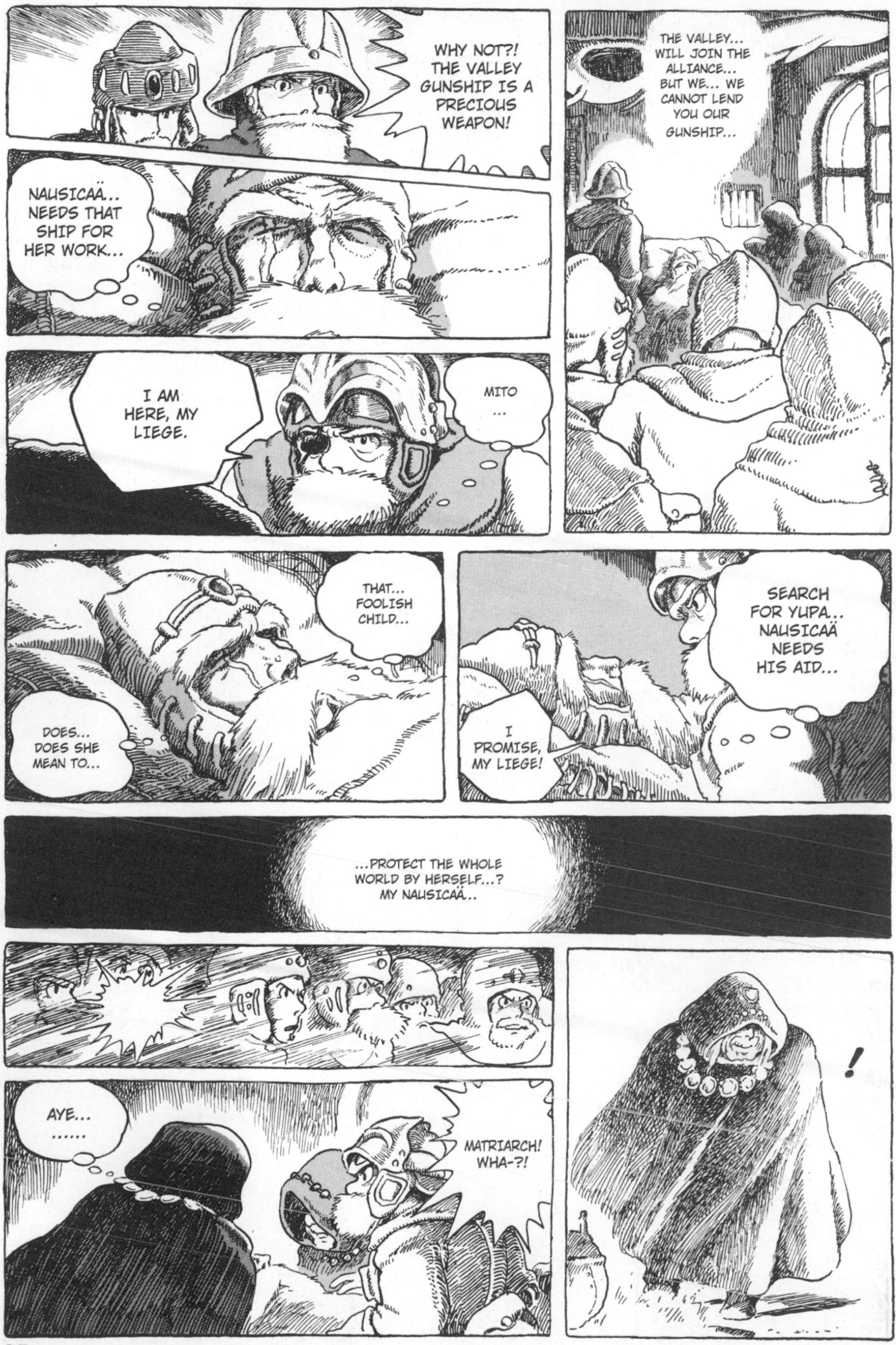
THE VALLEY... WILL JOIN THE ALLIANCE... BUT WE... WE CANNOT LEND YOU OUR GUNSHIP...
WHY NOT?! THE VALLEY GUNSHIP IS A PRECIOUS WEAPON!
NAUSICAÄ... NEEDS THAT SHIP FOR HER WORK...
MITO ...
I AM HERE, MY LIEGE.
SEARCH FOR YUPA... NAUSICAÄ NEEDS HIS AID...
I PROMISE, MY LIEGE!
THAT... FOOLISH CHILD...
DOES... DOES SHE MEAN TO...
...PROTECT THE WHOLE WORLD BY HERSELF...? MY NAUSICAÄ...
!
MATRIARCH! WHA-?!
AYE... ......

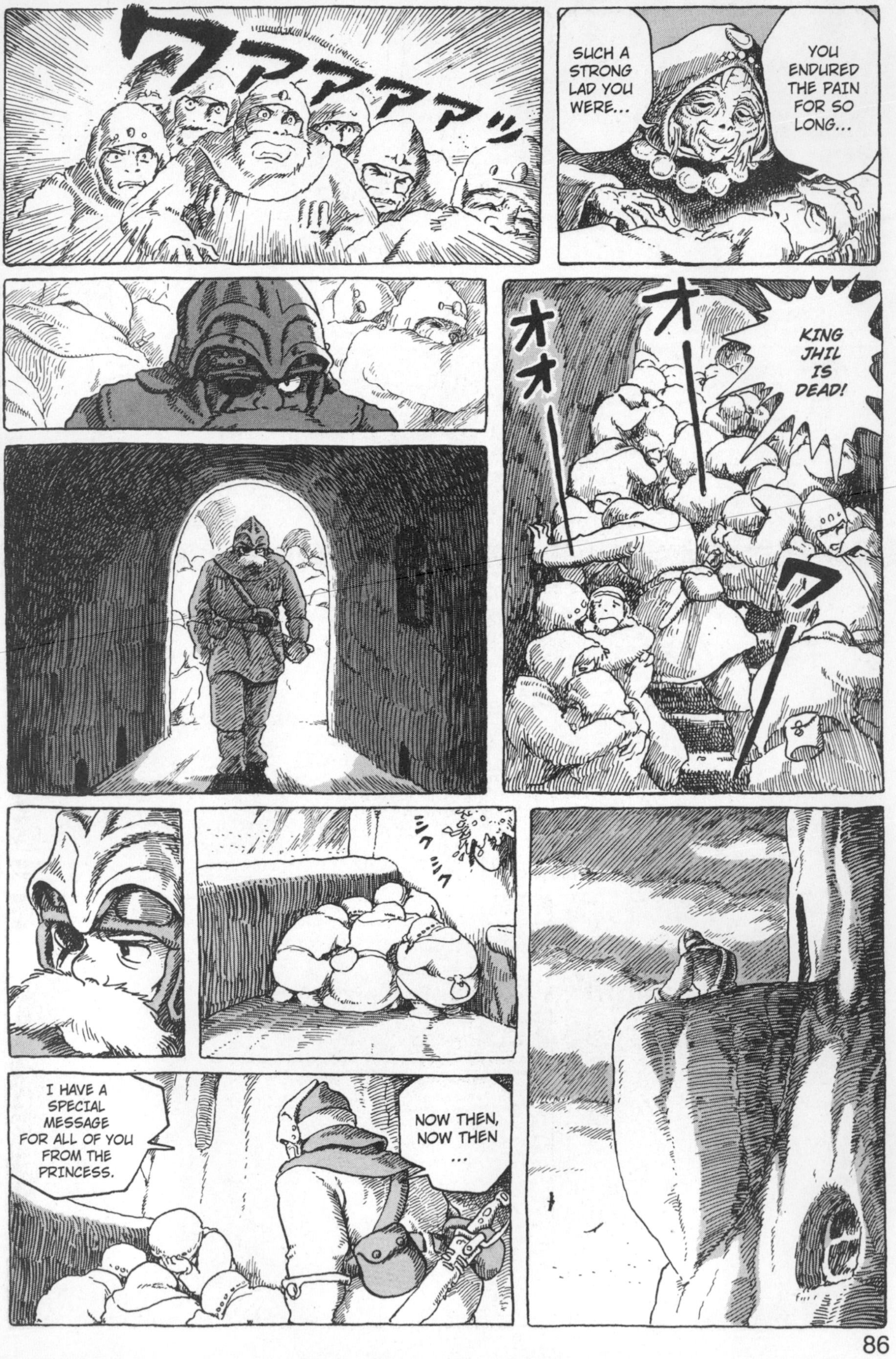
YOU ENDURED THE PAIN FOR SO LONG...
SUCH A STRONG LAD YOU WERE...
KING JHIL IS DEAD!
NOW THEN, NOW THEN ...
I HAVE A SPECIAL MESSAGE FOR ALL OF YOU FROM THE PRINCESS.

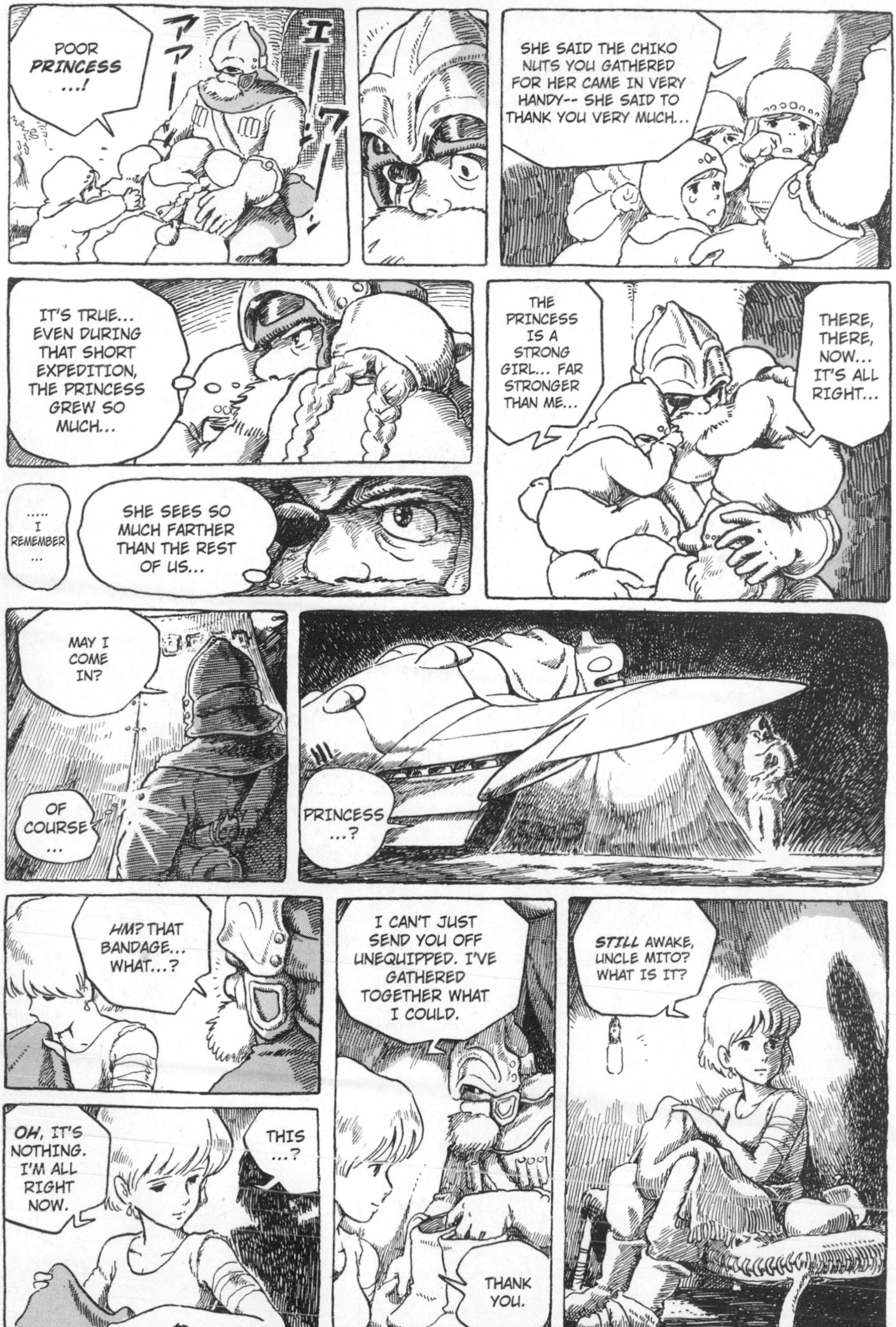
SHE SAID THE CHIKO NUTS YOU GATHERED FOR HER CAME IN VERY HANDY-- SHE SAID TO THANK YOU VERY MUCH...
POOR *PRINCESS* ...!
THERE, THERE, NOW... IT'S ALL RIGHT...
THE PRINCESS IS A STRONG GIRL... FAR STRONGER THAN ME...
IT'S TRUE... EVEN DURING THAT SHORT EXPEDITION, THE PRINCESS GREW SO MUCH...
SHE SEES SO MUCH FARTHER THAN THE REST OF US...
..... I REMEMBER ...
PRINCESS ...?
MAY I COME IN?
OF COURSE ...
STILL AWAKE, UNCLE MITO? WHAT IS IT?
I CAN'T JUST SEND YOU OFF UNEQUIPPED. I'VE GATHERED TOGETHER WHAT I COULD.
THANK YOU.
HM? THAT BANDAGE... WHAT...?
THIS ...?
OH, IT'S NOTHING. I'M ALL RIGHT NOW.

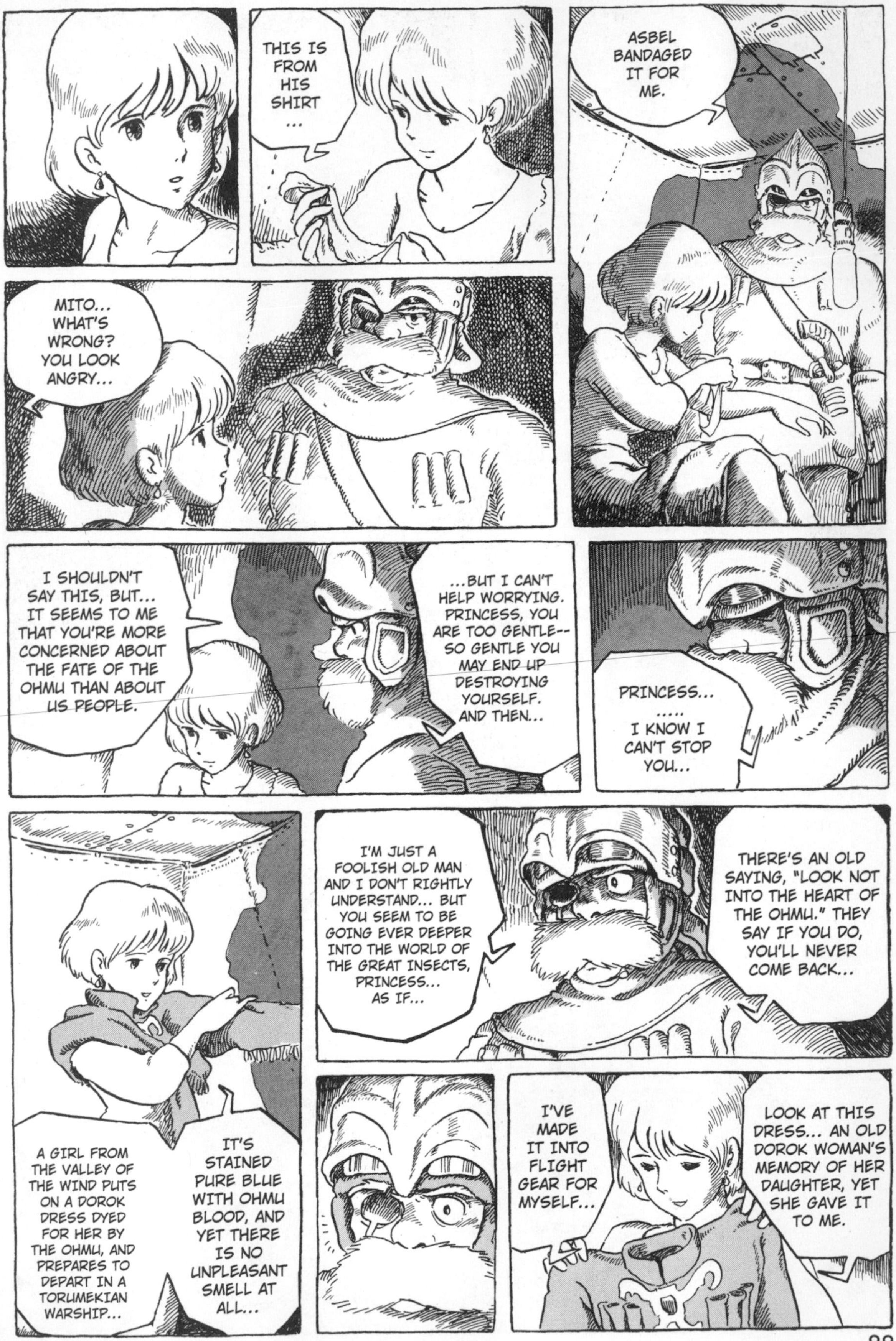
THIS IS FROM HIS SHIRT ...
ASBEL BANDAGED IT FOR ME.
MITO... WHAT'S WRONG? YOU LOOK ANGRY...
I SHOULDN'T SAY THIS, BUT... IT SEEMS TO ME THAT YOU'RE MORE CONCERNED ABOUT THE FATE OF THE OHMU THAN ABOUT US PEOPLE.
...BUT I CAN'T HELP WORRYING. PRINCESS, YOU ARE TOO GENTLE-- SO GENTLE YOU MAY END UP DESTROYING YOURSELF. AND THEN...
PRINCESS... ..... I KNOW I CAN'T STOP YOU...
A GIRL FROM THE VALLEY OF THE WIND PUTS ON A DOROK DRESS DYED FOR HER BY THE OHMU, AND PREPARES TO DEPART IN A TORUMEKIAN WARSHIP...
IT'S STAINED PURE BLUE WITH OHMU BLOOD, AND YET THERE IS NO UNPLEASANT SMELL AT ALL...
I'M JUST A FOOLISH OLD MAN AND I DON'T RIGHTLY UNDERSTAND... BUT YOU SEEM TO BE GOING EVER DEEPER INTO THE WORLD OF THE GREAT INSECTS, PRINCESS... AS IF...
THERE'S AN OLD SAYING, "LOOK NOT INTO THE HEART OF THE OHMU." THEY SAY IF YOU DO, YOU'LL NEVER COME BACK...
LOOK AT THIS DRESS... AN OLD DOROK WOMAN'S MEMORY OF HER DAUGHTER, YET SHE GAVE IT TO ME.
I'VE MADE IT INTO FLIGHT GEAR FOR MYSELF...

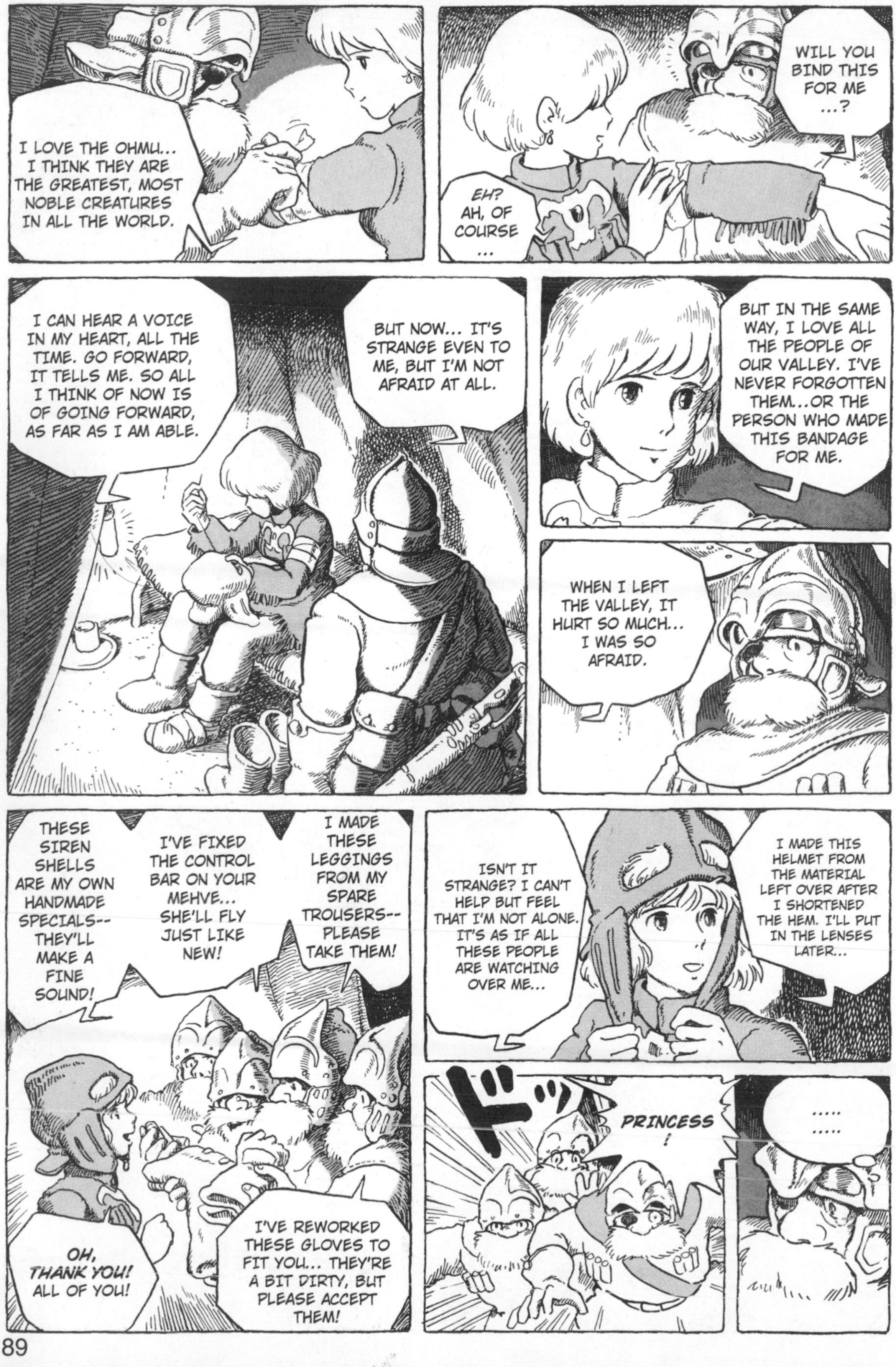
WILL YOU BIND THIS FOR ME ...?
EH? AH, OF COURSE ...
I LOVE THE OHMU... I THINK THEY ARE THE GREATEST, MOST NOBLE CREATURES IN ALL THE WORLD.
BUT IN THE SAME WAY, I LOVE ALL THE PEOPLE OF OUR VALLEY. I'VE NEVER FORGOTTEN THEM...OR THE PERSON WHO MADE THIS BANDAGE FOR ME.
WHEN I LEFT THE VALLEY, IT HURT SO MUCH... I WAS SO AFRAID.
BUT NOW... IT'S STRANGE EVEN TO ME, BUT I'M NOT AFRAID AT ALL.
I CAN HEAR A VOICE IN MY HEART, ALL THE TIME. GO FORWARD, IT TELLS ME. SO ALL I THINK OF NOW IS OF GOING FORWARD, AS FAR AS I AM ABLE.
I MADE THIS HELMET FROM THE MATERIAL LEFT OVER AFTER I SHORTENED THE HEM. I'LL PUT IN THE LENSES LATER...
ISN'T IT STRANGE? I CAN'T HELP BUT FEEL THAT I'M NOT ALONE. IT'S AS IF ALL THESE PEOPLE ARE WATCHING OVER ME...
....
ドッ
PRINCESS !
I MADE THESE LEGGINGS FROM MY SPARE TROUSERS-- PLEASE TAKE THEM!
I'VE FIXED THE CONTROL BAR ON YOUR MEHVE... SHE'LL FLY JUST LIKE NEW!
THESE SIREN SHELLS ARE MY OWN HANDMADE SPECIALS-- THEY'LL MAKE A FINE SOUND!
I'VE REWORKED THESE GLOVES TO FIT YOU... THEY'RE A BIT DIRTY, BUT PLEASE ACCEPT THEM!
OH, THANK YOU! ALL OF YOU!

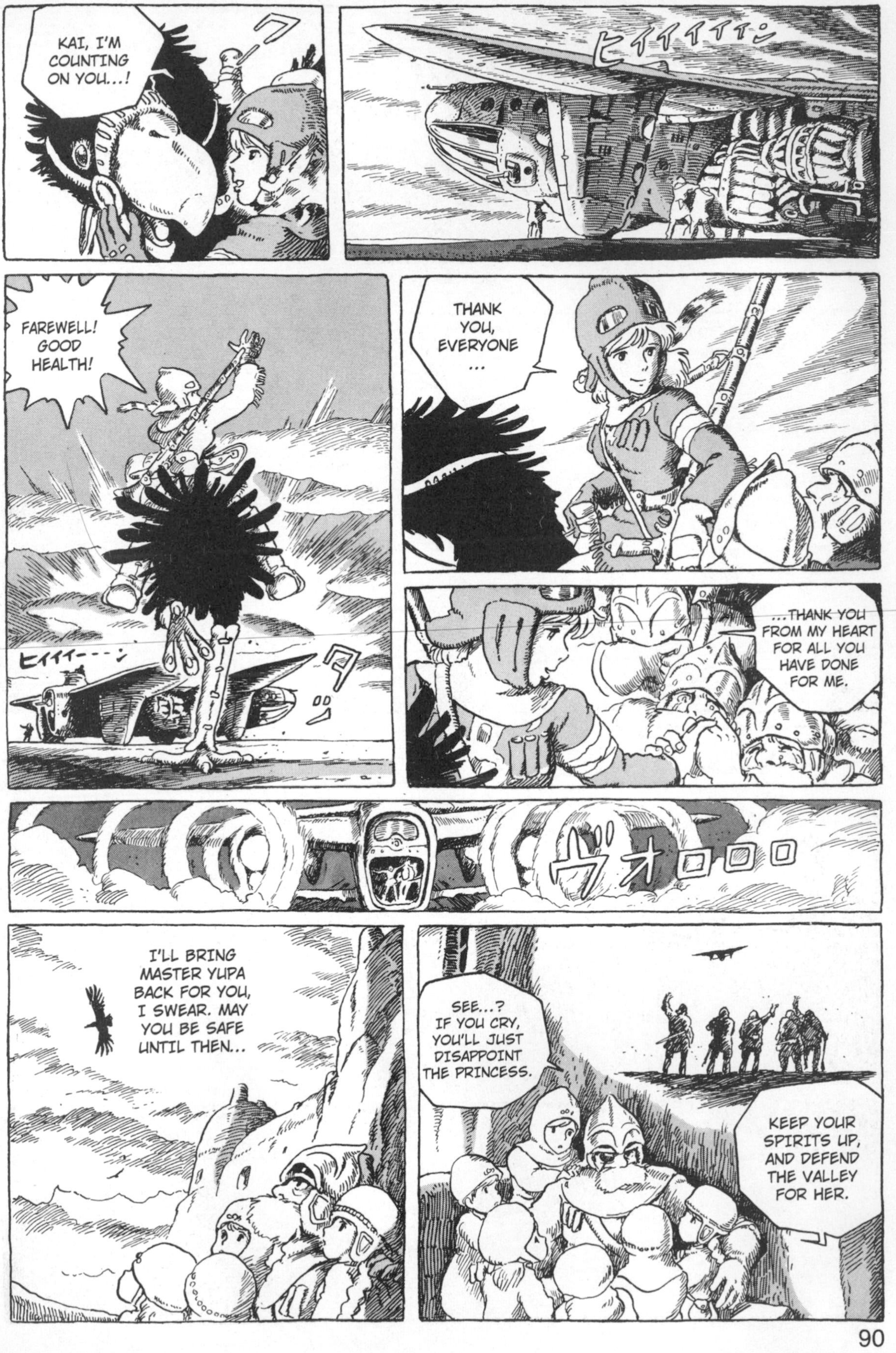
KAI, I'M COUNTING ON YOU...!
FAREWELL! GOOD HEALTH!
THANK YOU, EVERYONE ...
...THANK YOU FROM MY HEART FOR ALL YOU HAVE DONE FOR ME.
I'LL BRING MASTER YUPA BACK FOR YOU, I SWEAR. MAY YOU BE SAFE UNTIL THEN...
SEE...? IF YOU CRY, YOU'LL JUST DISAPPOINT THE PRINCESS.
KEEP YOUR SPIRITS UP, AND DEFEND THE VALLEY FOR HER.

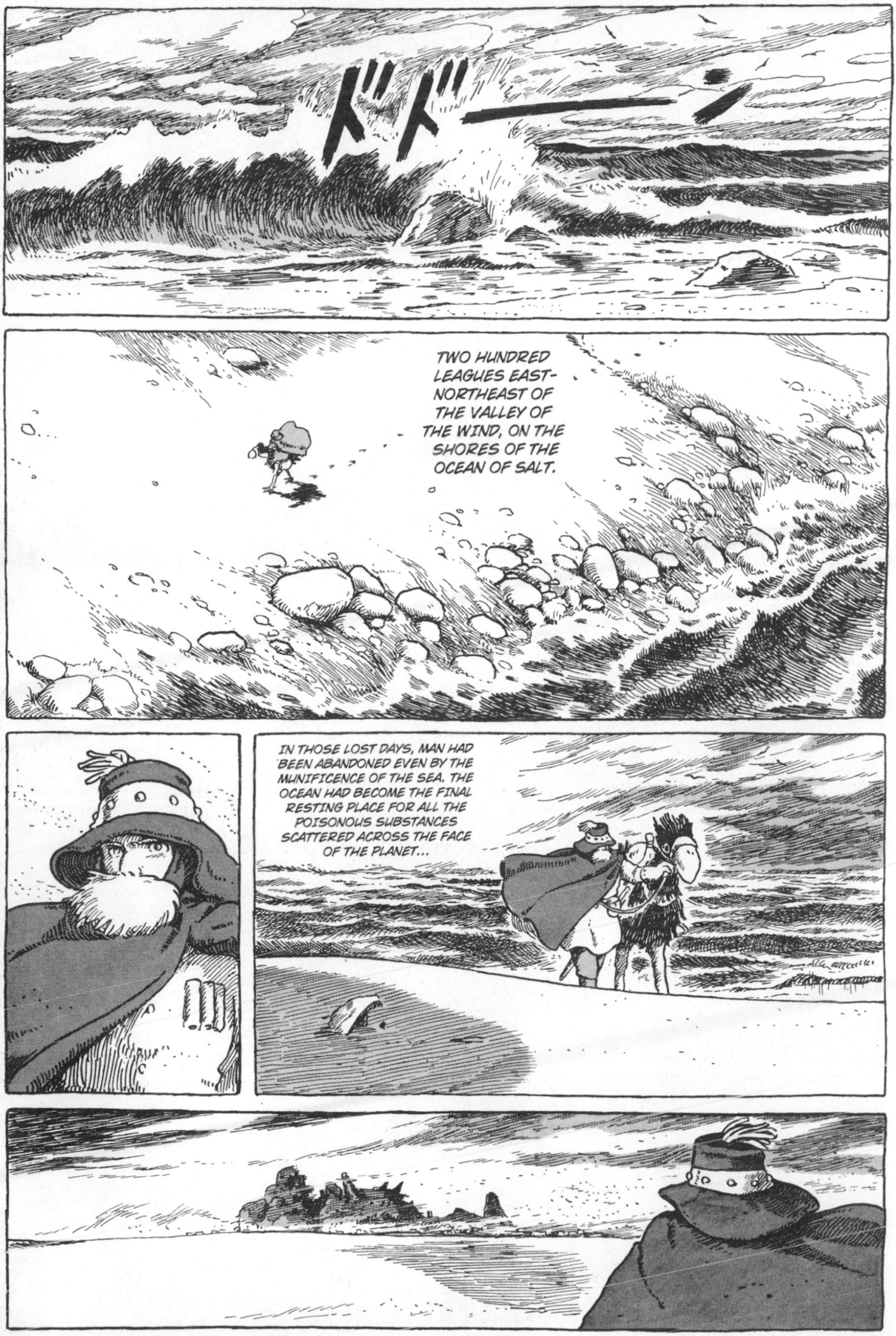
ドドーン
TWO HUNDRED LEAGUES EAST-NORTHEAST OF THE VALLEY OF THE WIND, ON THE SHORES OF THE OCEAN OF SALT.
IN THOSE LOST DAYS, MAN HAD BEEN ABANDONED EVEN BY THE MUNIFICENCE OF THE SEA. THE OCEAN HAD BECOME THE FINAL RESTING PLACE FOR ALL THE POISONOUS SUBSTANCES SCATTERED ACROSS THE FACE OF THE PLANET...

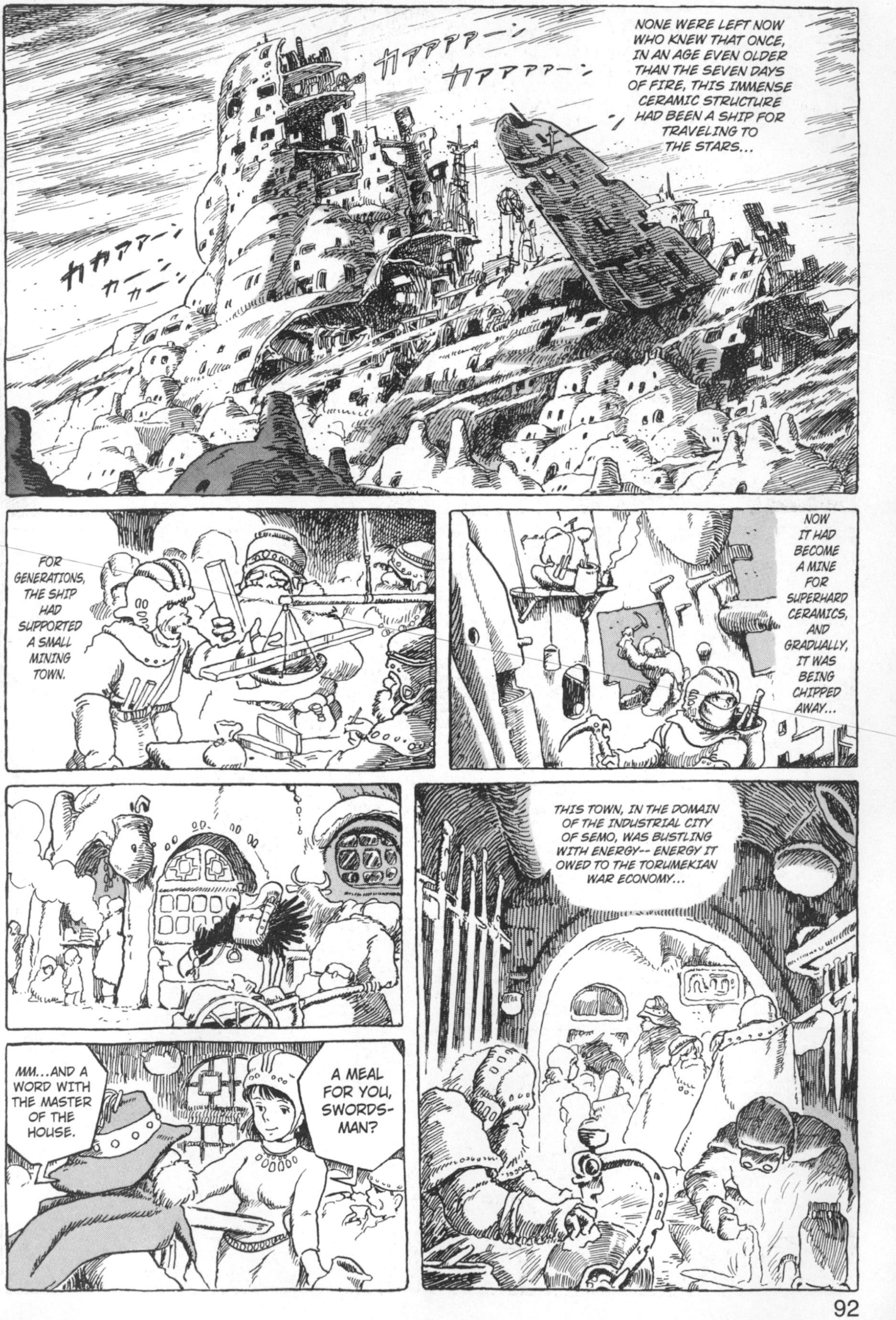
NONE WERE LEFT NOW WHO KNEW THAT ONCE, IN AN AGE EVEN OLDER THAN THE SEVEN DAYS OF FIRE, THIS IMMENSE CERAMIC STRUCTURE HAD BEEN A SHIP FOR TRAVELING TO THE STARS...
カァァァァーン
カァァァァーン
カァァァーン
カーン
カーン
NOW IT HAD BECOME A MINE FOR SUPERHARD CERAMICS, AND GRADUALLY, IT WAS BEING CHIPPED AWAY...
FOR GENERATIONS, THE SHIP HAD SUPPORTED A SMALL MINING TOWN.
THIS TOWN, IN THE DOMAIN OF THE INDUSTRIAL CITY OF SEMO, WAS BUSTLING WITH ENERGY-- ENERGY IT OWED TO THE TORUMEKIAN WAR ECONOMY...
A MEAL FOR YOU, SWORDS-MAN?
MM...AND A WORD WITH THE MASTER OF THE HOUSE.

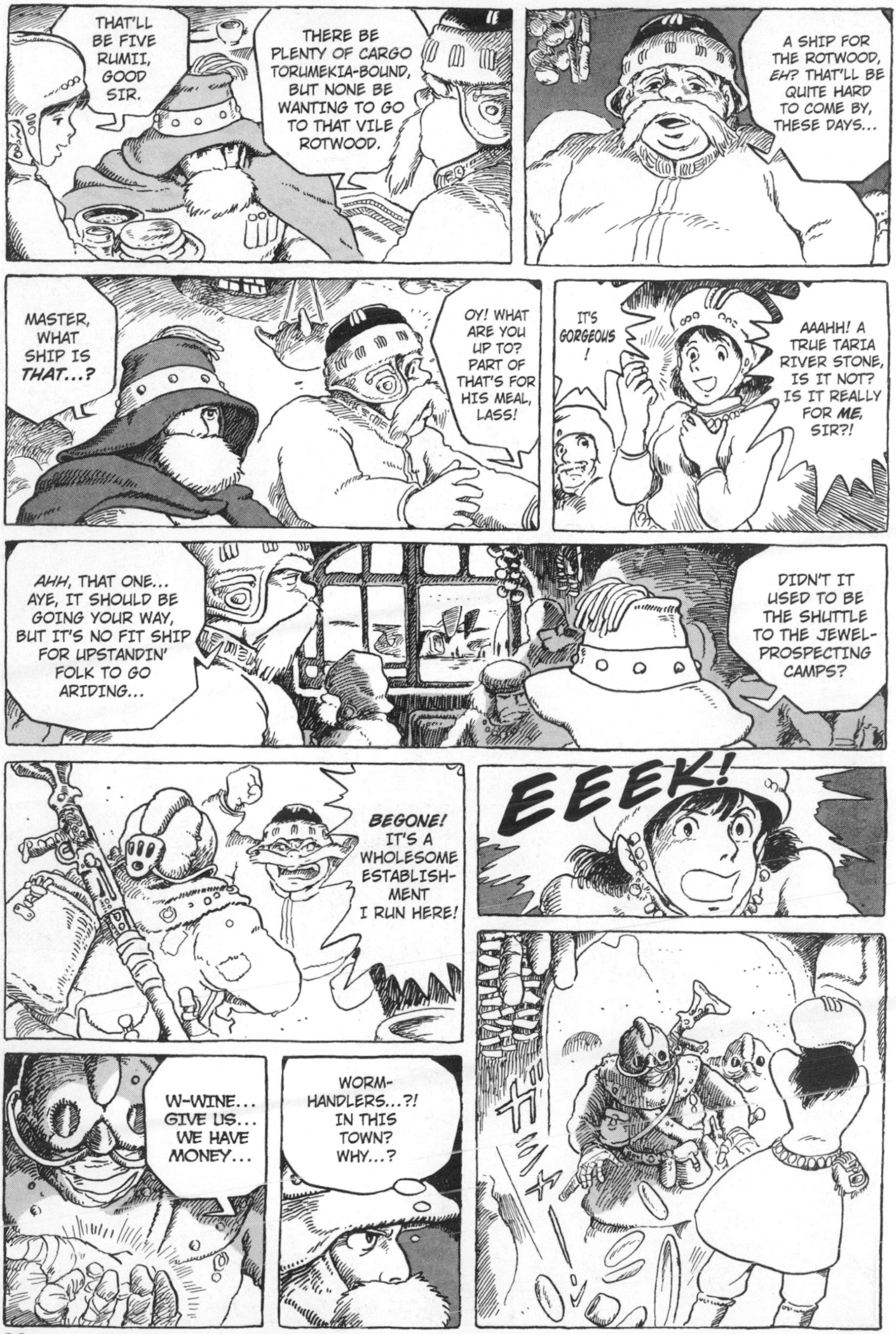
A SHIP FOR THE ROTWOOD, EH? THAT'LL BE QUITE HARD TO COME BY, THESE DAYS...
THERE BE PLENTY OF CARGO TORUMEKIA-BOUND, BUT NONE BE WANTING TO GO TO THAT VILE ROTWOOD.
THAT'LL BE FIVE RUMII, GOOD SIR.
AAAHH! A TRUE TARIA RIVER STONE, IS IT NOT? IS IT REALLY FOR ME, SIR?!
IT'S GORGEOUS!
OY! WHAT ARE YOU UP TO? PART OF THAT'S FOR HIS MEAL, LASS!
MASTER, WHAT SHIP IS THAT...?
DIDN'T IT USED TO BE THE SHUTTLE TO THE JEWEL-PROSPECTING CAMPS?
AHH, THAT ONE... AYE, IT SHOULD BE GOING YOUR WAY, BUT IT'S NO FIT SHIP FOR UPSTANDIN' FOLK TO GO ARIDING...
EEEK!
BEGONE! IT'S A WHOLESOME ESTABLISHMENT I RUN HERE!
WORM-HANDLERS...?! IN THIS TOWN? WHY...?
W-WINE... GIVE US... WE HAVE MONEY...

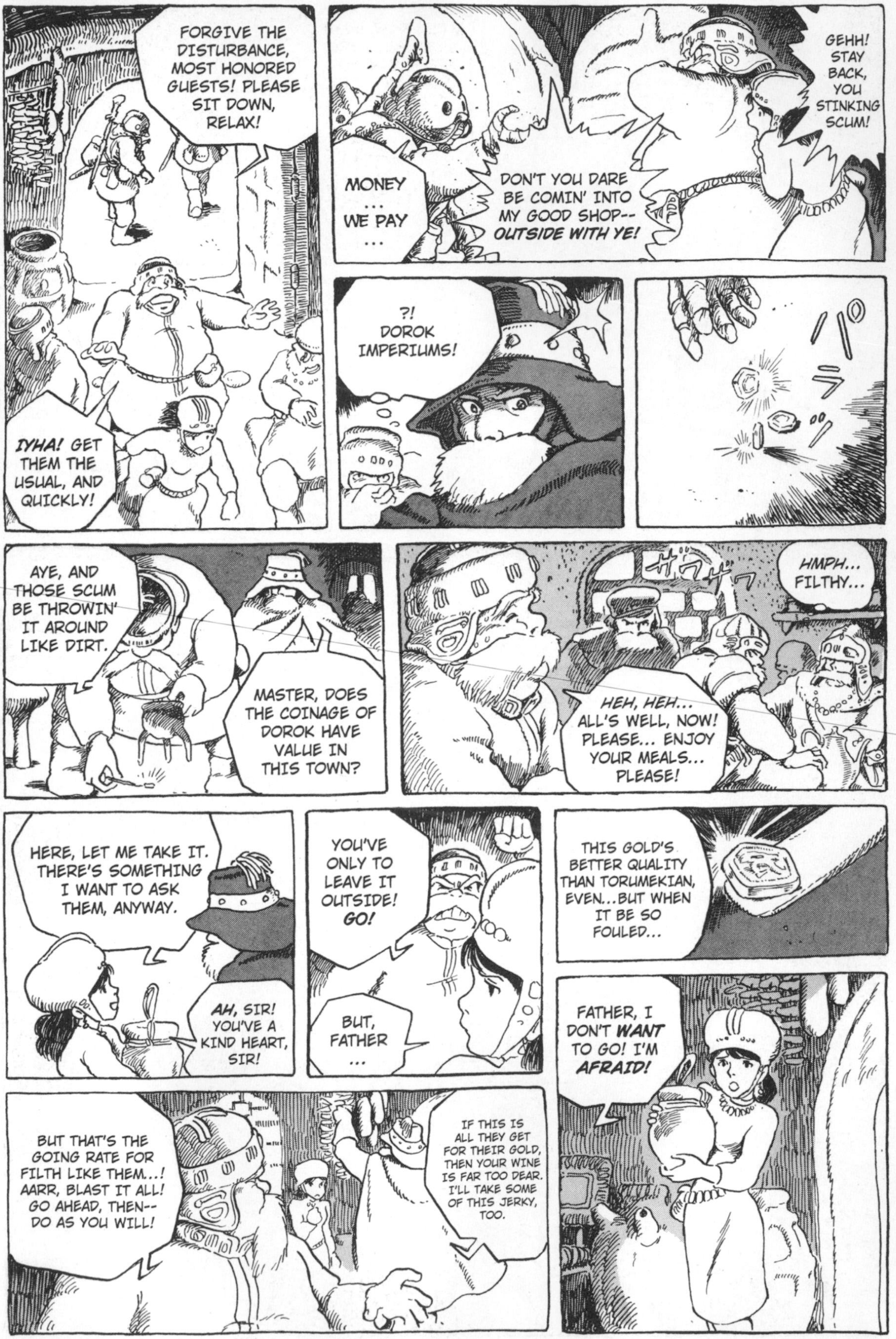
GEHH! STAY BACK, YOU STINKING SCUM!
DON'T YOU DARE BE COMIN' INTO MY GOOD SHOP-- ***OUTSIDE WITH YE!***
MONEY ... WE PAY ...
...
パラ
?! DOROK IMPERIUMS!
FORGIVE THE DISTURBANCE, MOST HONORED GUESTS! PLEASE SIT DOWN, RELAX!
IYHA! GET THEM THE USUAL, AND QUICKLY!
HMPH... FILTHY...
ザワザワ
HEH, HEH... ALL'S WELL, NOW! PLEASE... ENJOY YOUR MEALS... PLEASE!
AYE, AND THOSE SCUM BE THROWIN' IT AROUND LIKE DIRT.
MASTER, DOES THE COINAGE OF DOROK HAVE VALUE IN THIS TOWN?
THIS GOLD'S BETTER QUALITY THAN TORUMEKIAN, EVEN...BUT WHEN IT BE SO FOULED...
YOU'VE ONLY TO LEAVE IT OUTSIDE! ***GO!***
BUT, FATHER ...
FATHER, I DON'T ***WANT*** TO GO! I'M ***AFRAID!***
HERE, LET ME TAKE IT. THERE'S SOMETHING I WANT TO ASK THEM, ANYWAY.
AH, SIR! YOU'VE A KIND HEART, SIR!
IF THIS IS ALL THEY GET FOR THEIR GOLD, THEN YOUR WINE IS FAR TOO DEAR. I'LL TAKE SOME OF THIS JERKY, TOO.
BUT THAT'S THE GOING RATE FOR FILTH LIKE THEM...! AARR, BLAST IT ALL! GO AHEAD, THEN-- DO AS YOU WILL!

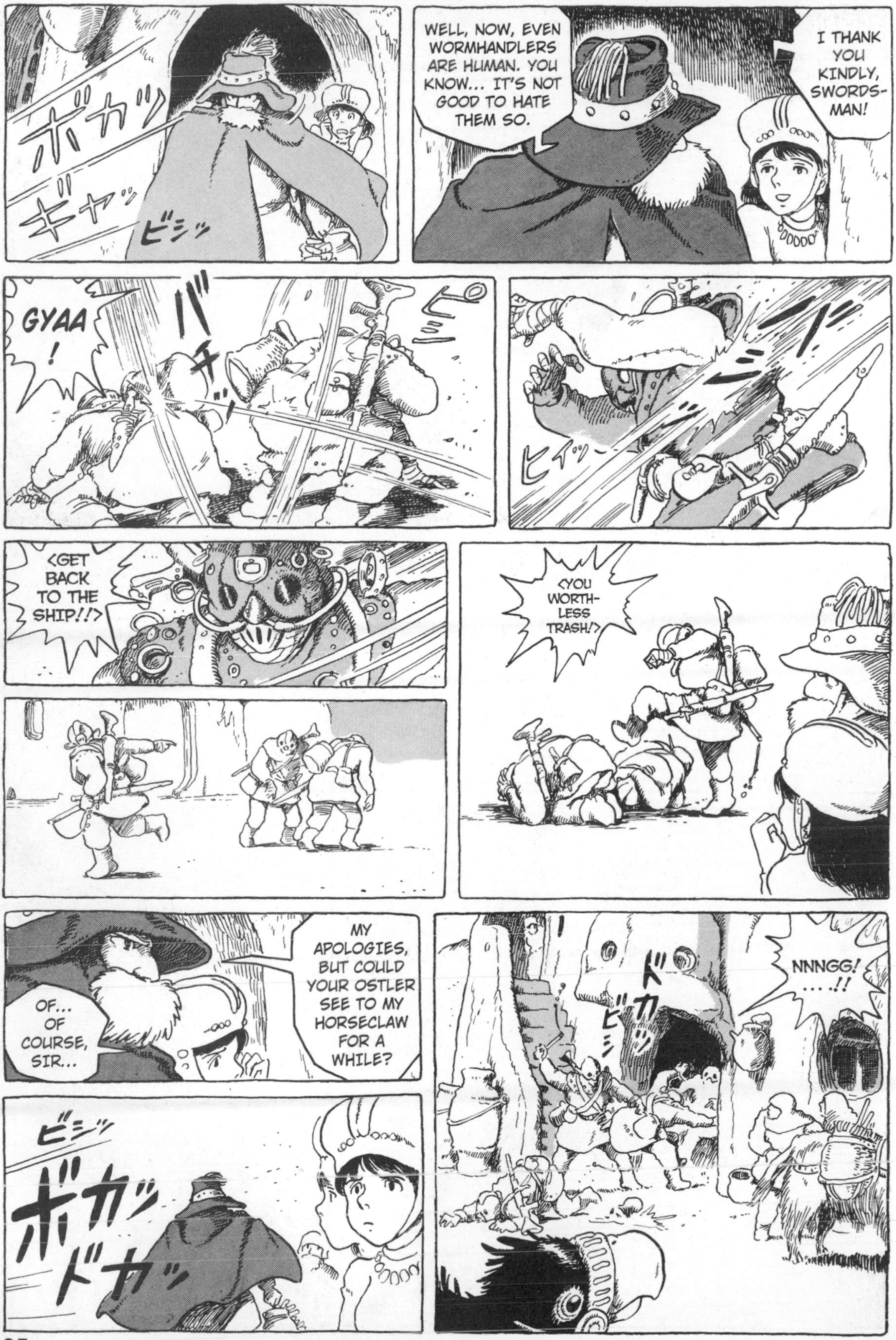
I THANK YOU KINDLY, SWORDSMAN!
WELL, NOW, EVEN WORMHANDLERS ARE HUMAN. YOU KNOW... IT'S NOT GOOD TO HATE THEM SO.
ボカッ
ギャッ
ビシッ
GYAA!
バチ
<YOU WORTHLESS TRASH!>
<GET BACK TO THE SHIP!!>
NNNGG! ...!!
ドカッ
ビシ
MY APOLOGIES, BUT COULD YOUR OSTLER SEE TO MY HORSECLAW FOR A WHILE?
OF... OF COURSE, SIR...
ビシッ
ボカッ
ドカッ

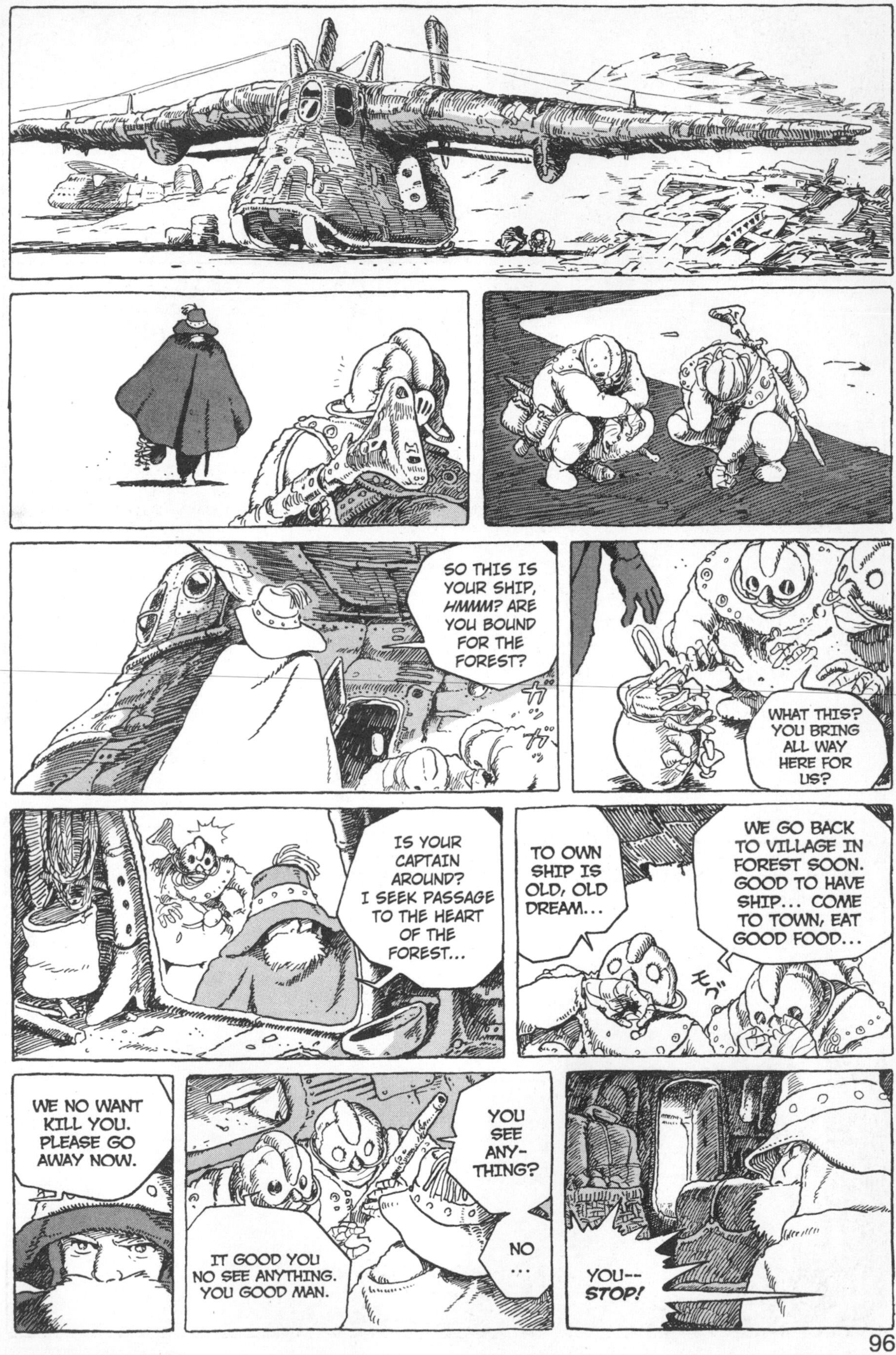
WHAT THIS? YOU BRING ALL WAY HERE FOR US?
SO THIS IS YOUR SHIP, *HMMM?* ARE YOU BOUND FOR THE FOREST?
WE GO BACK TO VILLAGE IN FOREST SOON. GOOD TO HAVE SHIP... COME TO TOWN, EAT GOOD FOOD...
モグ
TO OWN SHIP IS OLD, OLD DREAM...
IS YOUR CAPTAIN AROUND? I SEEK PASSAGE TO THE HEART OF THE FOREST...
YOU-- **STOP!**
YOU SEE ANYTHING?
NO ...
IT GOOD YOU NO SEE ANYTHING. YOU GOOD MAN.
WE NO WANT KILL YOU. PLEASE GO AWAY NOW.

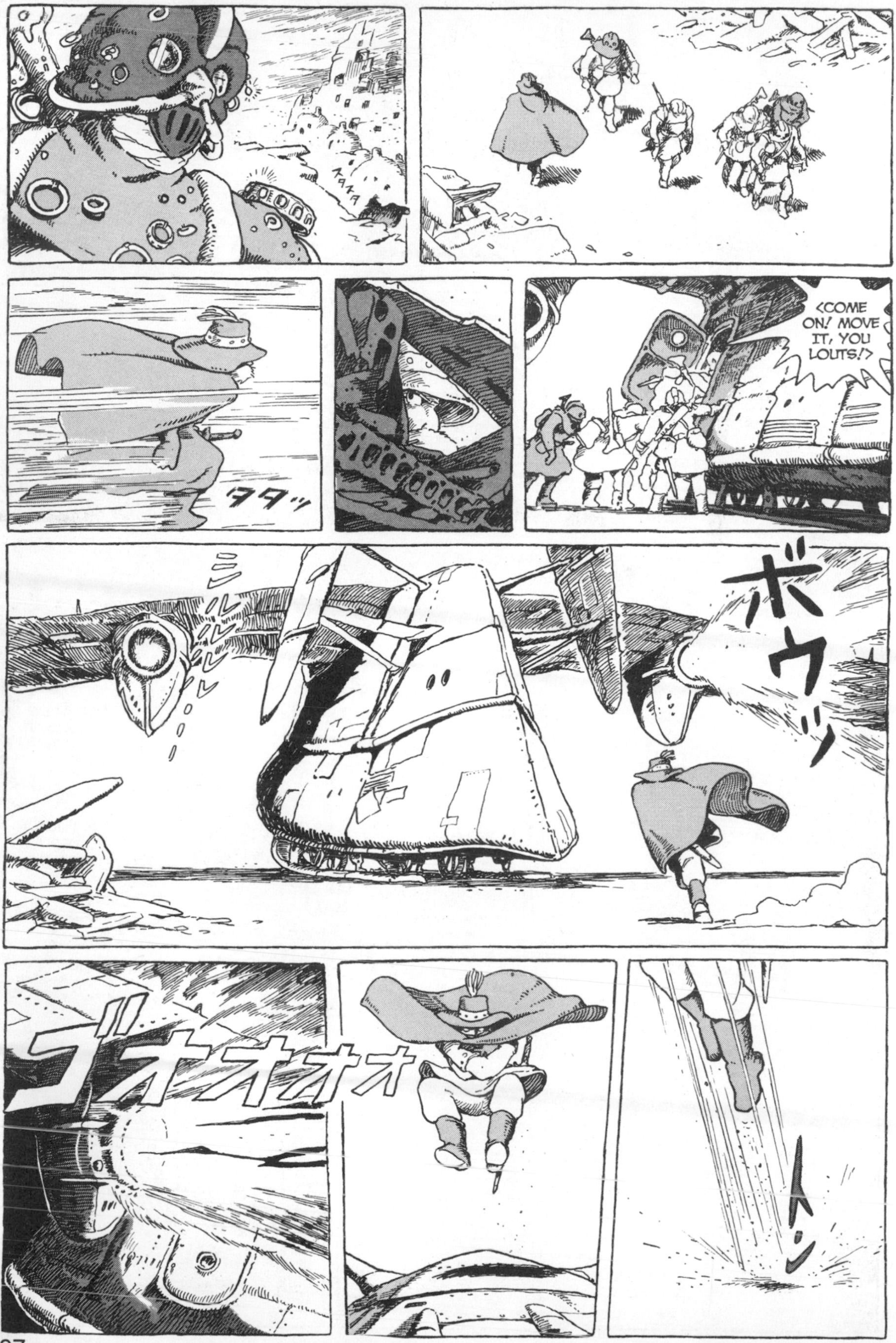
スタスタ
<COME ON! MOVE IT, YOU LOUTS!>
タタッ
ボウッ
シルルルル
ゴオオオオ

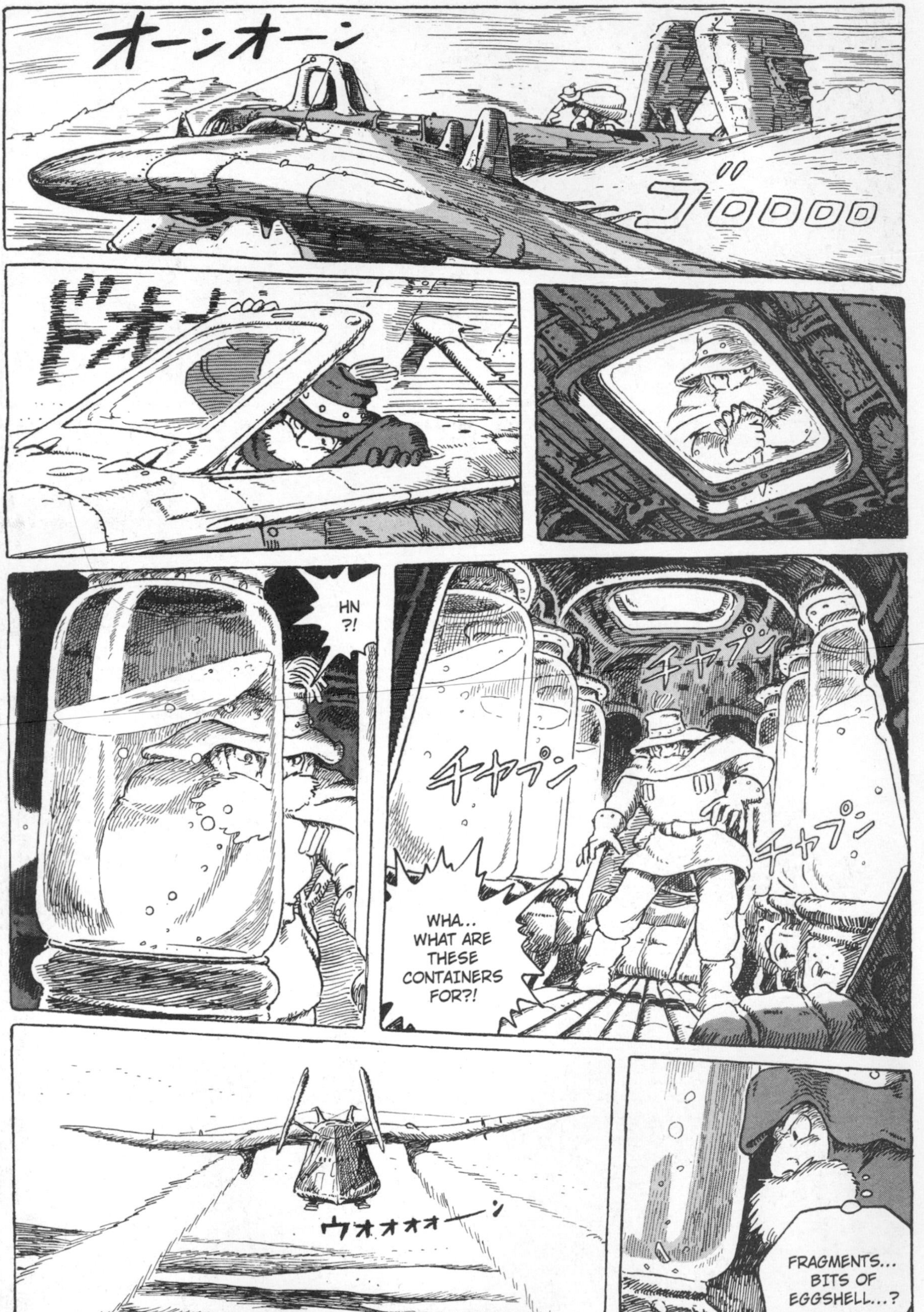

オーンオーン
ゴOOOOO
チャプン
チャプン
チャプン
WHA... WHAT ARE THESE CONTAINERS FOR?!
HN ?!
FRAGMENTS... BITS OF EGGSHELL...?
ウオオオオーン

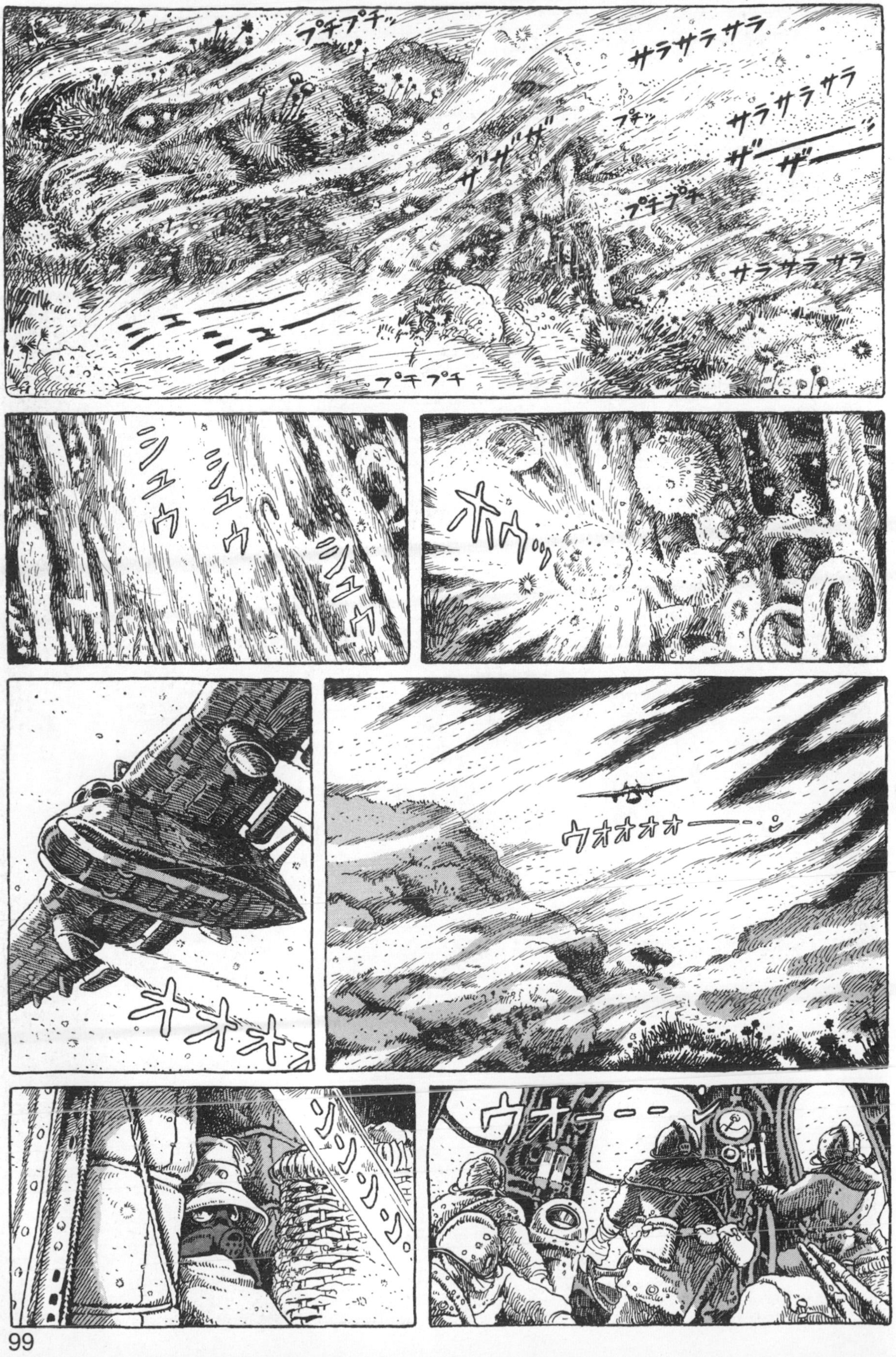
サラサラサラ
プチプチッ
サラサラサラ
ザーー
ザーー
プチッ
ザザザ
プチプチ
サラサラサラ
シューー
シューー
プチプチ
ホウッ
シュウ
シュウ
シュウ
ウオオオオー・・・ン
オオオオ
ウオーーー
ゾン・ン・ン

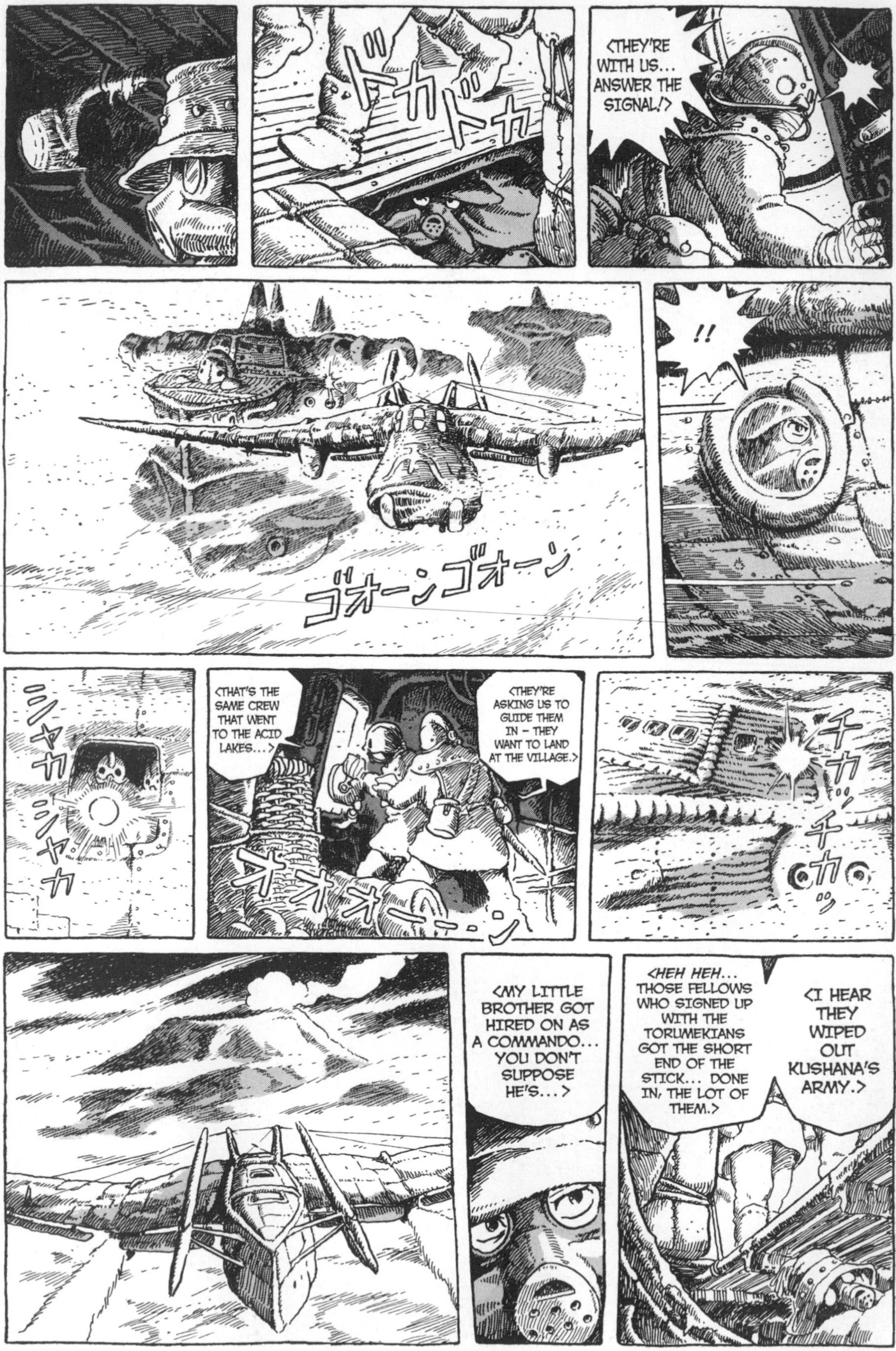
<THEY'RE WITH US... ANSWER THE SIGNAL!>
ドカドカ
!!
ゴォーンゴォーン
チカチカッ
<THEY'RE ASKING US TO GUIDE THEM IN – THEY WANT TO LAND AT THE VILLAGE.>
<THAT'S THE SAME CREW THAT WENT TO THE ACID LAKES...>
オオオーン
シャカシャカシャカ
<I HEAR THEY WIPED OUT KUSHANA'S ARMY.>
<HEH HEH... THOSE FELLOWS WHO SIGNED UP WITH THE TORUMEKIANS GOT THE SHORT END OF THE STICK... DONE IN, THE LOT OF THEM.>
<MY LITTLE BROTHER GOT HIRED ON AS A COMMANDO... YOU DON'T SUPPOSE HE'S...>

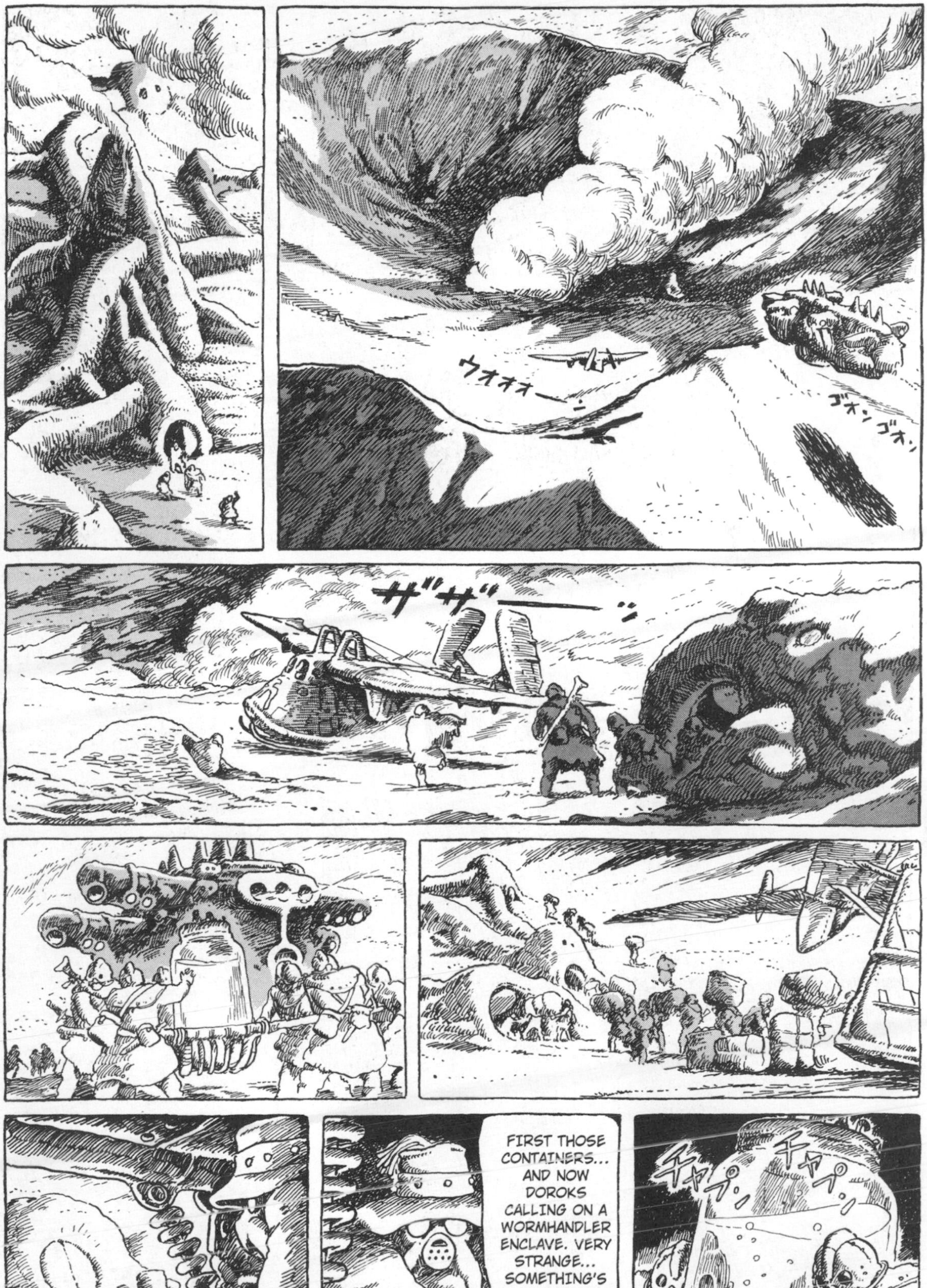
ウオオオーン
ゴオンゴオン
ザザーーッ
チャプンチャプン
FIRST THOSE CONTAINERS... AND NOW DOROKS CALLING ON A WORMHANDLER ENCLAVE. VERY STRANGE... SOMETHING'S GOING ON HERE...

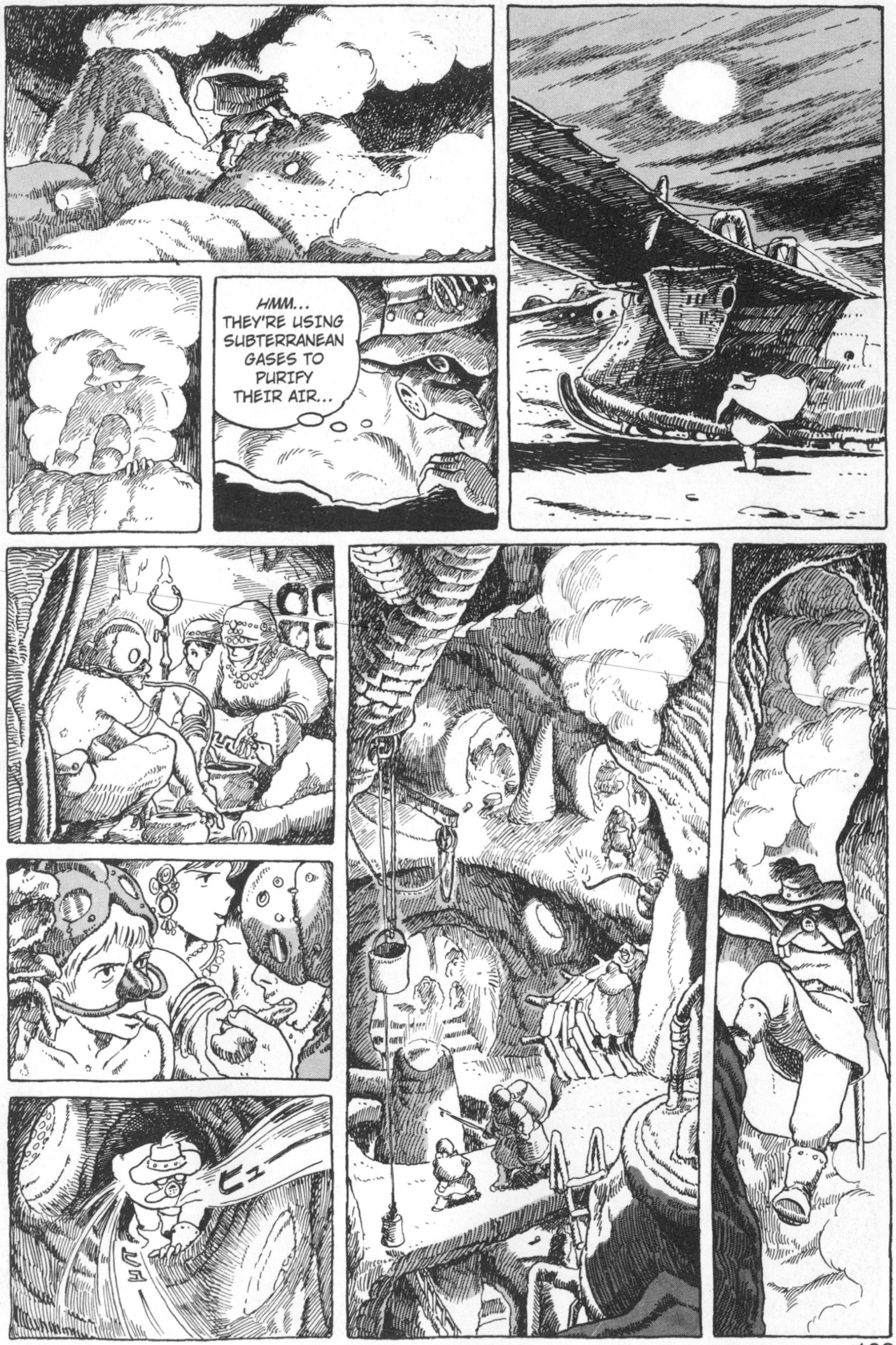
HMM... THEY'RE USING SUBTERRANEAN GASES TO PURIFY THEIR AIR...

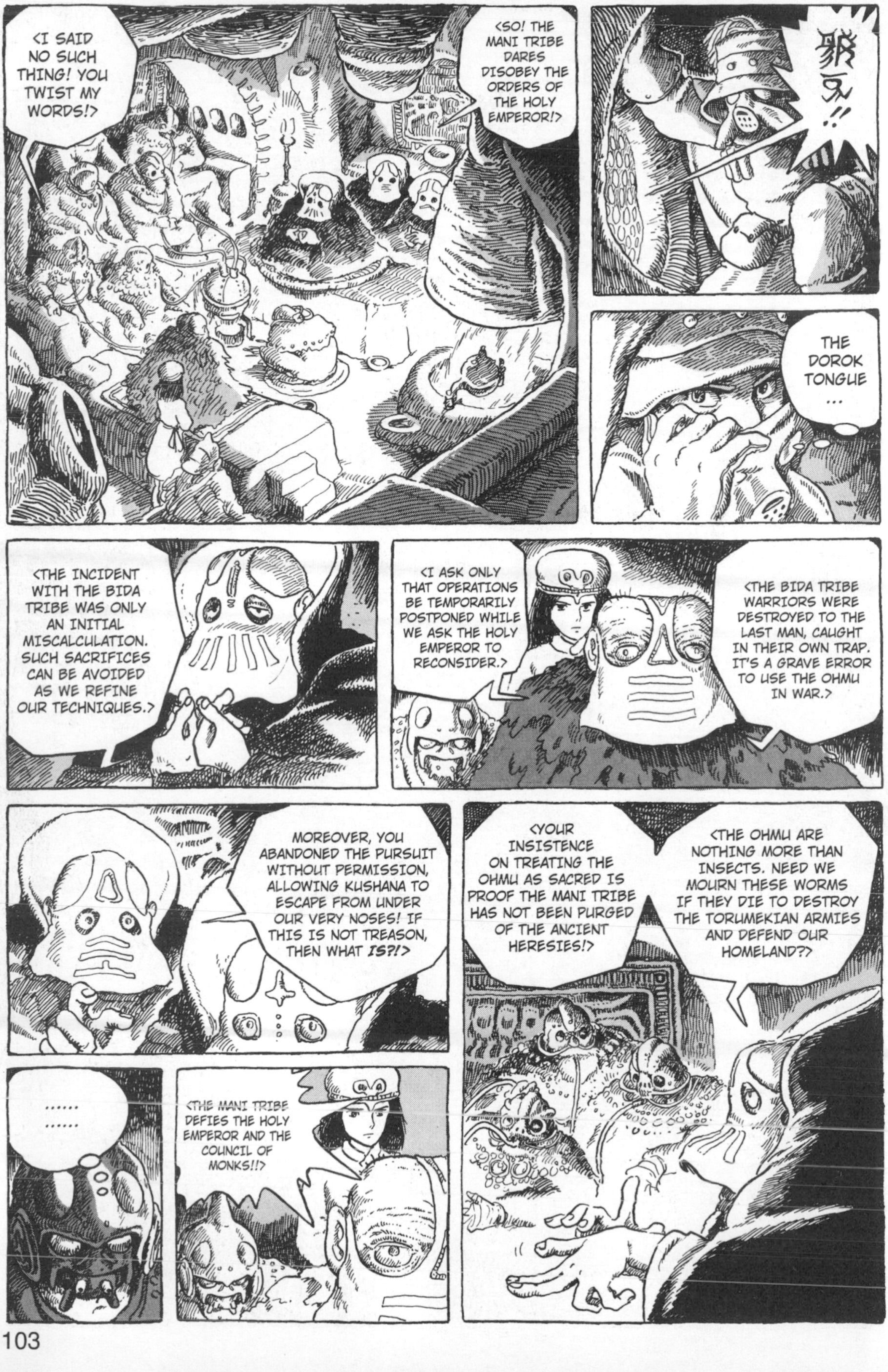
THE DOROK TONGUE ...
<SO! THE MANI TRIBE DARES DISOBEY THE ORDERS OF THE HOLY EMPEROR!>
<I SAID NO SUCH THING! YOU TWIST MY WORDS!>
<THE BIDA TRIBE WARRIORS WERE DESTROYED TO THE LAST MAN, CAUGHT IN THEIR OWN TRAP. IT'S A GRAVE ERROR TO USE THE OHMU IN WAR.>
<I ASK ONLY THAT OPERATIONS BE TEMPORARILY POSTPONED WHILE WE ASK THE HOLY EMPEROR TO RECONSIDER.>
<THE INCIDENT WITH THE BIDA TRIBE WAS ONLY AN INITIAL MISCALCULATION. SUCH SACRIFICES CAN BE AVOIDED AS WE REFINE OUR TECHNIQUES.>
<THE OHMU ARE NOTHING MORE THAN INSECTS. NEED WE MOURN THESE WORMS IF THEY DIE TO DESTROY THE TORUMEKIAN ARMIES AND DEFEND OUR HOMELAND?>
<YOUR INSISTENCE ON TREATING THE OHMU AS SACRED IS PROOF THE MANI TRIBE HAS NOT BEEN PURGED OF THE ANCIENT HERESIES!>
MOREOVER, YOU ABANDONED THE PURSUIT WITHOUT PERMISSION, ALLOWING KUSHANA TO ESCAPE FROM UNDER OUR VERY NOSES! IF THIS IS NOT TREASON, THEN WHAT *IS?!*>
<THE MANI TRIBE DEFIES THE HOLY EMPEROR AND THE COUNCIL OF MONKS!!>
....

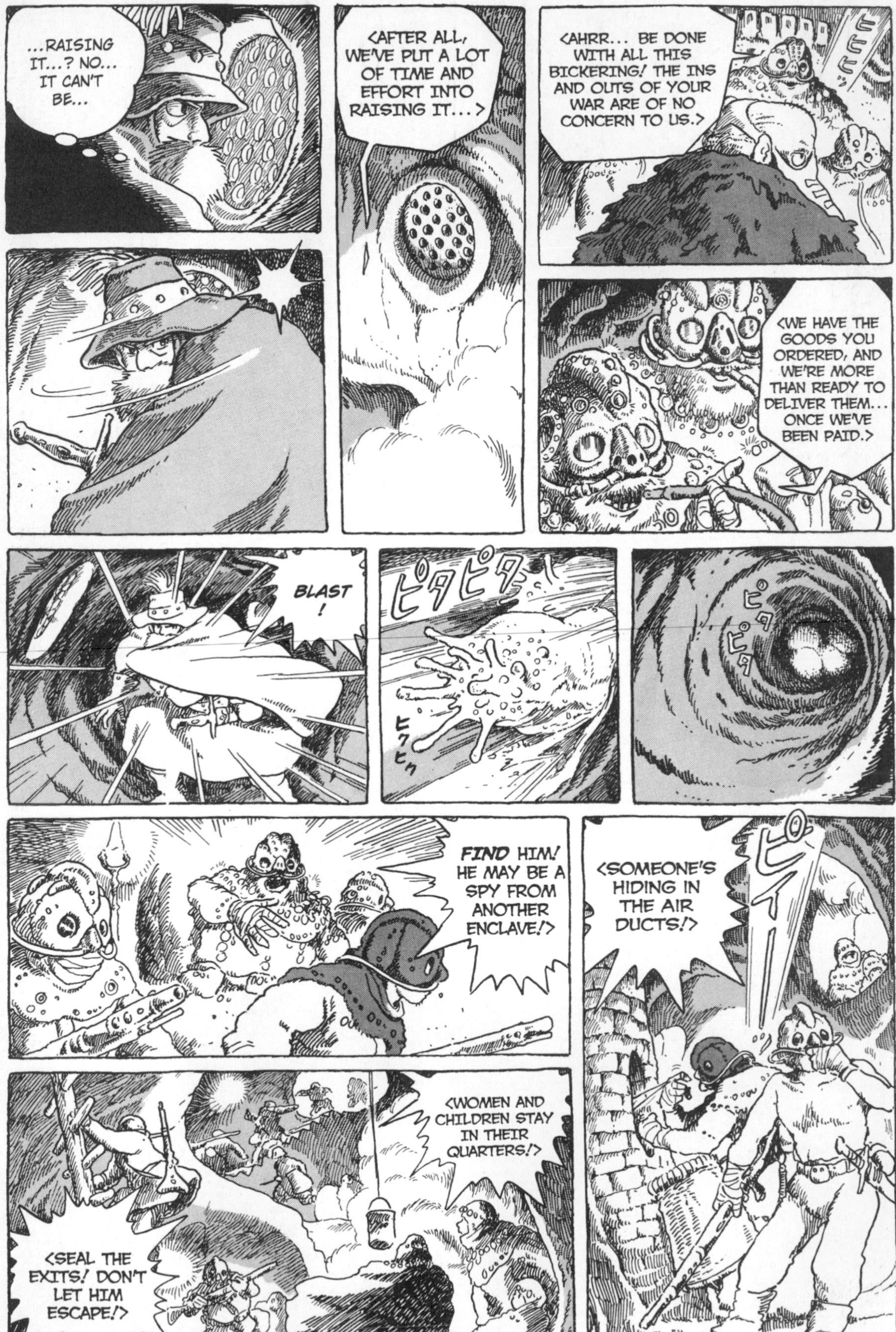
<AHRR... BE DONE WITH ALL THIS BICKERING! THE INS AND OUTS OF YOUR WAR ARE OF NO CONCERN TO US.>
<WE HAVE THE GOODS YOU ORDERED, AND WE'RE MORE THAN READY TO DELIVER THEM... ONCE WE'VE BEEN PAID.>
<AFTER ALL, WE'VE PUT A LOT OF TIME AND EFFORT INTO RAISING IT...>
...RAISING IT...? NO... IT CAN'T BE...
ピタピタ
ピタピタ
BLAST!
ピィー
<SOMEONE'S HIDING IN THE AIR DUCTS!>
FIND HIM! HE MAY BE A SPY FROM ANOTHER ENCLAVE!>
<WOMEN AND CHILDREN STAY IN THEIR QUARTERS!>
<SEAL THE EXITS! DON'T LET HIM ESCAPE!>

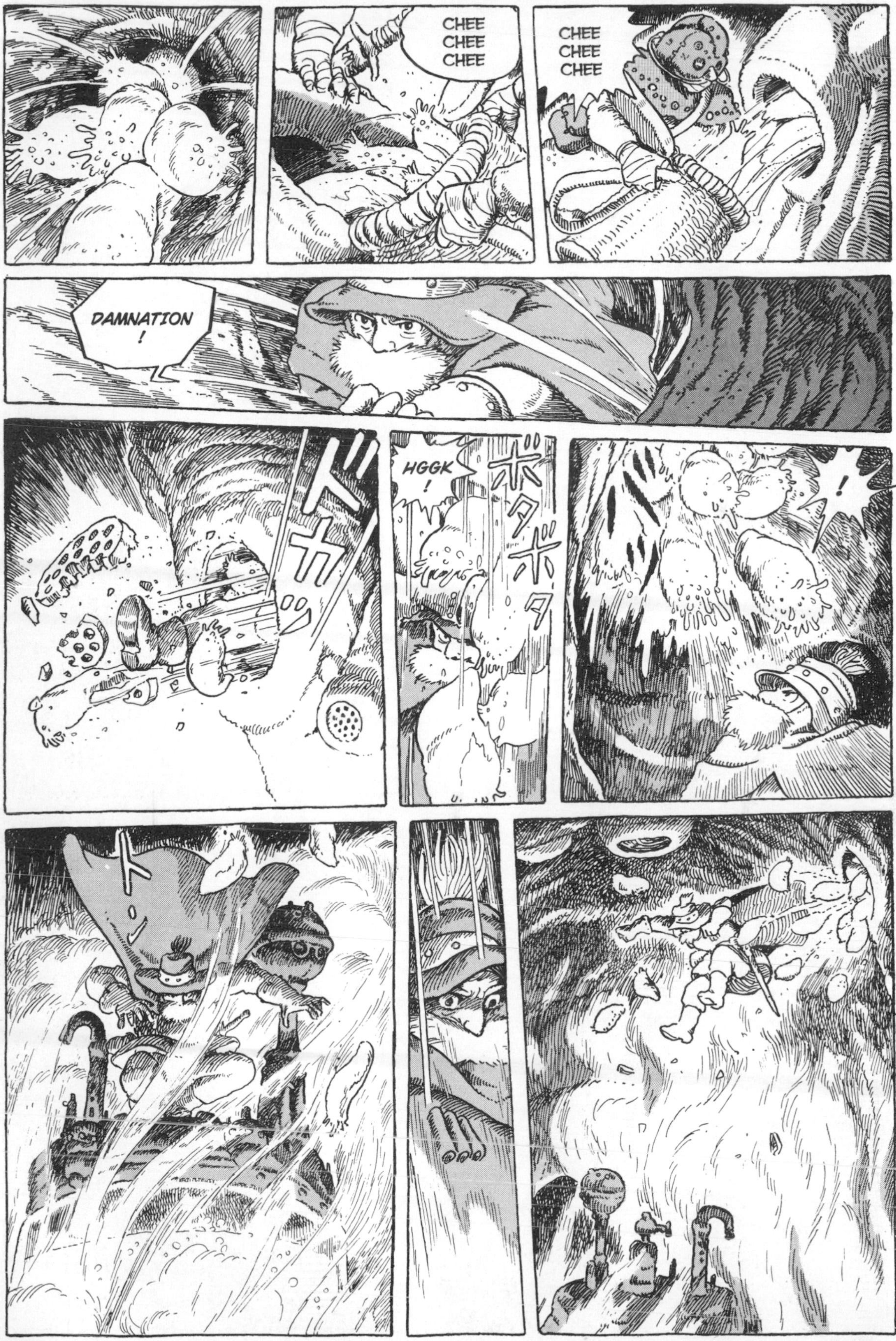
CHEE
CHEE
CHEE
CHEE
CHEE
CHEE
DAMNATION
!
!
HGGK
!
ボタボタ
ドカッ

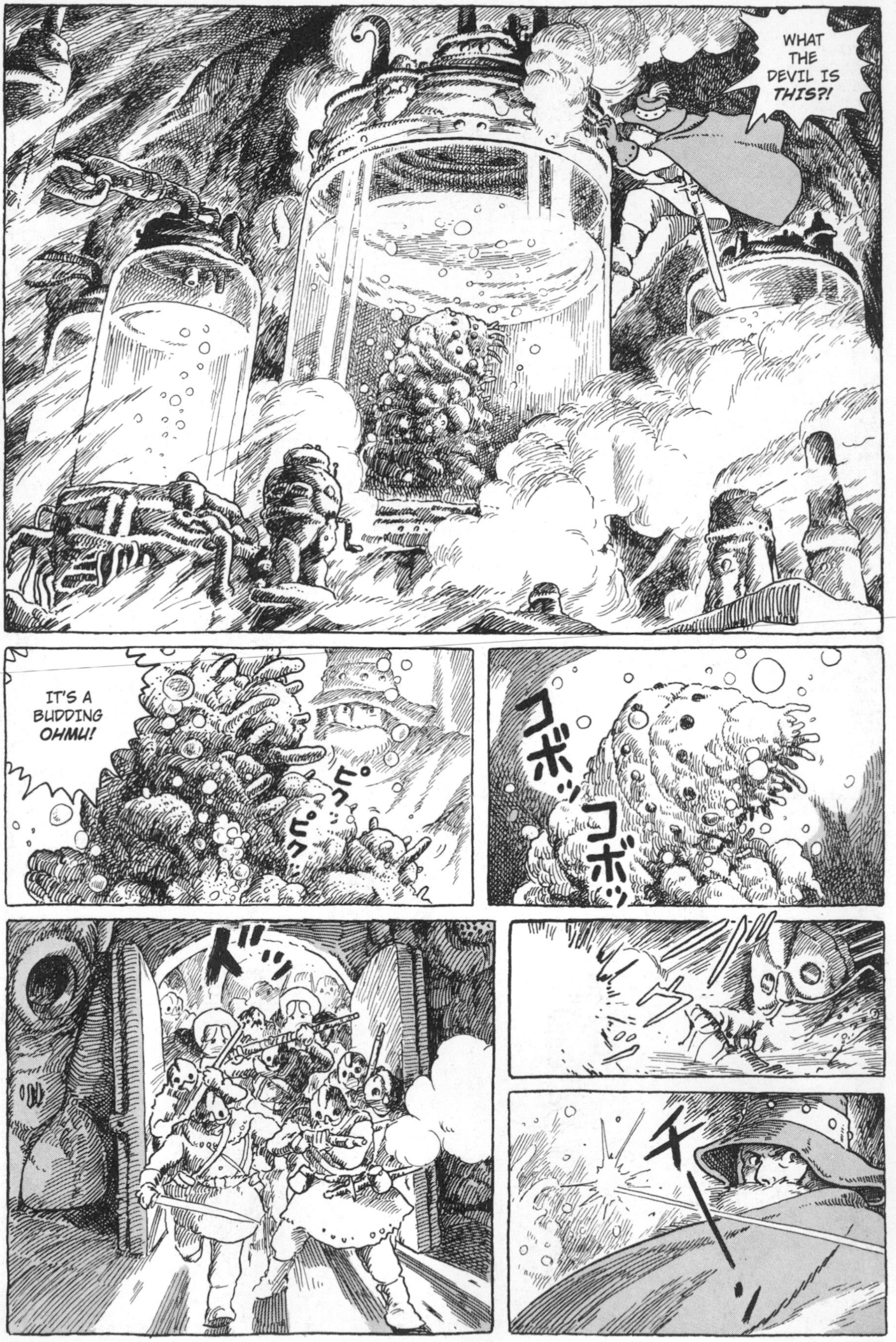
WHAT THE DEVIL IS THIS?!
IT'S A BUDDING OHMU!
ピクッ ピクッ
コポッ コポッ
ドッ

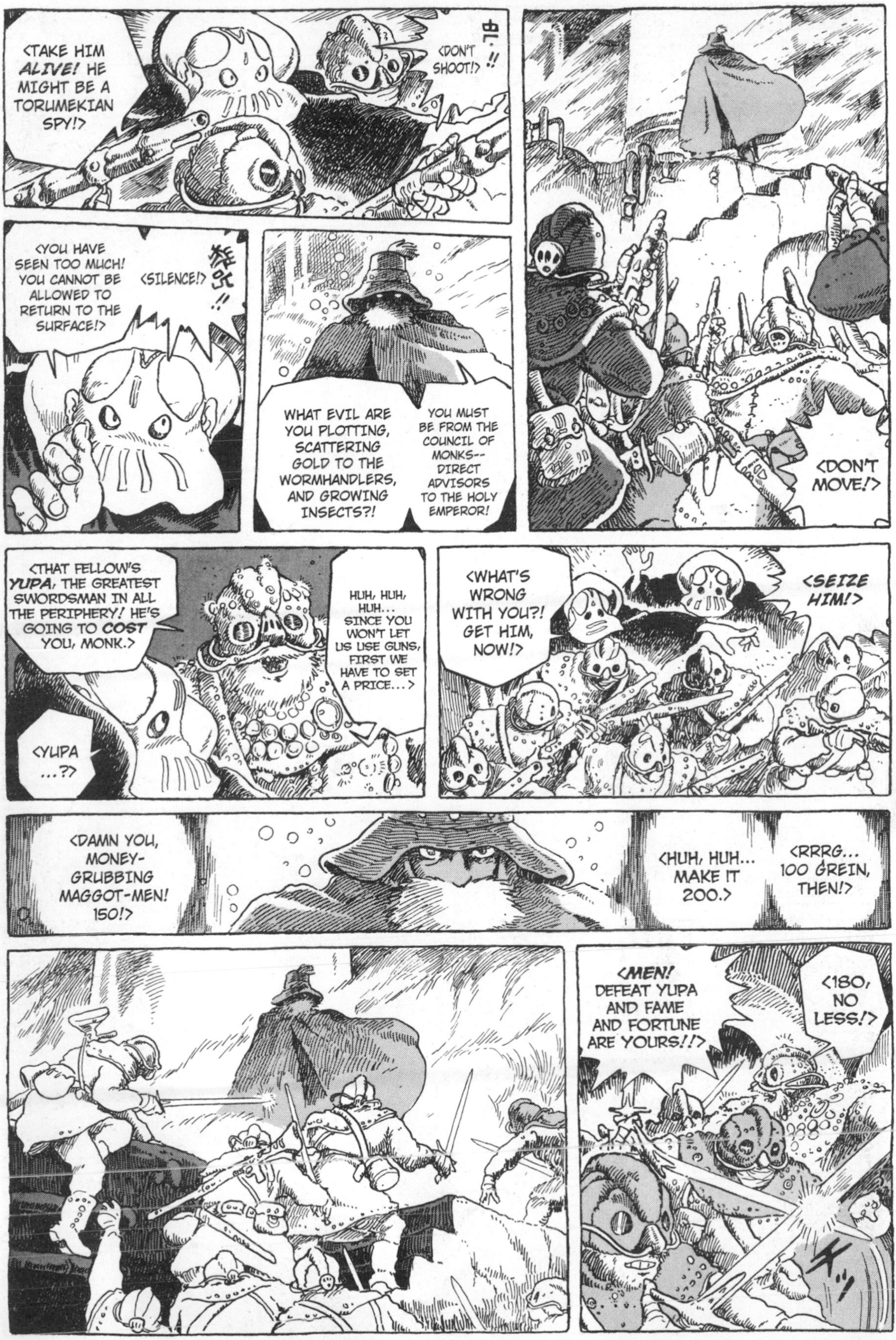

<DON'T MOVE!>
<DON'T SHOOT!>
<TAKE HIM *ALIVE!* HE MIGHT BE A TORUMEKIAN SPY!>
YOU MUST BE FROM THE COUNCIL OF MONKS-- DIRECT ADVISORS TO THE HOLY EMPEROR!
WHAT EVIL ARE YOU PLOTTING, SCATTERING GOLD TO THE WORMHANDLERS, AND GROWING INSECTS?!
<SILENCE!>
<YOU HAVE SEEN TOO MUCH! YOU CANNOT BE ALLOWED TO RETURN TO THE SURFACE!>
<*SEIZE HIM!*>
<WHAT'S WRONG WITH YOU?! GET HIM, NOW!>
HUH, HUH, HUH... SINCE YOU WON'T LET US USE GUNS, FIRST WE HAVE TO SET A PRICE...>
<THAT FELLOW'S *YUPA*, THE GREATEST SWORDSMAN IN ALL THE PERIPHERY! HE'S GOING TO *COST* YOU, MONK.>
<YUPA ...?>
<RRRG... 100 GREIN, THEN!>
<HUH, HUH... MAKE IT 200.>
<DAMN YOU, MONEY-GRUBBING MAGGOT-MEN! 150!>
<180, NO LESS!>
<*MEN!* DEFEAT YUPA AND FAME AND FORTUNE ARE YOURS!!>

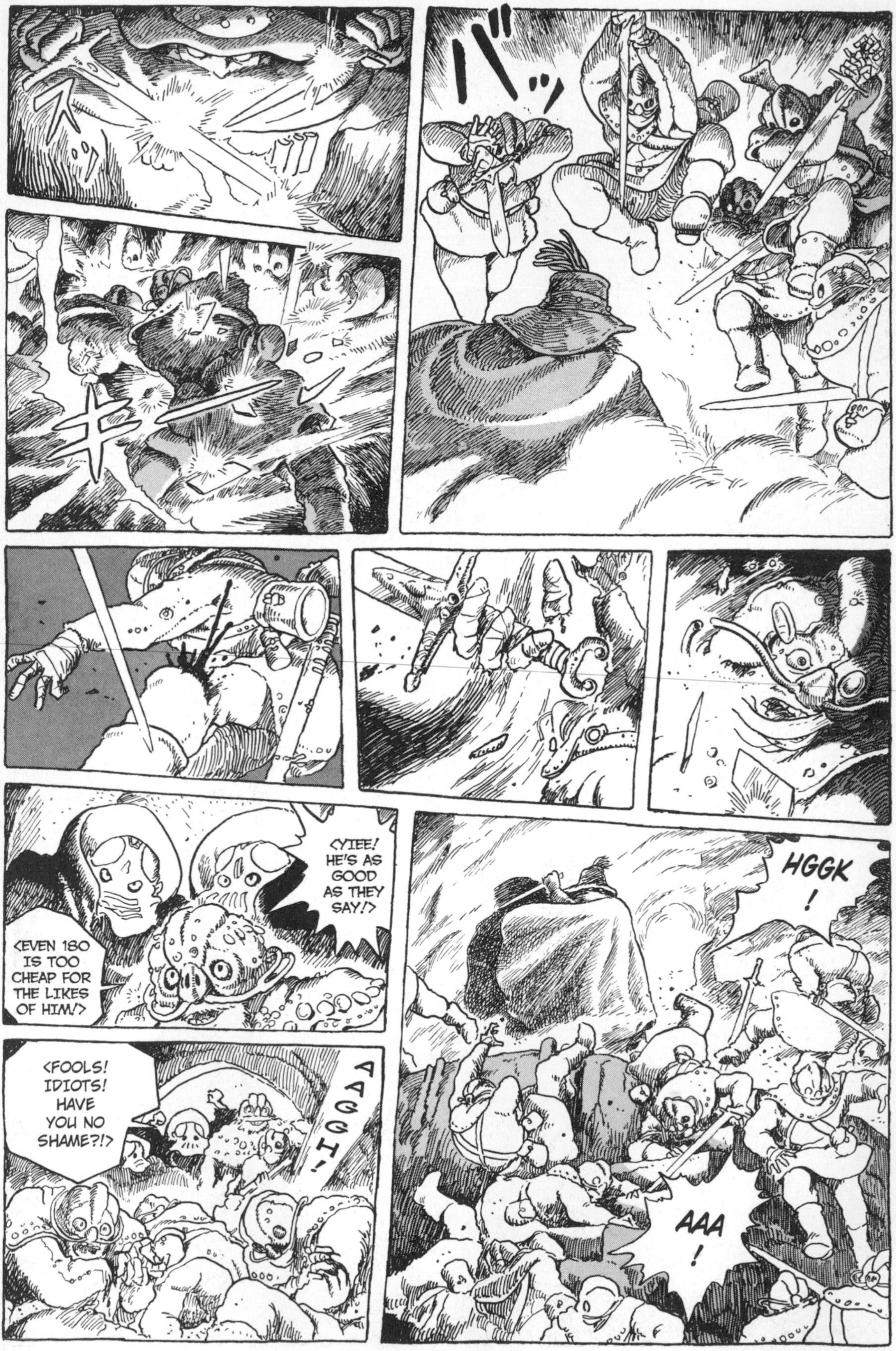

バッ
HGGK!
AAA!
<YIEE! HE'S AS GOOD AS THEY SAY!>
<EVEN 180 IS TOO CHEAP FOR THE LIKES OF HIM!>
AAGGH!
<FOOLS! IDIOTS! HAVE YOU NO SHAME?!>

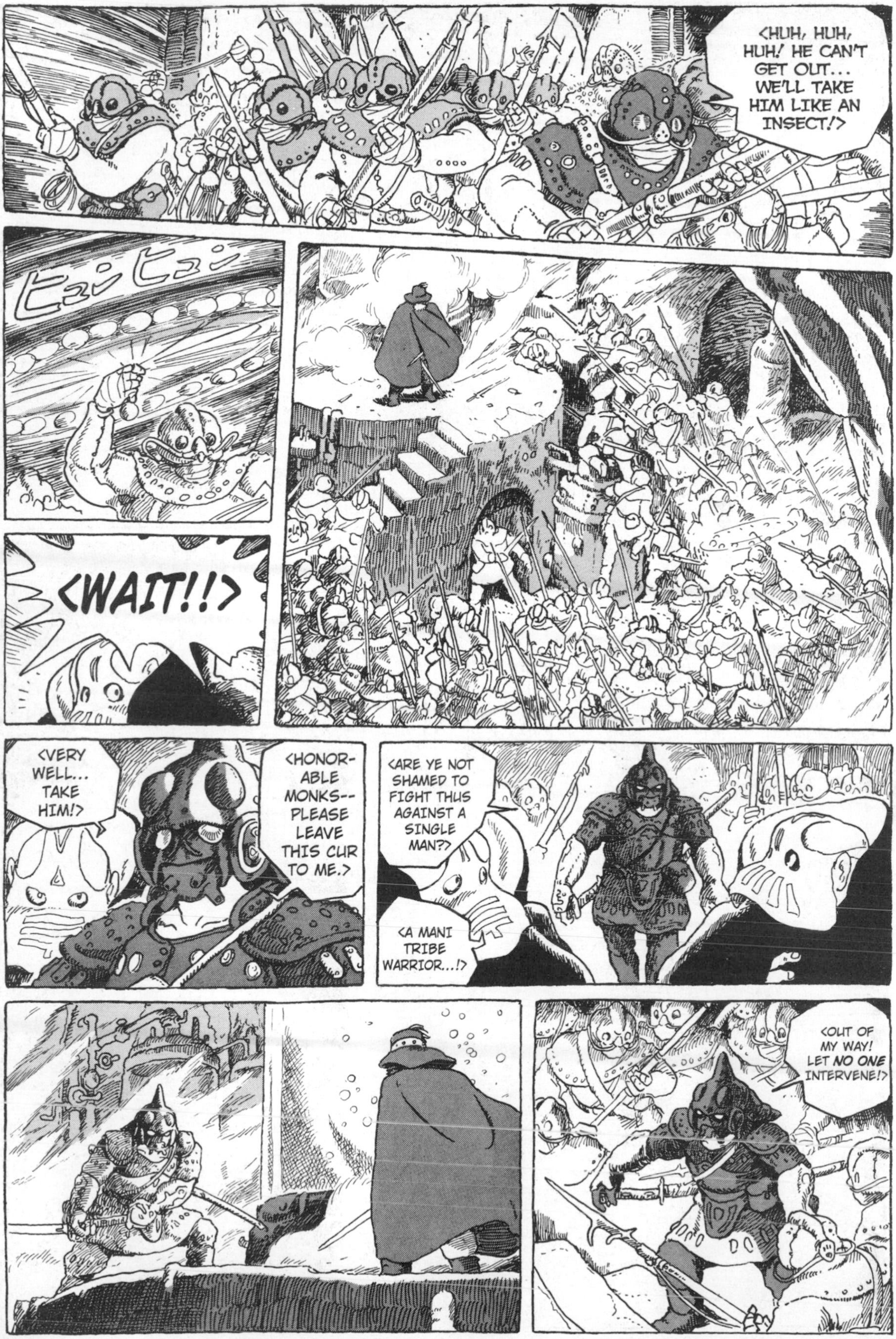
<HUH, HUH, HUH! HE CAN'T GET OUT... WE'LL TAKE HIM LIKE AN INSECT!>
ヒュンヒュン
<WAIT!!>
<ARE YE NOT SHAMED TO FIGHT THUS AGAINST A SINGLE MAN?>
<A MANI TRIBE WARRIOR...!>
<HONORABLE MONKS--PLEASE LEAVE THIS CUR TO ME.>
<VERY WELL... TAKE HIM!>
<OUT OF MY WAY! LET ***NO ONE*** INTERVENE!>

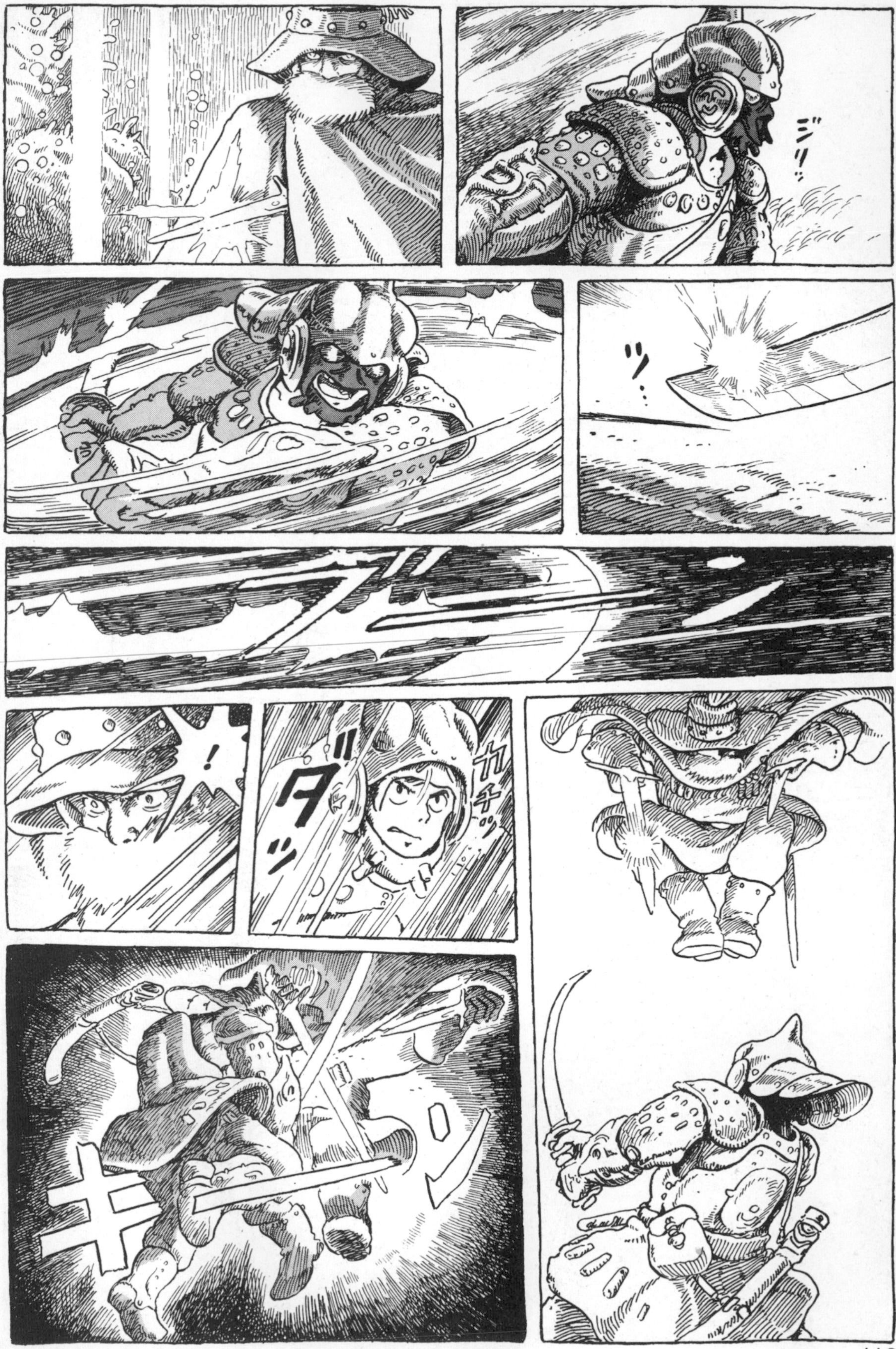
ジリッ
ツ…
ブーン
カチッ
ダッ
!
キーン

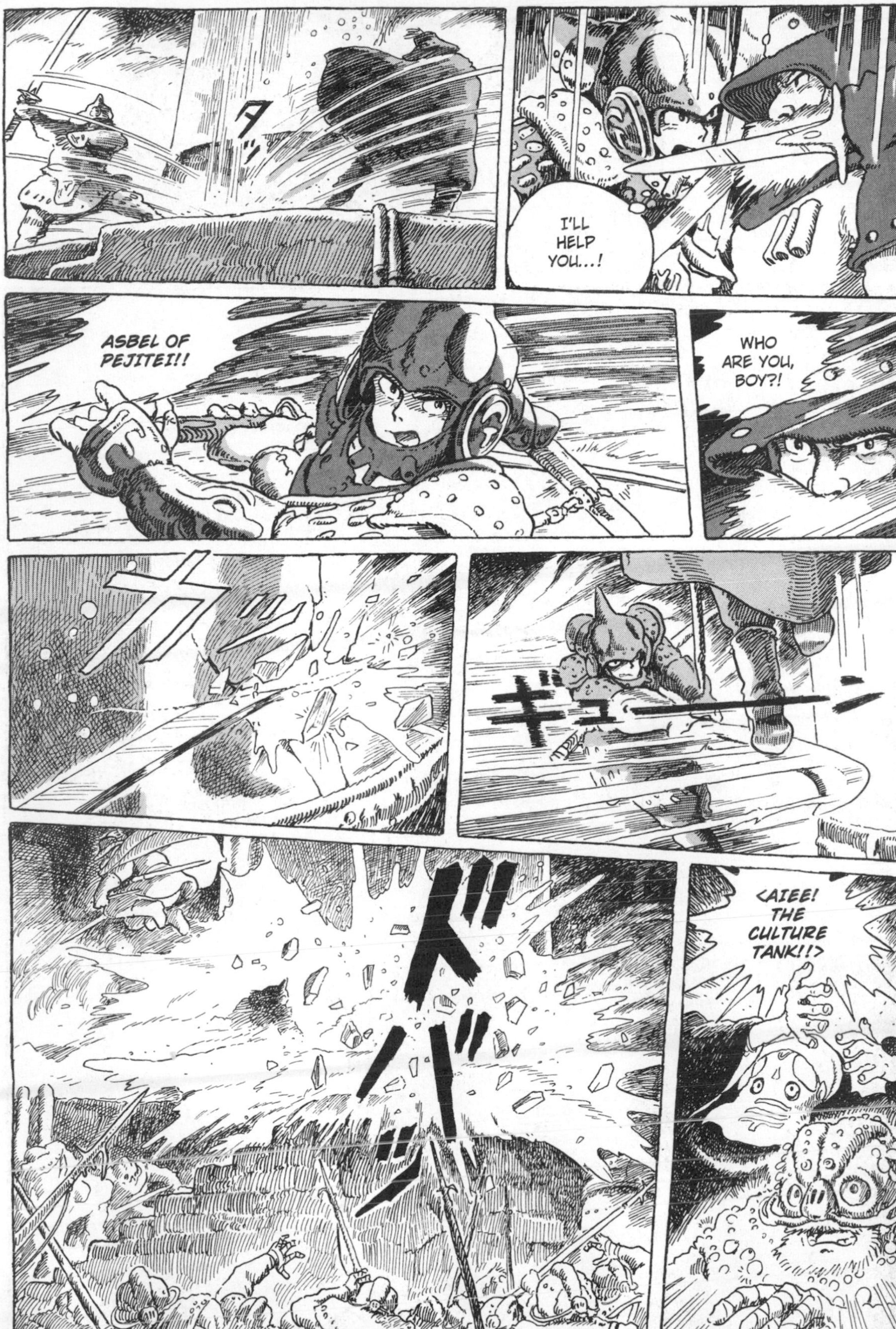

I'LL HELP YOU...!
タ
WHO ARE YOU, BOY?!
ASBEL OF PEJITEI!!
ギュ
カッ
<AIEE! THE CULTURE TANK!!>
ドバ

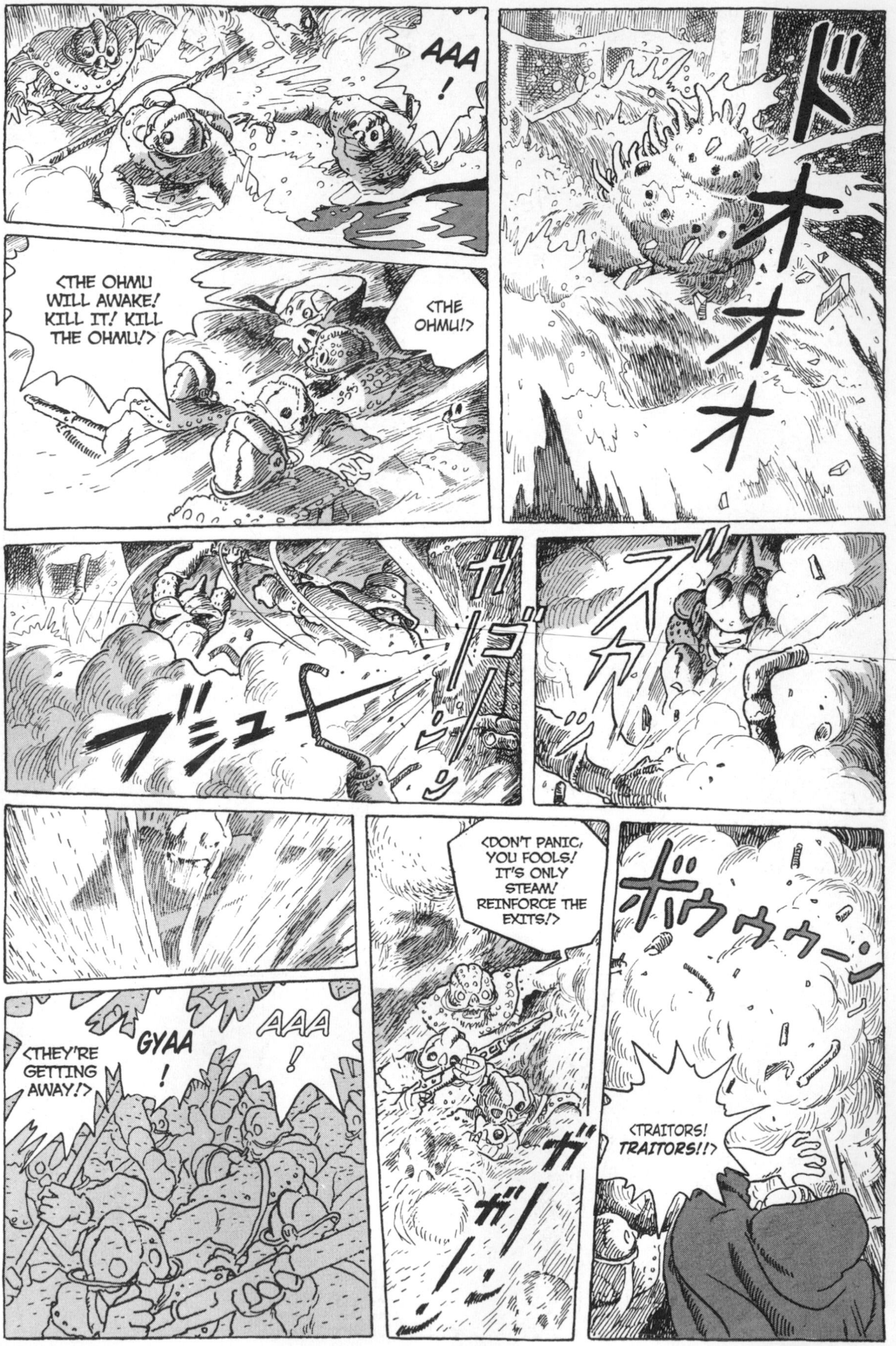
ドオオオ
AAA!
<THE OHMU!>
<THE OHMU WILL AWAKE! KILL IT! KILL THE OHMU!>
ズイカン
ガゴン
ブシュー
ボウウウー
<TRAITORS! TRAITORS!!>
<DON'T PANIC, YOU FOOLS! IT'S ONLY STEAM! REINFORCE THE EXITS!>
ガガン
AAA!
GYAA!
<THEY'RE GETTING AWAY!>

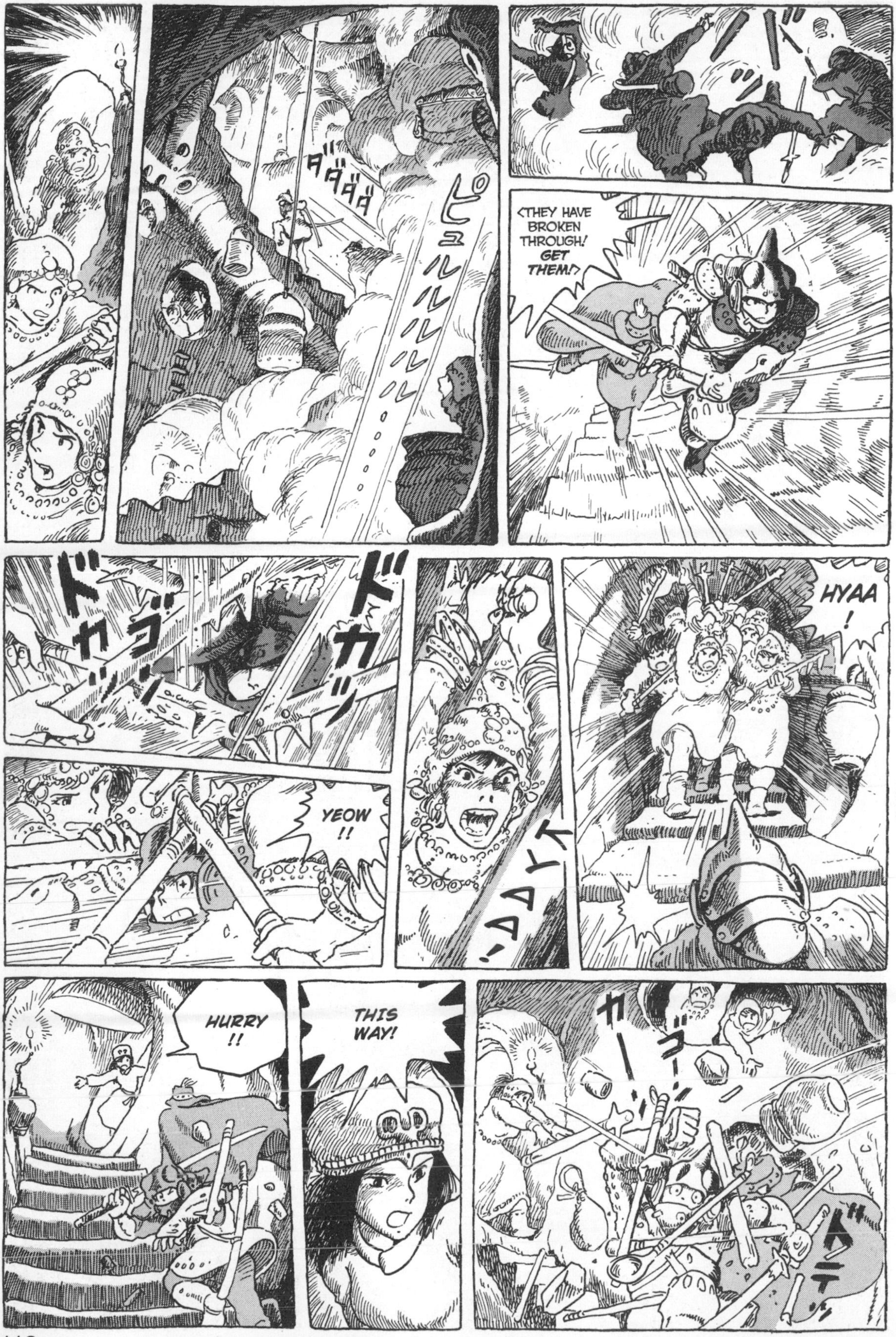

<THEY HAVE BROKEN THROUGH! GET THEM!>
HYAA!
YEOW!!
THIS WAY!
HURRY!!

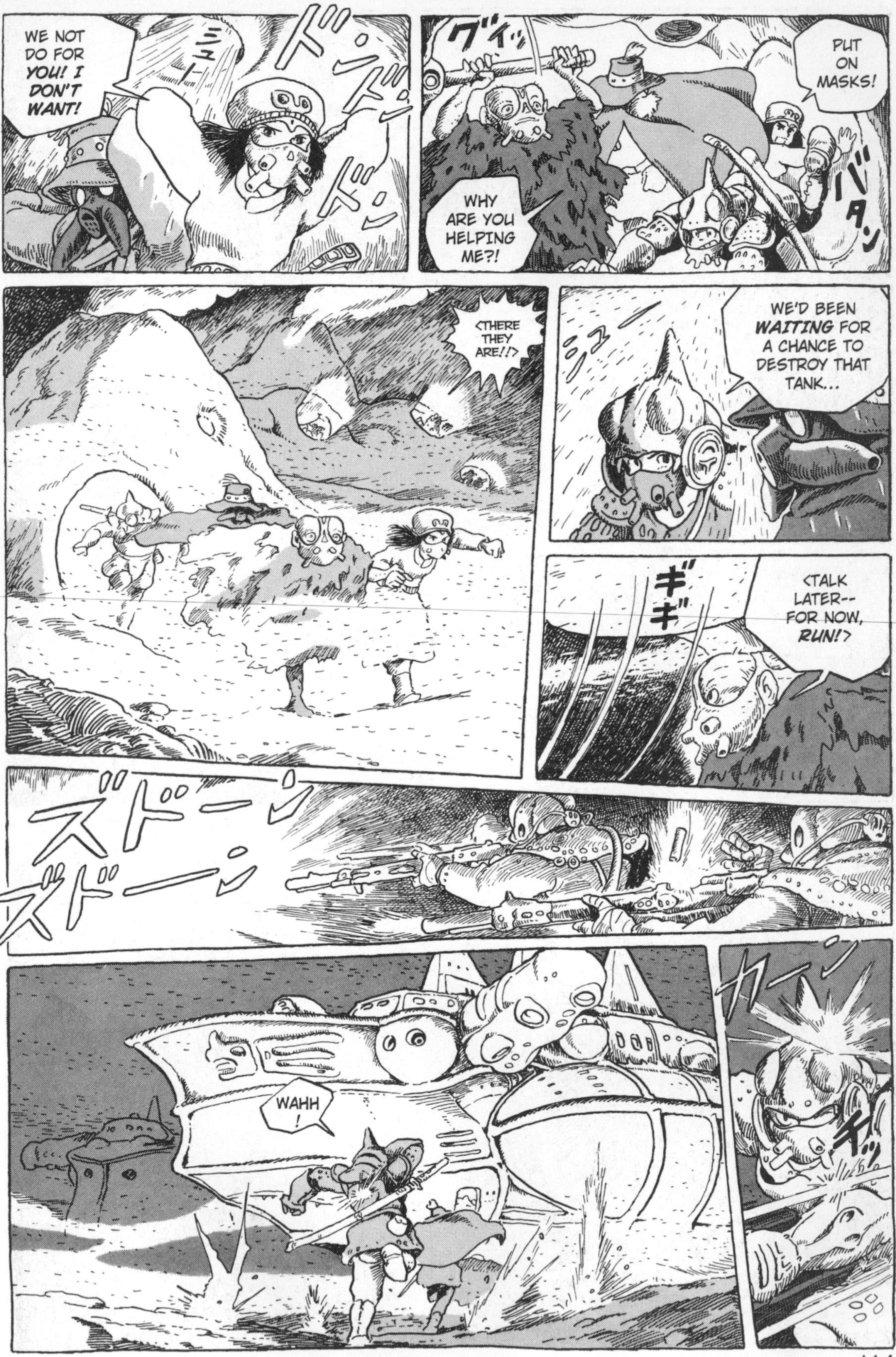
PUT ON MASKS!
WHY ARE YOU HELPING ME?!
WE NOT DO FOR YOU! I DON'T WANT!
WE'D BEEN WAITING FOR A CHANCE TO DESTROY THAT TANK...
<TALK LATER-- FOR NOW, RUN!>
<THERE THEY ARE!!>
ズドーン
ズドーン
WAHH!

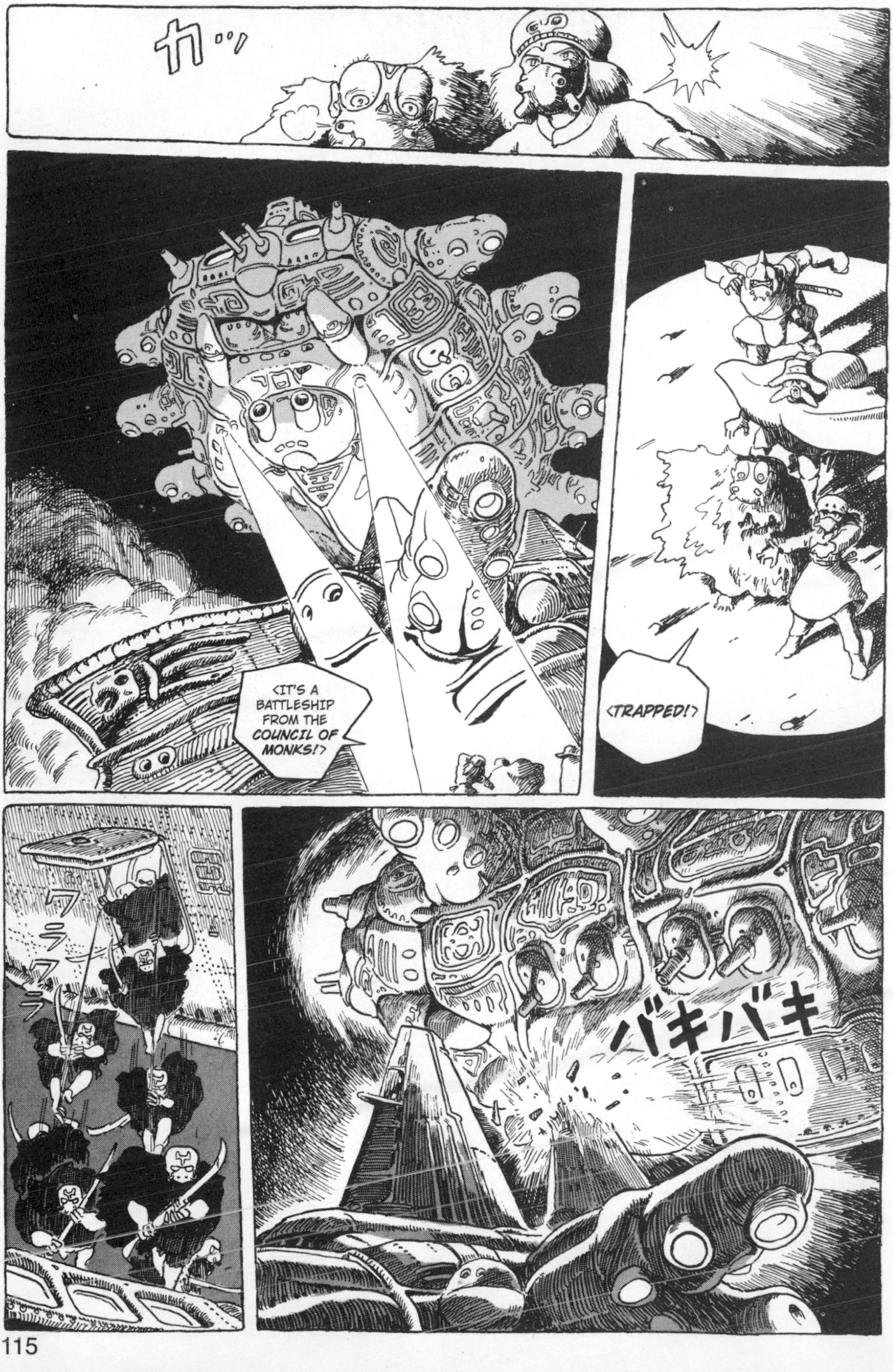
カッ
<TRAPPED!>
<IT'S A BATTLESHIP FROM THE COUNCIL OF MONKS!>
バキバキ
ワラワラ

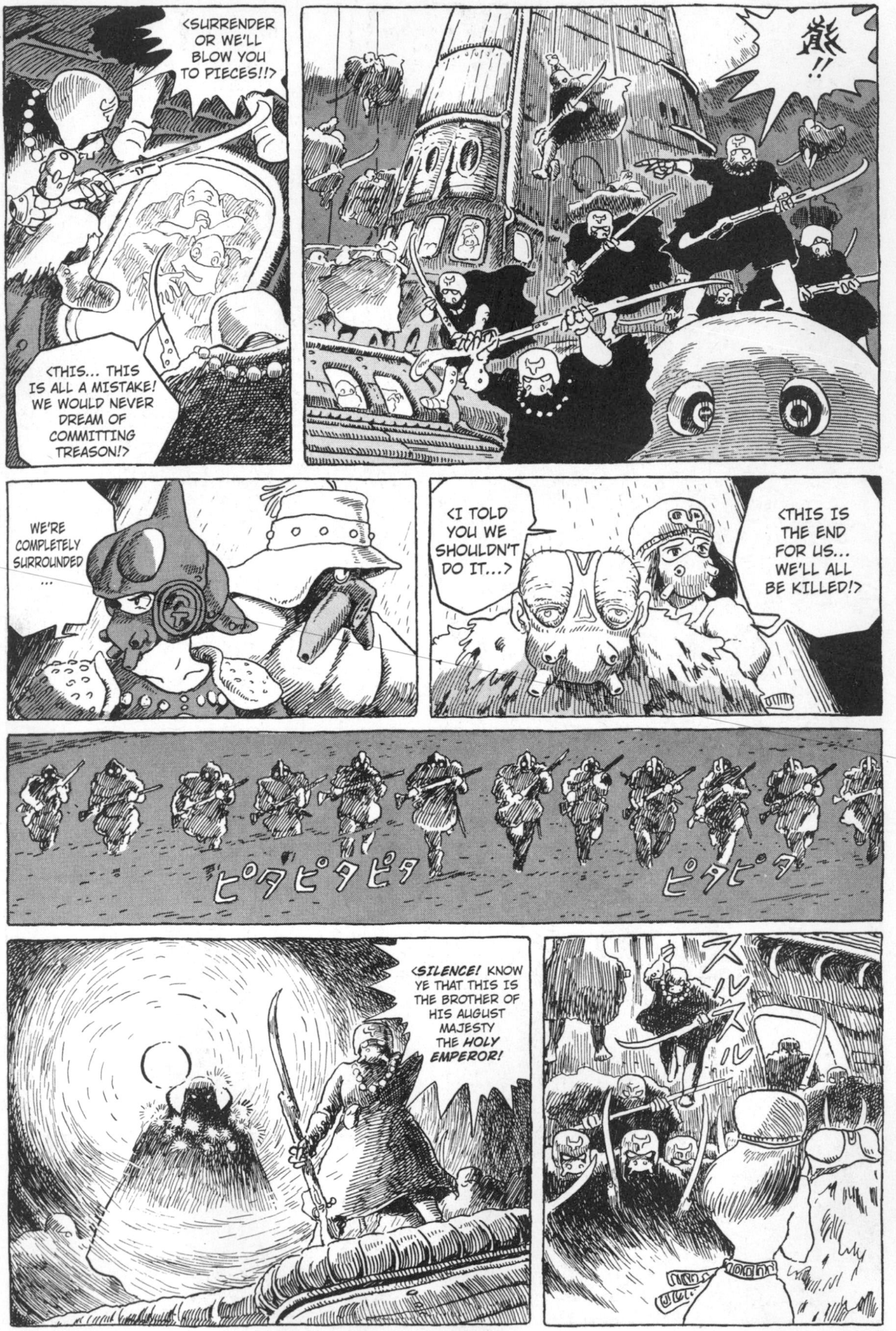
!!
<SURRENDER OR WE'LL BLOW YOU TO PIECES!!>
<THIS... THIS IS ALL A MISTAKE! WE WOULD NEVER DREAM OF COMMITTING TREASON!>
<THIS IS THE END FOR US... WE'LL ALL BE KILLED!>
<I TOLD YOU WE SHOULDN'T DO IT...>
WE'RE COMPLETELY SURROUNDED ...
ピタピタ
ピタピタピタ
スルスル
<*SILENCE!* KNOW YE THAT THIS IS THE BROTHER OF HIS AUGUST MAJESTY THE *HOLY EMPEROR!*>

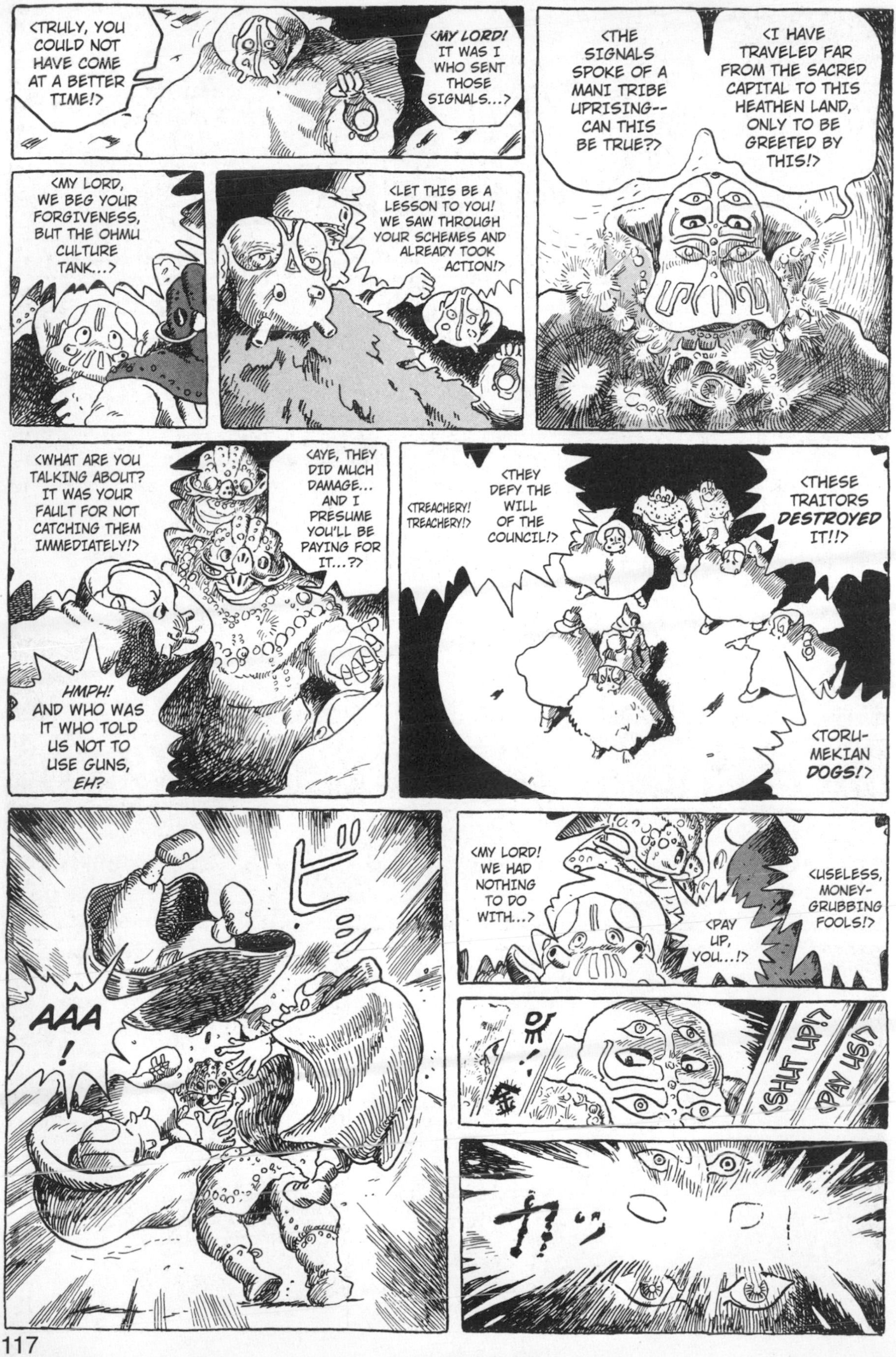

<I HAVE TRAVELED FAR FROM THE SACRED CAPITAL TO THIS HEATHEN LAND, ONLY TO BE GREETED BY THIS!>
<THE SIGNALS SPOKE OF A MANI TRIBE UPRISING-- CAN THIS BE TRUE?>
<MY LORD! IT WAS I WHO SENT THOSE SIGNALS...>
<TRULY, YOU COULD NOT HAVE COME AT A BETTER TIME!>
<LET THIS BE A LESSON TO YOU! WE SAW THROUGH YOUR SCHEMES AND ALREADY TOOK ACTION!>
<MY LORD, WE BEG YOUR FORGIVENESS, BUT THE OHMU CULTURE TANK...>
<THESE TRAITORS DESTROYED IT!!>
<THEY DEFY THE WILL OF THE COUNCIL!>
<TREACHERY! TREACHERY!>
<TORU-MEKIAN DOGS!>
<AYE, THEY DID MUCH DAMAGE... AND I PRESUME YOU'LL BE PAYING FOR IT...?>
<WHAT ARE YOU TALKING ABOUT? IT WAS YOUR FAULT FOR NOT CATCHING THEM IMMEDIATELY!>
HMPH! AND WHO WAS IT WHO TOLD US NOT TO USE GUNS, EH?
<USELESS, MONEY-GRUBBING FOOLS!>
<PAY UP, YOU...!>
<MY LORD! WE HAD NOTHING TO DO WITH...>
<SHUT UP!?
<PAY US!?
AAA !

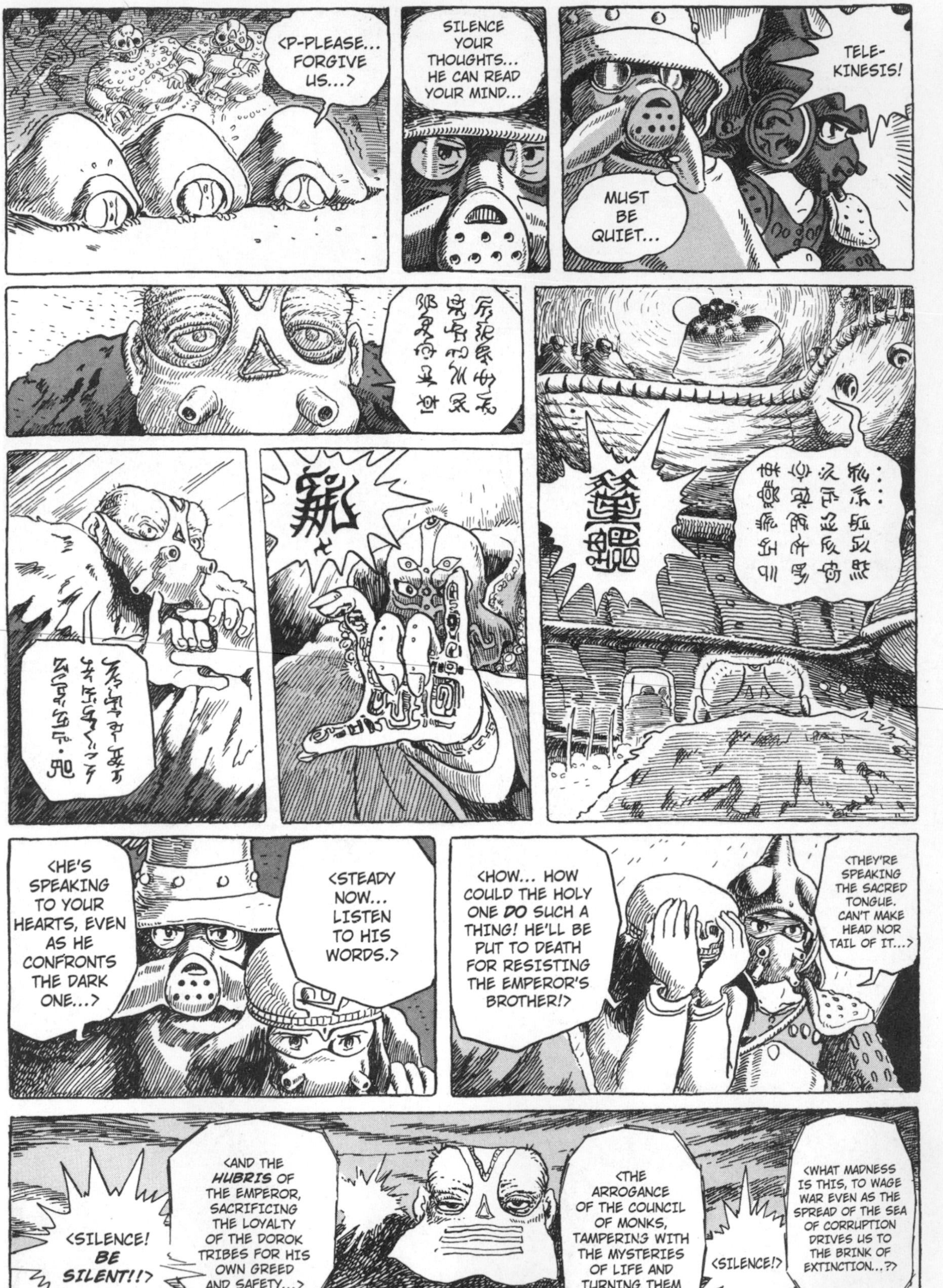
TELE-KINESIS!
MUST BE QUIET...
SILENCE YOUR THOUGHTS... HE CAN READ YOUR MIND...
<P-PLEASE... FORGIVE US...>
<THEY'RE SPEAKING THE SACRED TONGUE. CAN'T MAKE HEAD NOR TAIL OF IT...>
<HOW... HOW COULD THE HOLY ONE **DO** SUCH A THING! HE'LL BE PUT TO DEATH FOR RESISTING THE EMPEROR'S BROTHER!>
<STEADY NOW... LISTEN TO HIS WORDS.>
<HE'S SPEAKING TO YOUR HEARTS, EVEN AS HE CONFRONTS THE DARK ONE...>
<WHAT MADNESS IS THIS, TO WAGE WAR EVEN AS THE SPREAD OF THE SEA OF CORRUPTION DRIVES US TO THE BRINK OF EXTINCTION...?>
<SILENCE!>
<THE ARROGANCE OF THE COUNCIL OF MONKS, TAMPERING WITH THE MYSTERIES OF LIFE AND TURNING THEM TO WAR...>
<AND THE ***HUBRIS*** OF THE EMPEROR, SACRIFICING THE LOYALTY OF THE DOROK TRIBES FOR HIS OWN GREED AND SAFETY...>
<SILENCE! ***BE SILENT!!***>

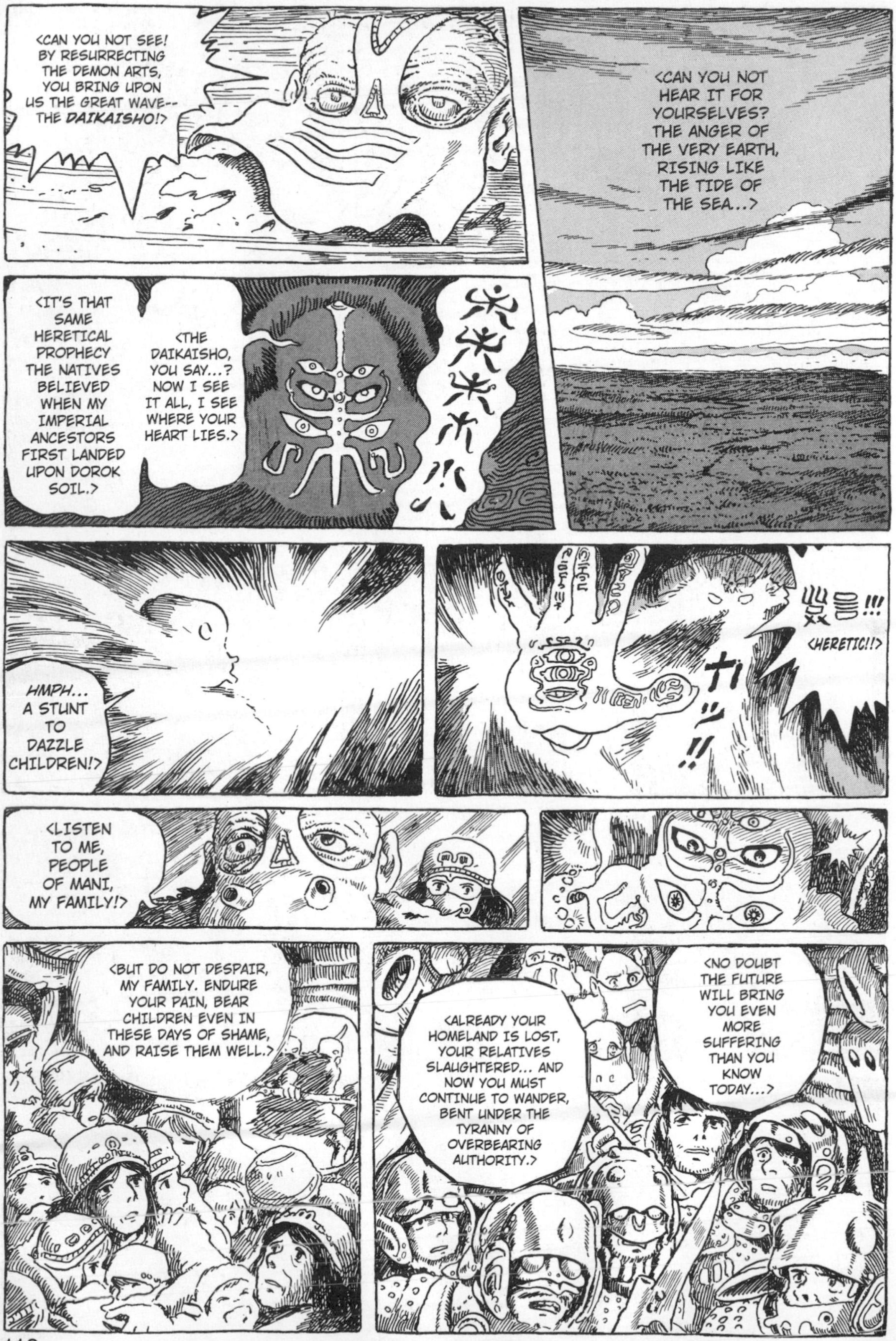
<CAN YOU NOT HEAR IT FOR YOURSELVES? THE ANGER OF THE VERY EARTH, RISING LIKE THE TIDE OF THE SEA...>
<CAN YOU NOT SEE! BY RESURRECTING THE DEMON ARTS, YOU BRING UPON US THE GREAT WAVE--THE *DAIKAISHO*!>
<THE DAIKAISHO, YOU SAY...? NOW I SEE IT ALL, I SEE WHERE YOUR HEART LIES.>
<IT'S THAT SAME HERETICAL PROPHECY THE NATIVES BELIEVED WHEN MY IMPERIAL ANCESTORS FIRST LANDED UPON DOROK SOIL.>
異端!!!
<HERETIC!!>
ガッ!!
HMPH... A STUNT TO DAZZLE CHILDREN!>
<LISTEN TO ME, PEOPLE OF MANI, MY FAMILY!>
<NO DOUBT THE FUTURE WILL BRING YOU EVEN MORE SUFFERING THAN YOU KNOW TODAY...>
<ALREADY YOUR HOMELAND IS LOST, YOUR RELATIVES SLAUGHTERED... AND NOW YOU MUST CONTINUE TO WANDER, BENT UNDER THE TYRANNY OF OVERBEARING AUTHORITY.>
<BUT DO NOT DESPAIR, MY FAMILY. ENDURE YOUR PAIN, BEAR CHILDREN EVEN IN THESE DAYS OF SHAME, AND RAISE THEM WELL.>

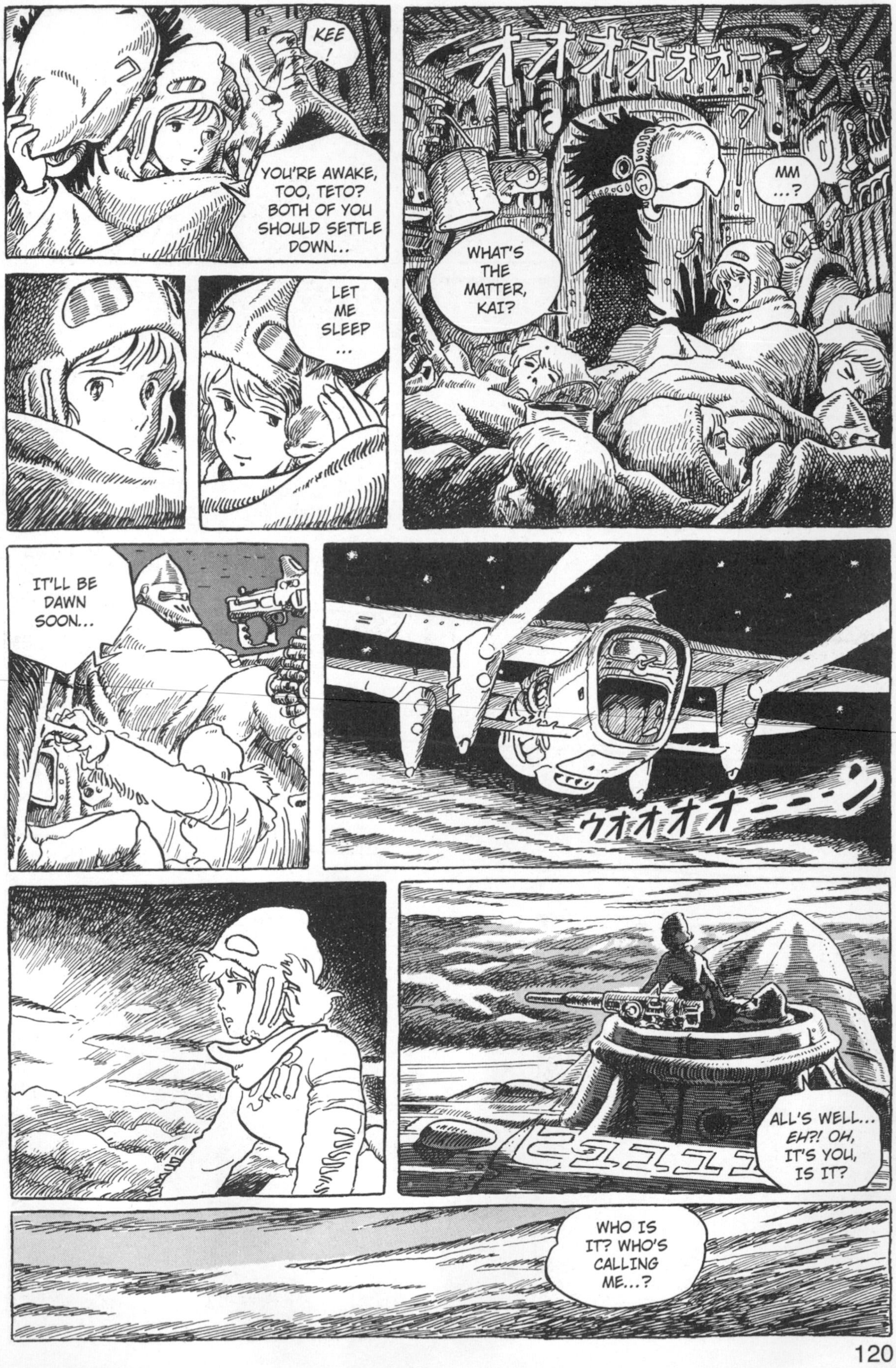

オオオオオオーーン
MM ...?
WHAT'S THE MATTER, KAI?
KEE!
YOU'RE AWAKE, TOO, TETO? BOTH OF YOU SHOULD SETTLE DOWN...
LET ME SLEEP ...
ウオオオオーーン
IT'LL BE DAWN SOON...
ALL'S WELL... *EH?!* OH, IT'S YOU, IS IT?
WHO IS IT? WHO'S CALLING ME...?

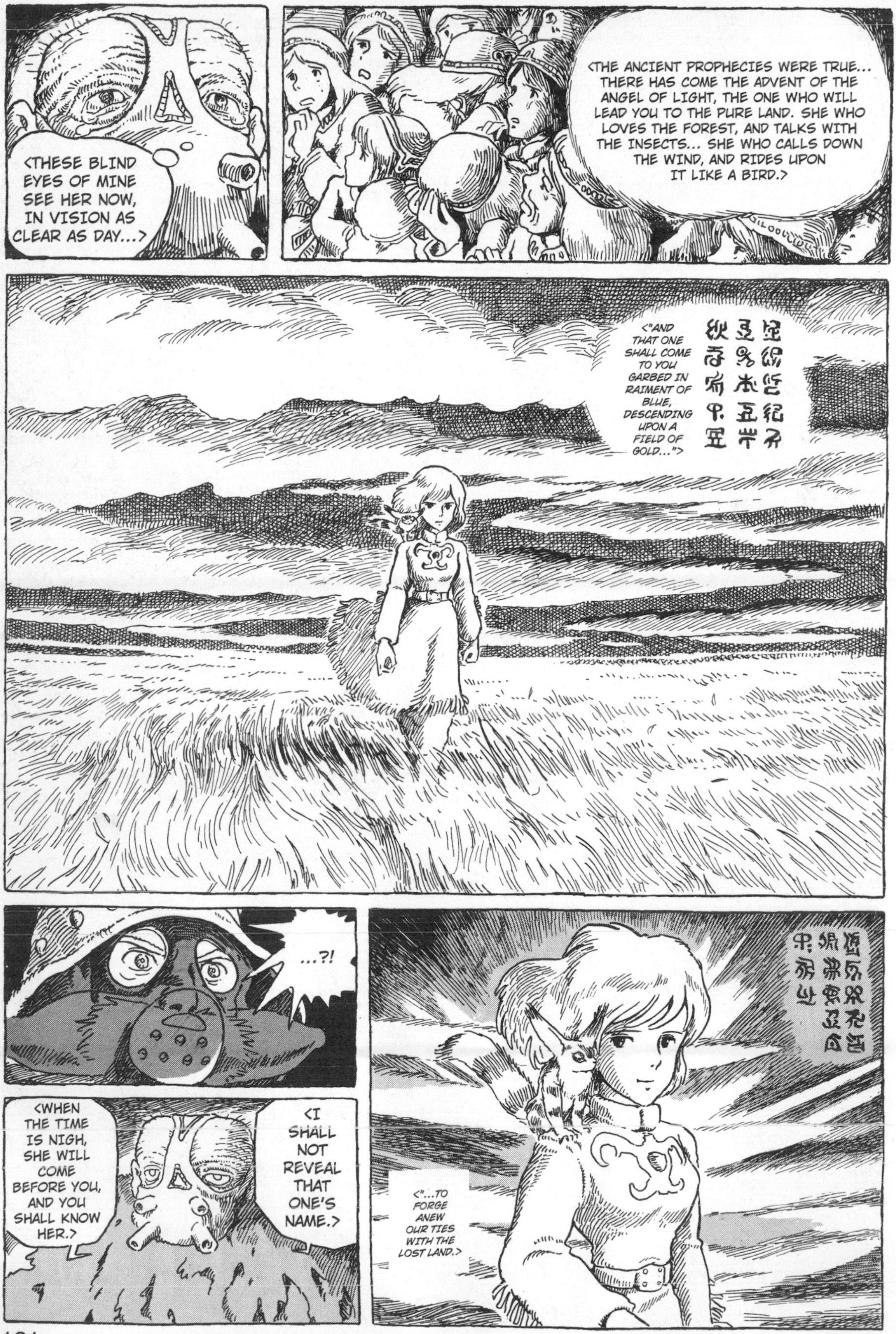
<THE ANCIENT PROPHECIES WERE TRUE... THERE HAS COME THE ADVENT OF THE ANGEL OF LIGHT, THE ONE WHO WILL LEAD YOU TO THE PURE LAND. SHE WHO LOVES THE FOREST, AND TALKS WITH THE INSECTS... SHE WHO CALLS DOWN THE WIND, AND RIDES UPON IT LIKE A BIRD.>
<THESE BLIND EYES OF MINE SEE HER NOW, IN VISION AS CLEAR AS DAY...>
<"AND THAT ONE SHALL COME TO YOU GARBED IN RAIMENT OF BLUE, DESCENDING UPON A FIELD OF GOLD...">
<"...TO FORGE ANEW OUR TIES WITH THE LOST LAND.>
...?!
<I SHALL NOT REVEAL THAT ONE'S NAME.>
<WHEN THE TIME IS NIGH, SHE WILL COME BEFORE YOU, AND YOU SHALL KNOW HER.>

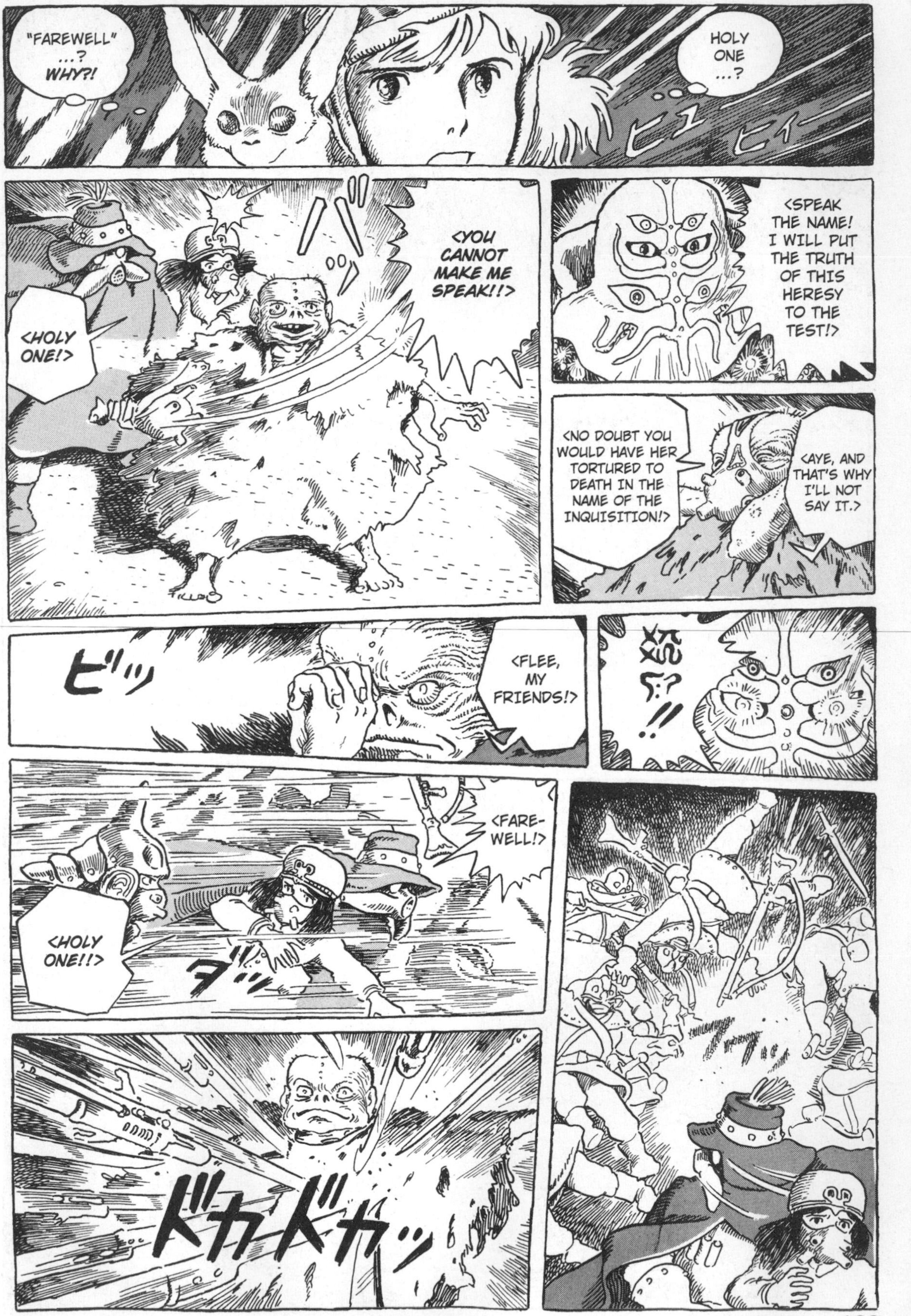
HOLY ONE ...?
ヒュ ヒイー
"FAREWELL" ...? WHY?!
<SPEAK THE NAME! I WILL PUT THE TRUTH OF THIS HERESY TO THE TEST!>
<NO DOUBT YOU WOULD HAVE HER TORTURED TO DEATH IN THE NAME OF THE INQUISITION!>
<AYE, AND THAT'S WHY I'LL NOT SAY IT.>
<YOU CANNOT MAKE ME SPEAK!!>
<HOLY ONE!>
<FLEE, MY FRIENDS!>
ビッ
<FARE-WELL!>
<HOLY ONE!!>
ダッ
ドカドカッ

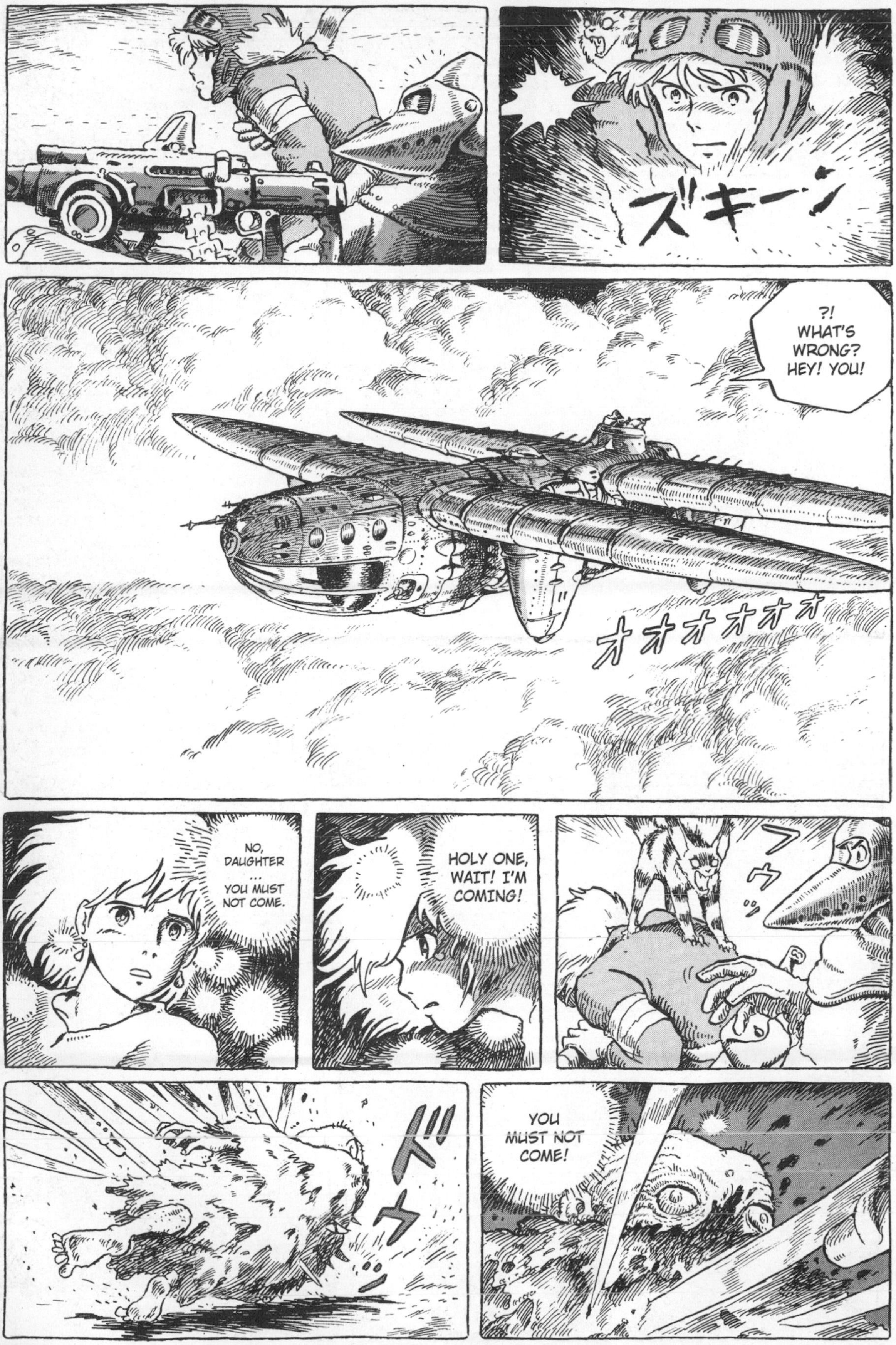
ズギーン
?! WHAT'S WRONG? HEY! YOU!
オオオオオオ
フウッ
HOLY ONE, WAIT! I'M COMING!
NO, DAUGHTER ... YOU MUST NOT COME.
YOU MUST NOT COME!
ドッ

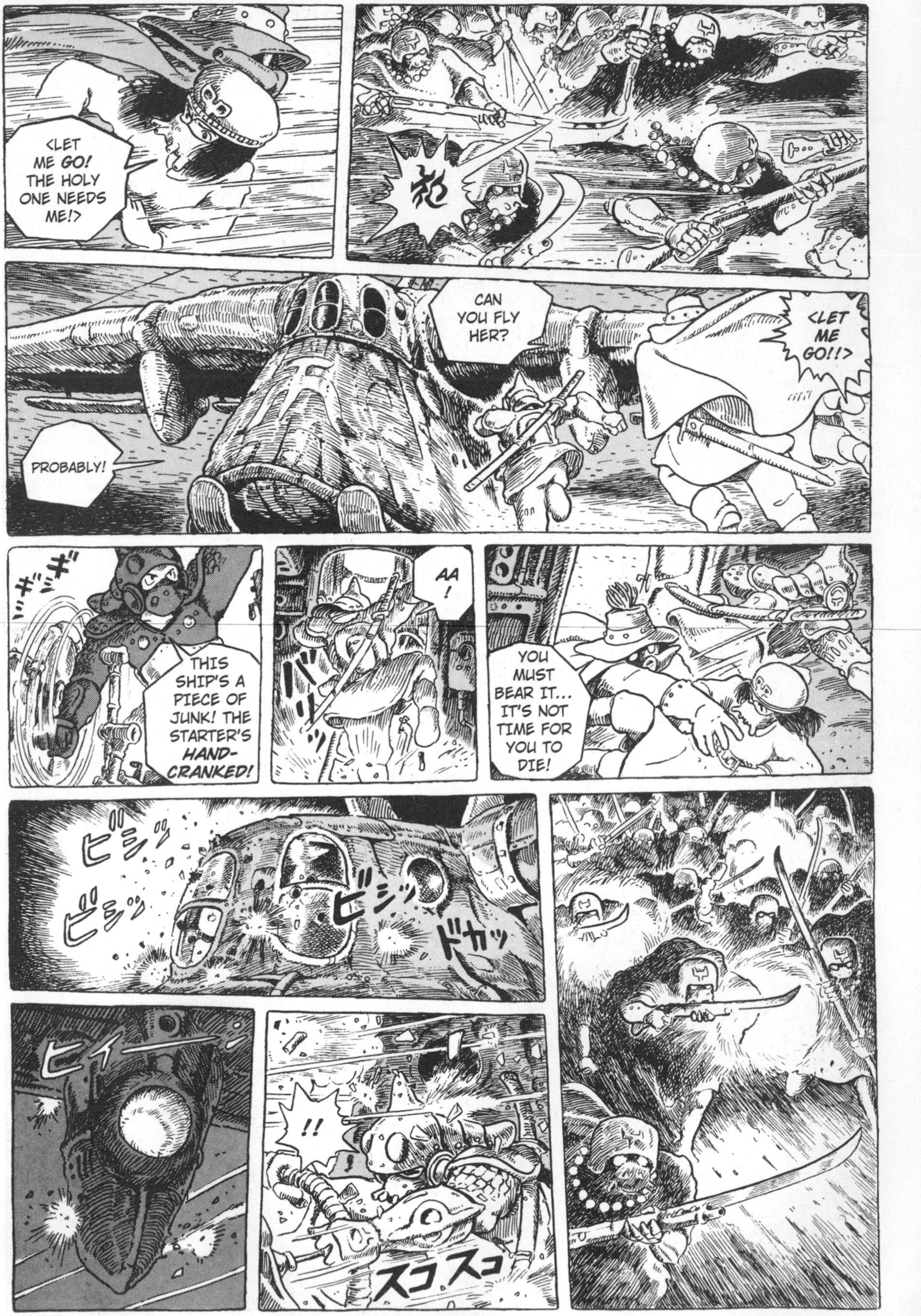
<LET ME GO! THE HOLY ONE NEEDS ME!>
<LET ME GO!!>
CAN YOU FLY HER?
PROBABLY!
YOU MUST BEAR IT... IT'S NOT TIME FOR YOU TO DIE!
AA!
バッ
ギ ギ
THIS SHIP'S A PIECE OF JUNK! THE STARTER'S HAND-CRANKED!
ビシッ ビシッ
ビシッ
ドカッ
!!
スコ スコ
ヒィー

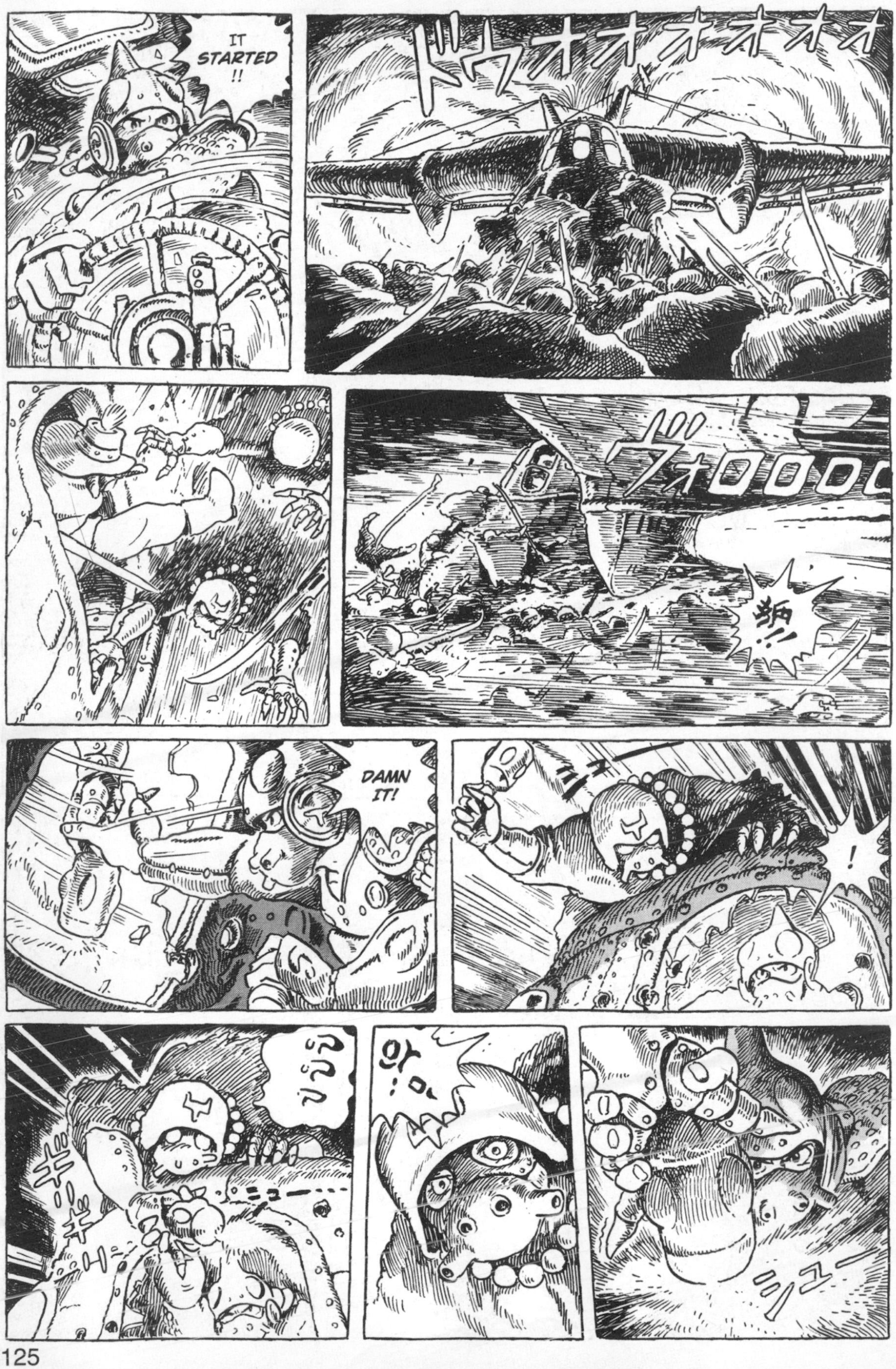
IT STARTED !!
!
DAMN IT!

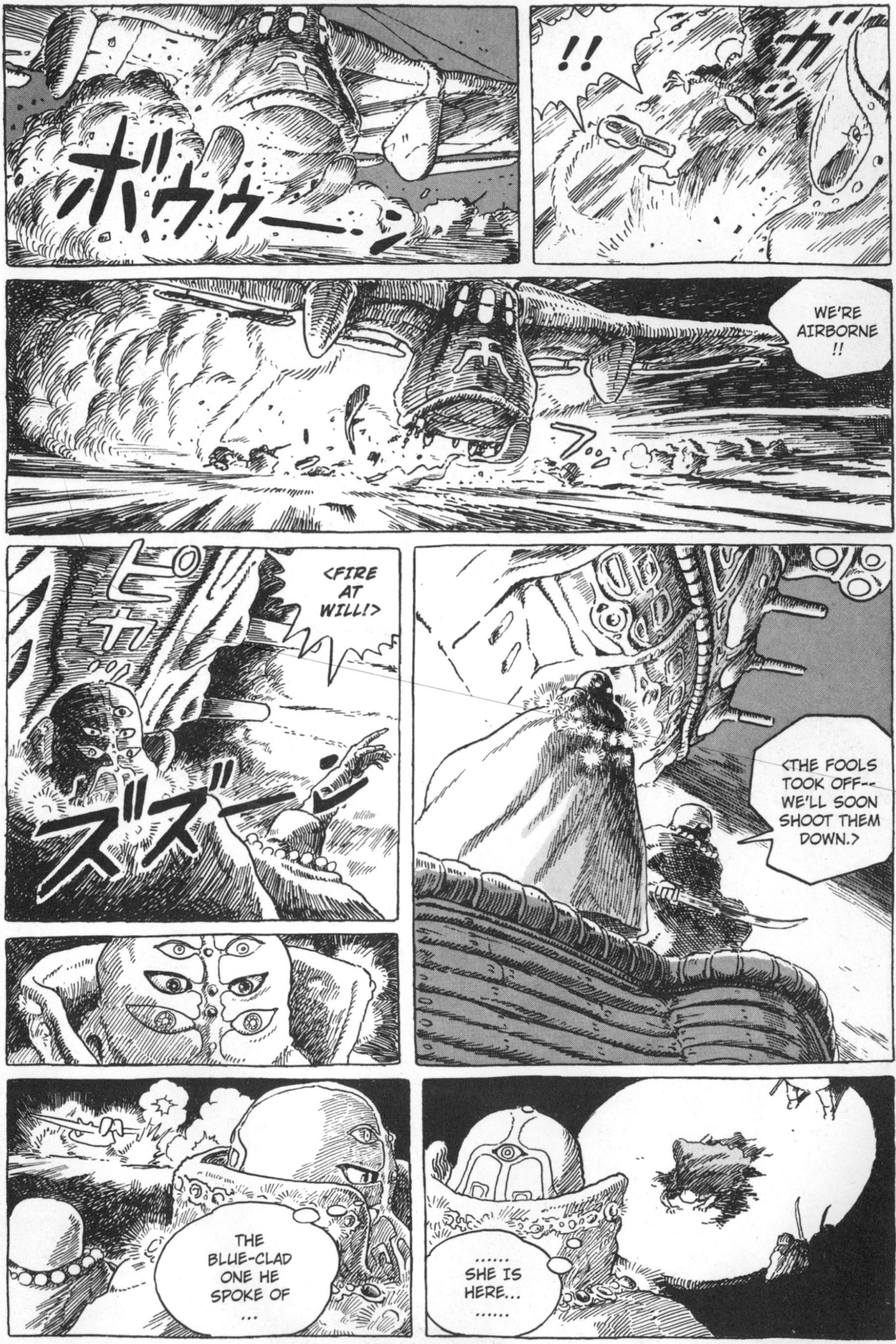

!!
ガ
ボヴウーン
WE'RE AIRBORNE !!
<THE FOOLS TOOK OFF-- WE'LL SOON SHOOT THEM DOWN.>
ピカ
<FIRE AT WILL!>
ズズーン
...... SHE IS HERE... ......
THE BLUE-CLAD ONE HE SPOKE OF ...

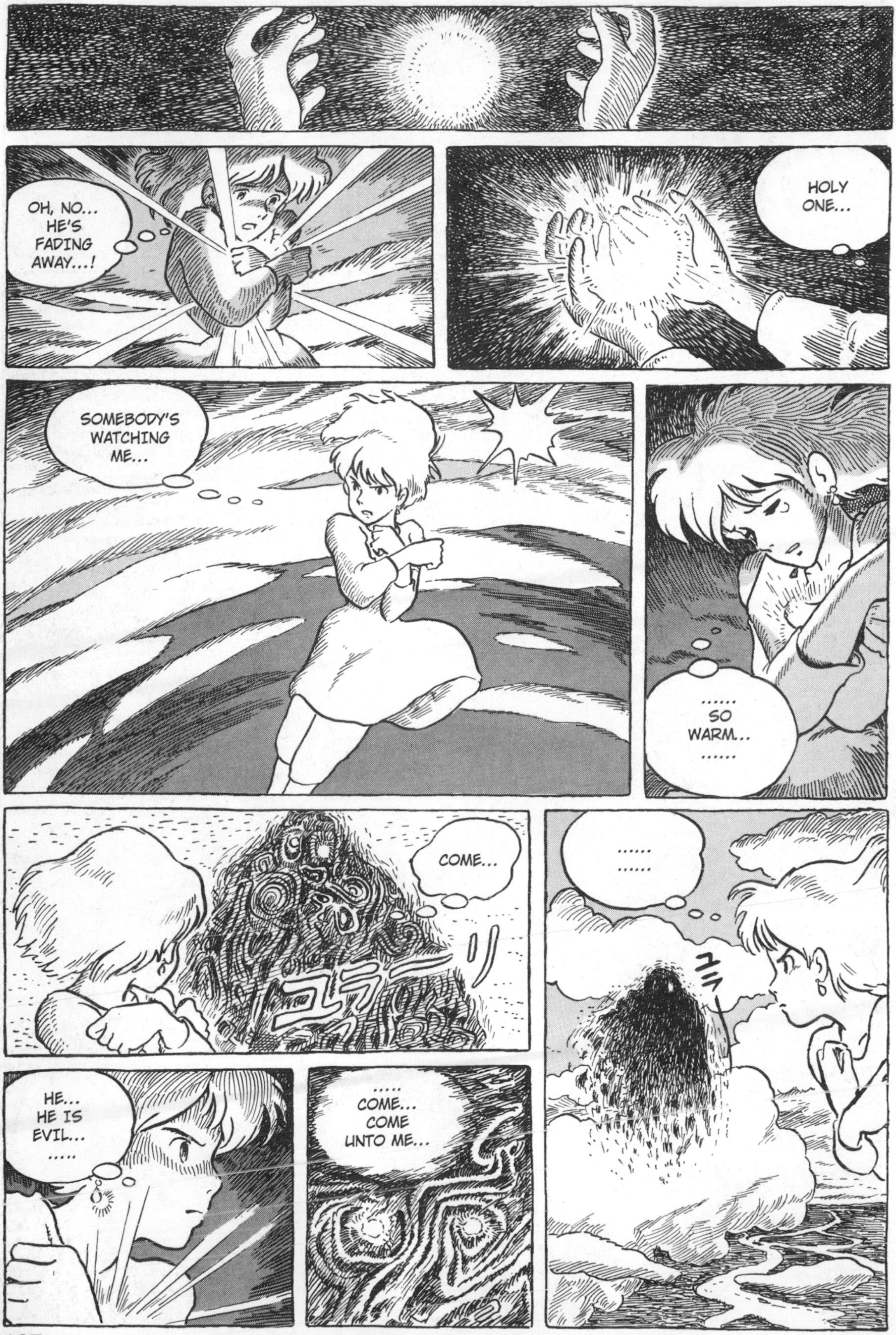

HOLY ONE...
OH, NO... HE'S FADING AWAY...!
...... SO WARM... ......
SOMEBODY'S WATCHING ME...
....
COME...
..... COME... COME UNTO ME...
HE... HE IS EVIL... .....

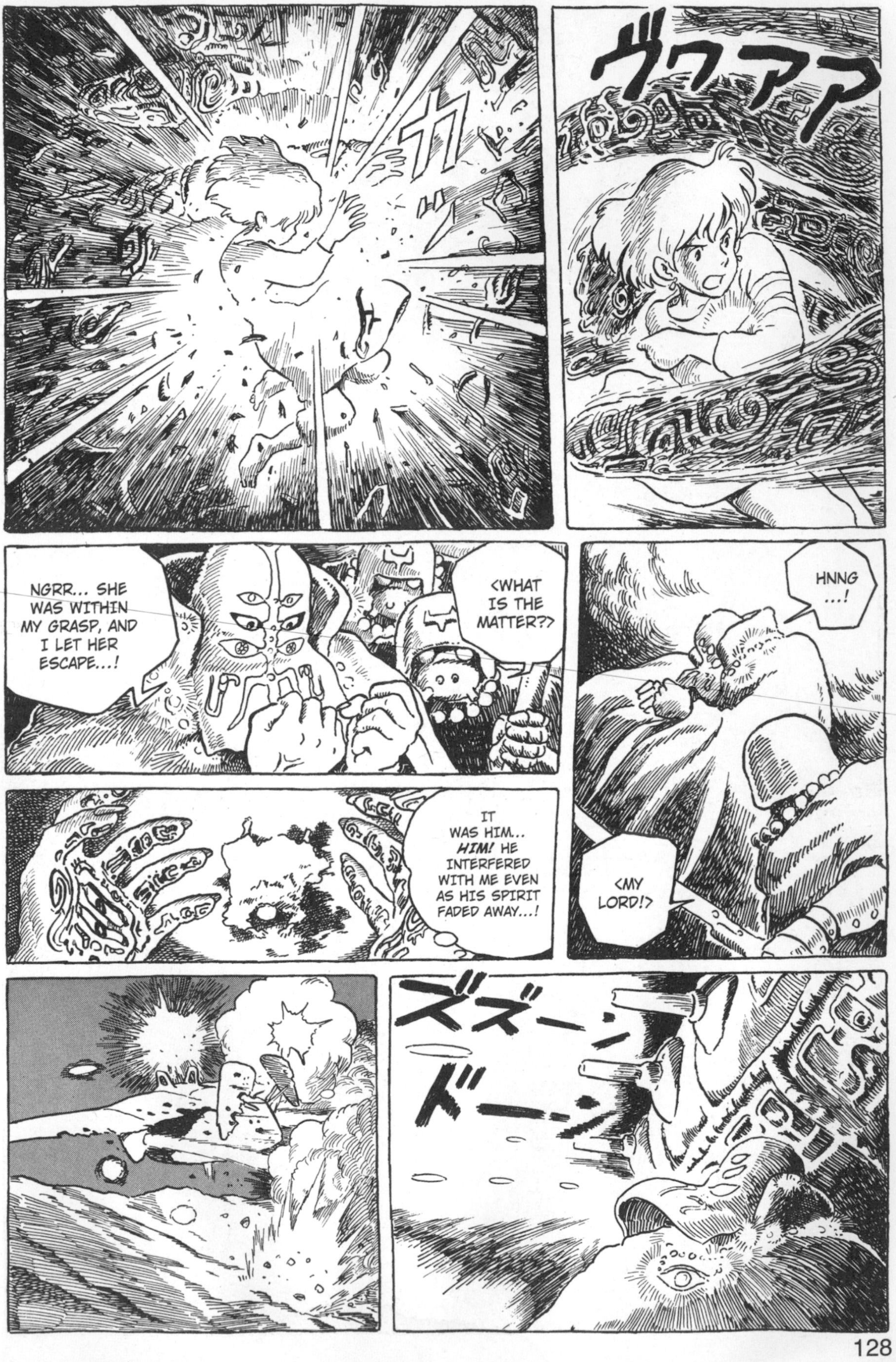
ヴワアア
カッ
HNNG ...!
<MY LORD!>
<WHAT IS THE MATTER?>
NGRR... SHE WAS WITHIN MY GRASP, AND I LET HER ESCAPE...!
IT WAS HIM... HIM! HE INTERFERED WITH ME EVEN AS HIS SPIRIT FADED AWAY...!
ズズーン
ドーン

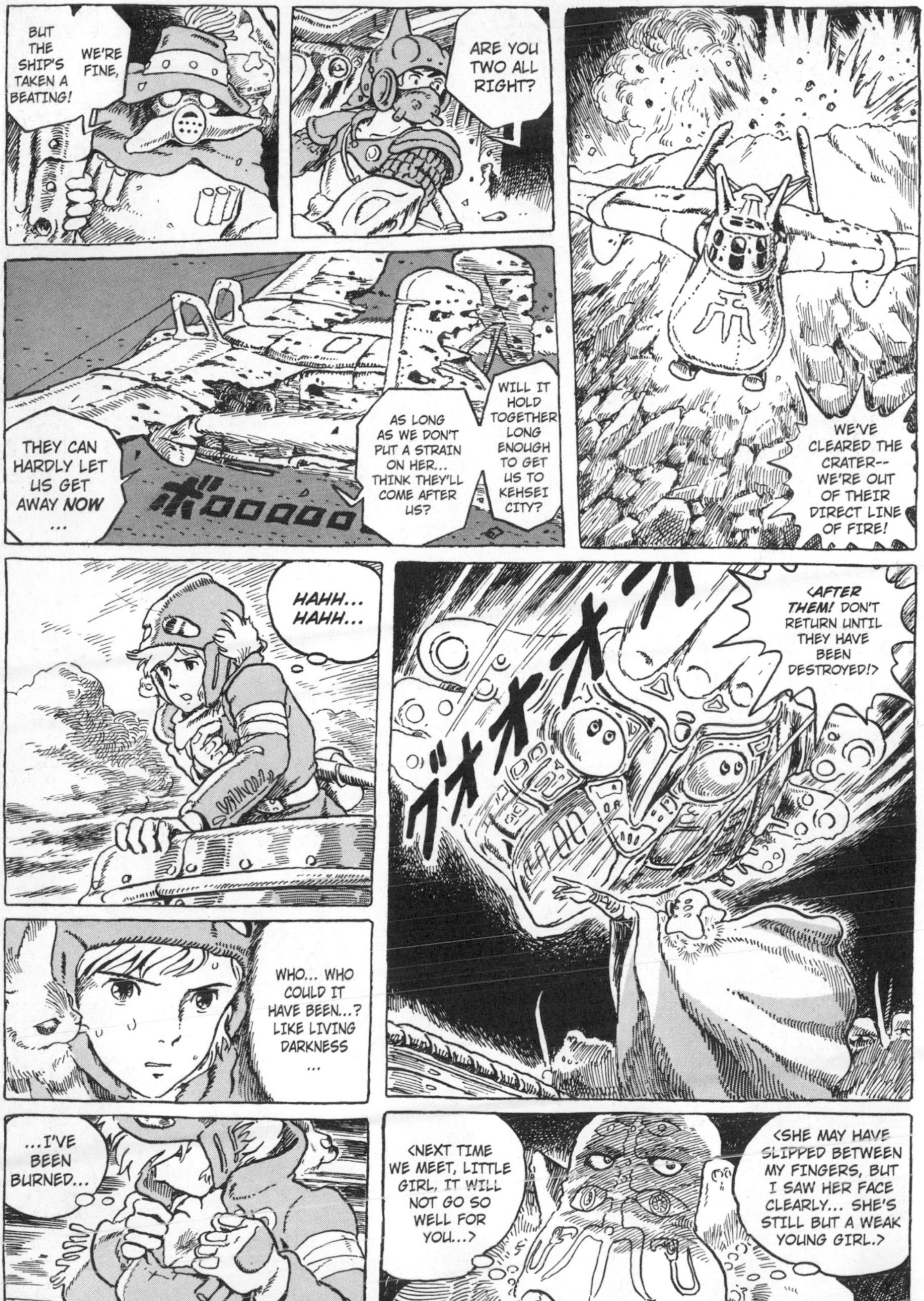
WE'VE CLEARED THE CRATER-- WE'RE OUT OF THEIR DIRECT LINE OF FIRE!
ARE YOU TWO ALL RIGHT?
WE'RE FINE,
BUT THE SHIP'S TAKEN A BEATING!
WILL IT HOLD TOGETHER LONG ENOUGH TO GET US TO KEHSEI CITY?
AS LONG AS WE DON'T PUT A STRAIN ON HER... THINK THEY'LL COME AFTER US?
THEY CAN HARDLY LET US GET AWAY *NOW* ...
<*AFTER THEM!* DON'T RETURN UNTIL THEY HAVE BEEN DESTROYED!>
HAHH... HAHH...
WHO... WHO COULD IT HAVE BEEN...? LIKE LIVING DARKNESS ...
<SHE MAY HAVE SLIPPED BETWEEN MY FINGERS, BUT I SAW HER FACE CLEARLY... SHE'S STILL BUT A WEAK YOUNG GIRL.>
<NEXT TIME WE MEET, LITTLE GIRL, IT WILL NOT GO SO WELL FOR YOU...>
...I'VE BEEN BURNED...

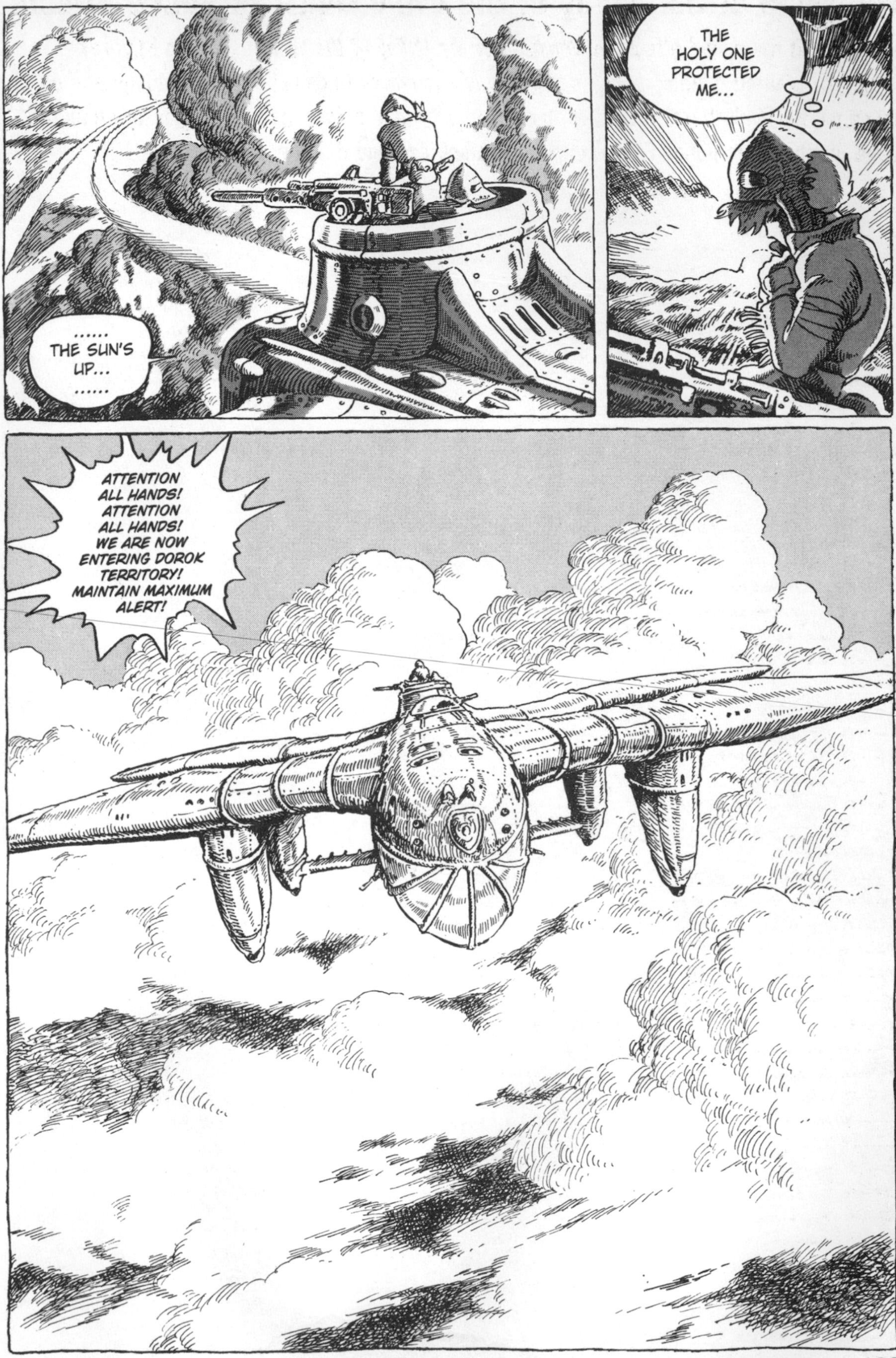
THE HOLY ONE PROTECTED ME...
...... THE SUN'S UP... ......
ATTENTION ALL HANDS! ATTENTION ALL HANDS! WE ARE NOW ENTERING DOROK TERRITORY! MAINTAIN MAXIMUM ALERT!

Nausicaä of the Valley of the Wind Guide to Sound Effects

VIZ has left the sound effects in *Nausicaä of the Valley of the Wind* as Hayao Miyazaki originally created them – in Japanese. Use this glossary to decipher, page-by-page and panel-by-panel, what all those foreign words and background noises mean. The glossary lists the page number then panel. For example, 6.1 indicates page 6, panel 1.

34.3——FX: Lululululu (rrrrrrr)
34.7——FX: Hyulululu (whirrrrr)
34.8——FX: Tou tou (pow pow)
34.9——FX: Bau (vwoosh)
34.11——FX: Saaa (shaaa)
35.1——FX: Dodooon (kabooom)
35.2——FX: Lululu lulululu (skree shree)
——FX: Hiiiin (hweee)
——FX: Hylululu (whirrrr)
——FX: Zuuuun (zaboom)
35.3——FX: Guwaaan (grabooom)
35.4——FX: Lululu (skree)
——FX: Bou (bom)
35.5——FX: Gaan gagaan gaan gaaan
         (bang ba-bang bang bang)
35.6——FX: Ba (dash)
36.1——FX: Gaan gaan (bang bang)
36.3——FX: Gooo gooo (gwhoooh gwoooh)
36.4——FX: Gaan (bang)
——FX: Doka baki (thwak whak)
——FX: Bau (boom)
36.5——FX: Shuu (fwoosh)
36.6——FX: Guwaaan (kabooom)
36.7——FX: Waa waa (crowd yelling, screaming)
37.6——FX: Dodododo (bwatatata)
37.10——FX: Dodododo (rumble rumble)
38.1——FX: Dodododo (rumble rumble)
38.2——FX: Hyuuuun (whiz)
38.3——FX: Bau (boom)
38.4——FX: Dolo dolo dolo (rumble rumble rumble)
——FX: Gooo (gwhoooh)
38.5——FX: Ddodo (rumble)
38.6——FX: Ba (vwish)
39.2——FX: Dou (dwom)
39.3——FX: Lululu (whir)
——FX: Shuuu shuuu (fwoosh fwoosh)
39.4——FX: Tatatata (pow pow pow pow)
39.5——FX: Ka (flash)
——FX: Doka doka (boom boom)
——FX: Bau (vwip)
39.6——FX: Dou dou (bom bom bom)
39.7——FX: Zaaa (zshaa)
39.8——FX: Hilululu (whir)
40.1——FX: Gyuuuuun (gwroooosh)
40.2——FX: Uiiiiin (vweeeeeen)
40.3——FX: Buchi (snap)
40.5——FX: Lululu (whirrr)
40.8——FX: Dadada (bwatatata)
40.9——FX: Hyuuu (hwooosh)
40.10——FX: Pau (pow)

21.1——FX: Gogooo on on on (gwroooh vrm vrm)
21.8——FX: Yoro (falter)
22.5——FX: Ooooooooon (wrrrrrroooooom)
23.8——FX: Za (zash)
24.2——FX: Zuzuuun (zaboom)
24.3——FX: Dodooon (dabooom)
24.4——FX: Zuzuuun (zaboom)
——FX: Dooon dodooon zuun
         (booom kaboom zaboom)
——FX: Zuzuuun (zaboom)
——FX: Ooon oooooon (wrrroom wrrooom)
24.5——FX: Pau pau (bam bam)
24.6——FX: Kiiin (shree)
25.1——FX: Dou (daboom)
——FX: Bau (boom)
25.3——FX: Zuzuuun (zaboom)
——FX: Hylululu (hwroosh)
25.4——FX: Ka (koom)
25.6——FX: Gyaaaan (shoom)
25.7——FX: Fu (fwah)
25.8——FX: Ooooooooon (wrrooooooom)
25.9——FX: Tatata (tump tump tump)
26.8——FX: Ba (fling)
26.9——FX: Ta (dash)
27.8——FX: Kiiiiin (vweeeeeeh)
27.9——FX: Hiiii (hweeeeeen)
28.1——FX: Uooooooon (vwroooooooom)
28.2——FX: Hiiii (hwooosh)
28.5——FX: Ba (vwip)
28.6——FX: Gyaaaa (gweeeen)
29.1——FX: Uooooon (vwoooooh)
29.2——FX: Chika chika chika (flash flash flash)
29.4——FX: Chika chika (flash flash)
——FX: Oooo (wroooom)
29.5——FX: Goooo (gwhoooh)
29.6——FX: Ooo (wrooom)
30.4——FX: Sa (swoosh)
30.6——FX: Da (dash)
30.7——FX: Bau (shoom)
30.12——FX: Boka doka boki (bonk whack thud)
31.3——FX: Gooon gooon (gwoom gwoom)
31.5——FX: Shuuu (shwoooosh)
31.8——FX: Goooo (gwhooooh)
32.1——FX: Viiiii (vweeeeeeh)
32.6——FX: Hiii (hweeee)
33.2——FX: Dodododo (rumble rumble rumble)
33.3——FX: Zazazaza (zzzzshhaaa)
33.5——FX: Zazazaza (zzzzshhaaa)
——FX: Dododo (rumble rumble)
34.1——FX: Hyulululu (whirrr)

3.2——FX: Shuuu (fwoosh)
3.4——FX: Hyuuu hyuuu (hwoooosh hwooosh)
3.6——FX: Bau (vom)
4.1——FX: Saaa (fwoosh)
4.2——FX: Uooo (vwoom)
4.4——FX: Gui (yank)
4.5——FX: Zaza (zshh)
5.1——FX: Dodododo (d-d-dagoom)
5.2——FX: Uoooo (vwoom)
5.3——FX: Goooo (gwooh)
5.5——FX: Papau (bam bam)
5.6——FX: Gagaaan (gaboom)
5.7——FX: Fu (shift)
6.1——FX: On on on (vwoom vwoom vwoom)
——FX: Goo (gwooh)
6.2——FX: Shuuu shuu (fwoosh fwoosh)
7.5——FX: Ka (whack)
7.9——FX: Goho goho (gack cough)
8.1——FX: Kiiin (klang)
8.9——FX: Hyoko hyoko (hobble hobble)
10.2——FX: Shuu shuu (fwoosh fwoosh)
10.7——FX: Gogogogogo (gwogwogwogwoh)
10.8——FX: Uoo (vwoooom)
11.1——FX: Uooooon (vwwwooooon)
11.2——FX: Uoooon (vwwwooomm)
12.2——FX: Kasha gasha gasha
         (crunch scrunch scrunch)
12.5——FX: Gan gan (kang kang)
——FX: Bibibibi (bwttt)
12.9——FX: Gaya gaya (chatter chatter)
14.6——FX: Kuuu kueee (coo kree)
15.4——FX: Wahahahahaha (bwahahaha)
15.13——FX: Tatata (tump tump)
16.4——FX: Ba (bam)
16.6——FX: Zaaaa (zash)
16.7——FX: Doka doka (dwak dwak)
17.1——FX: Pau (blam)
——FX: Uooo (vwooosh)
17.2——FX: Dou (dwwwom)
17.3——FX: Guooooooon (gwroom)
17.5——FX: Golo (klink)
18.7——FX: Goon goon goon
         (gwhum gwhum gwhum)
18.8——FX: Gooo (gwhooh)
19.1——FX: Biiiin (vweeeeeen)
19.4——FX: Olololololo (vrrrroomm)
19.5——FX: Gon gon gon (gwhum gwhum gwhum)
19.6——FX: Ooooon (wroooom)
19.8——FX: Ki (kree)
20.1——FX: Ton (toom)
20.8——FX: Ooooooooon (wrooooooom)

———FX: Byu (spurt)
59.2 ———FX: Uiiiiiin (vwooooosh)
59.3 ———FX: Hilululu (hwrrrrr)
59.4 ———FX: Zu (zash)
59.5 ———FX: Zu zu zu (zash zash zash)
59.6 ———FX: Zu (zash)
59.7 ———FX: Jyulululu (sizzle)
59.8 ———FX: Shuu shuu (fwoosh fwoosh)
60.1 ———FX: Dosa (whud)
60.5 ———FX: Ozu ozu (slink)
60.6 ———FX: Uooooon (wrooooon)
60.8 ———FX: Zazaza (zshaa)
———FX: Zaba (splash)
60.9-10 ———FX: Juuu Julululu (sizzle sssizzzle)
61.1 ———FX: Shuuu shuuu (fwoosh fwoosh)
———FX: Jyulululululu (sizzle)
———FX: Jyuu jyuu jyuu (sizzle sizzle sizzle)
61.5 ———FX: Goooo (gwhooh)
62.4 ———FX: Zazaza (zshhhh)
62.6 ———FX: Ka (flash)
63.4 ———FX: Gogogogo goon gon gon (gwooohm gwm gmgm)
63.5 ———FX: Dou (dwom)
63.7 ———FX: Hyuun (hwoooooosh)
63.8 ———FX: Guuu (gshhh)
63.9 ———FX: Shaa (shwoosh)
64.1 ———FX: Fuwa (fwoh)
64.5 ———FX: Uooooon (wrooooon)
64.8 ———FX: Ba (bwah)
64.9 ———FX: Hyuuun (hwoooosh)
65.1 ———FX: Batan (slam)
65.7 ———FX: Chi (chik)
65.8 ———FX: Ki (kree)
66.2 ———FX: Hyuu (hwoooh)
66.9 ———FX: Uooooon (wroooon)
67.1 ———FX: Lululu (whirrr)
67.2 ———FX: Duo duo (davom davom)
67.3 ———FX: Gagagaga (ggggshhh)
67.5 ———FX: Zazaza (zwoosh)
67.6 ———FX: Zuzuzu (zggshh)
67.7 ———FX: Gugu (shhhh)
67.8 ———FX: Uoooooon (wrooooon)
68.5 ———FX: Yota yota (wobble wobble)
68.7 ———FX: Zuzu zulu (drag drag)
68.8 ———FX: Hyulululu (hwrrrr)
68.9 ———FX: Hyulululu (hwrrrr)
69.4 ———FX: Hyulululu (hwrrrr)
70.1 ———FX: Zulu zulu (slide slide)
70.4 ———FX: Shulu shulu (shwrl shwrl)
70.5 ———FX: Sawasawa (sha sha)
70.8 ———FX: Sala sala (sssshhhhaaa)
71.1 ———FX: Su (lift)
71.7 ———FX: Sawasawa sawasawa (sha sha sha sha)
73.2 ———FX: Wana wana (tremble tremble)
73.9 ———FX: Zawa zawa (shuffle shuffle)
———FX: Dolo dolo (rumble rumble)
74.1 ———FX: Zawa zawa zawa (shuffle shuffle shuffle)
74.2 ———FX: Zazaza (zshhh)

(rumble rumble rumble rumble rumble)
———FX: Dooooo (roooooaaar)
48.4 ———FX: Dodooooo (dgwrooooh)
48.7 ———FX: Waa waa waa (crowd yelling)
———FX: Dodododo (rumble rumble)
49.1 ———FX: Zazazaza zazaza (zshhashasha zshashasha)
49.2 ———FX: Dooo (rumble)
49.4 ———FX: Waa waa waa (crowd yelling)
49.7 ———FX: Dada (bwatata)
49.8 ———FX: Dadadada (bwatatatata)
49.10 ———FX: Vulooooo (vwroooooooh)
50.1 ———FX: Ooooo (vroooooom)
———FX: Waaaa waa (crowd screaming, yelling)
50.5 ———FX: Ka (bam)
50.6 ———FX: Gaan (gaboom)
———FX: Gi (screech)
50.8 ———FX: Za (whud)
50.9 ———FX: Dodo (rumble)
———FX: Doulu doulululu (rumble rumble)
51.1 ———FX: Uoooo (vwooooh)
51.2 ———FX: Gooo (gwooooh)
———FX: Dododo (rumble rumble)
51.3 ———FX: Waaa waa waa (crowd screaming, yelling)
51.4 ———FX: Zazaza (rumble rumble)
———FX: Gooo (gwooooh)
52.1 ———FX: Gogogo (ggroooh)
52.2 ———FX: Gyaaa (gaaaaah)
52.3 ———FX: Dokaaan (booom)
52.5 ———FX: Meki meki meki (crush crush crush)
———FX: Bali bali bali (crunch crunch crunch)
52.6 ———FX: Buchi (bwach)
52.7 ———FX: Boumn (babooom)
53.1 ———FX: Dodo (rumble)
53.2 ———FX: Gooo (gwooooh)
———FX: Zazaza (zshhhaa)
53.4 ———FX: Zuzuuun (zaboom)
54.1 ———FX: Dododo (rumble)
54.3 ———FX: Dododo (rumble)
54.5 ———FX: Gooo (gwhooh)
———FX: Pa (fwip)
54.6 ———FX: Gyaa (aaagh)
54.7 ———FX: Dodododo doo dooo (rumble rumble rumble)
55.1 ———FX: Dolo dolo dolo (rumble rumble rumble)
55.2 ———FX: Oooo (whooooh)
55.6 ———FX: Bashi (smack)
55.10 ———FX: Sa (swish)
56.1 ———FX: Ozu ozu (shuffle shuffle)
56.3 ———FX: Uooooon (wrooooon)
———FX: Hyuuu (hwooosh)
56.4 ———FX: Bata bata (fwap fwap)
56.9 ———FX: Ba (slice)
57.3 ———FX: Dooo dodoo dooo (rumble rumble rumble)
57.7 ———FX: Zun (zagoom)
57.8 ———FX: Zun zun zun zun (zagoom zagoom zagoom zagoom)
57.9 ———FX: Dosa (thud)
58.3 ———FX: Dokun dokun (ba-dump ba-dump)
58.4 ———FX: Dokku dokku dokku (pump pump pump)
58.7 ———FX: Yoro yoro (wobble wobble)

40.11 ———FX: Bishi (fwip)
41.1 ———FX: Gaan gaan (bang bang)
41.2 ———FX: Dodon (daboom)
———FX: Babababa (bang bang bang)
———FX: Lululululu (whirrrr)
41.3 ———FX: Zuzuun (th-thud)
41.4 ———FX: Gula (wobble)
41.5 ———FX: Gugu (jerk)
41.6 ———FX: Bili bili (shake shake)
41.7 ———FX: Ba (bwah)
41.10 ———FX: Zushiiin (zzgmm)
———FX: Jyuu jyuu (sizzle sizzle)
42.1 ———FX: Shuu shuu (ssss ssss)
42.4 ———FX: Za (zash)
42.8 ———FX: Zuzu (drag)
42.9 ———FX: Zulu zulu (drag drag)
42.10 ———FX: Dokun dokun (da-bump da-bump)
43.1 ———FX: Byuu (spurt)
———FX: Bu (gush)
43.2 ———FX: Dodooo (spray)
43.3 ———FX: Hiku hiku (twitch twitch)
43.7 ———FX: Za (zsh)
43.8 ———FX: Ba (bwah)
———FX: Dokaan (kaboom)
43.9 ———FX: Ga (chok)
44.1 ———FX: Zuuun zudoon (zaboom zaboom)
———FX: Gaaan gagaaan (bang ba-bang)
———FX: Dadada (rumble rumble)
44.2 ———FX: Bau bau baaan (bang bang boom)
44.3 ———FX: Gaaan (boom)
44.10 ———FX: Kiiiin (vweeesh)
45.1 ———FX: Bau bau (bam bam)
45.2 ———FX: Gyulululuuuun (gwrooooooomh)
45.3 ———FX: Zubau zuzuun (zabooom kaboom)
45.5 ———FX: Hiiii (hweeee)
———FX: Waa waa (crowd yelling)
45.6 ———FX: Goooo (gwooooh)
45.9 ———FX: Zaza (zgwash)
46.1 ———FX: Waa waa waa (crowd yelling)
———FX: Gooo gooo (gwhoooh gwoooh)
46.5 ———FX: Goto goto (gatunk gatunk)
46.6 ———FX: Dododo dodododo (rumble rumble rumble)
———FX: Ha ha (huff huff)
46.7 ———FX: Ha ha (huff huff)
46.8 ———FX: Duoooo (dwrooooogh)
46.9 ———FX: Vuooo (vrooom)
47.1 ———FX: Gau gau (bam bam)
47.2 ———FX: Kiin kiin (klang klang)
47.4 ———FX: Ka (whud)
47.5 ———FX: Uooooon (vwooom)
47.6 ———FX: Ba (bwah)
47.7 ———FX: Dadada (rumble rumble)
47.8 ———FX: Dadada (rumble rumble)
47.10 ———FX: Guoooo (gwooooooh)
48.1 ———FX: Uoooooon uooooon uooo000n uoooo (wroooooon wroooooon wrooon wrooo)
48.2 ———FX: Dolo dolo dolo dolo dolo dolo (rumble rumble rumble rumble rumble rumble)
48.3 ———FX: Dolo dolo dolo dolo dolo dolo

113.7——FX: Doka gon doka (dwak gonk whack)
113.8——FX: Dote goon kaan (thud gonk klang)
114.1——FX: Batan (slam)
——FX: Gui (yank)
114.2——FX: Don don don (bam bam bam)
——FX: Shyuuu (fshhh)
114.3——FX: Shuu (fwoosh)
114.4——FX: Gigi (creak)
114.6——FX: Zudoon zudooon (zaboom zaboom)
114.7——FX: Kaan (klaaang)
——FX: Chi (ach)
115.1——FX: Ka (flash)
115.4——FX: Baki baki (bwakrak)
115.5——FX: Walawala (whrsh whrsh)
116.5——FX: Pita pita pita pita pita (slink slink slink slink slink)
116.6——FX: Sulu sulu (shwrl shwrl)
117.9——FX: Ka (flash)
117.10——FX: Bishi (vwip)
119.4——FX: Ka (kraah)
120.1——FX: Oooouun (wroooooom)
——FX: Kuuu (coo)
120.2——FX: Kuuu (coo)
120.5——FX: Uoooooon (wroooon)
120.7——FX: Hyuuu (hwooosh)
122.1——FX: Hyuuu hiiii (hwooosh hweee)
122.4——FX: Ba (bwah)
122.6——FX: Bi (vwip)
122.7——FX: Buwa (float)
122.8——FX: Da (dash)
122.9——FX: Doka doka (thud thud)
123.1——FX: Zukiiiin (ziing)
123.3——FX: Ooooo (vwmmm)
123.4——FX: Fu (hiss)
123.8——FX: Dou (whud)
124.5——FX: Bali (crack)
124.6——FX: Gishi gishi (crank crank)
124.8——FX: Doka bishi bishi bishi (daboom dwak dwak dwak)
124.9——FX: Suko suko (sksh sksh)
124.10——FX: Hiiiin (hweeeen)
125.1——FX: Duooooo (dvwroooom)
125.3——FX: Vulolololo (vwmvwmvwm)
125.5——FX: Shuuu (fshhh)
125.7——FX: Shuu (fshhh)
125.9——FX: Shuu (fshhh)
——FX: Gili gili (grip grip)
126.1——FX: Ga (gank)
126.2——FX: Bouuuun (kaboooom)
126.3——FX: Fu (float)
126.5——FX: Pika (flash)
——FX: Zuzuuun (zaboo)
127.6——FX: Yulaaa (wavering)
127.7——FX: Yulaaali (wavering)
128.1——FX: Vuwaaa (vwoooh)
128.2——FX: Ka (flash)
128.6——FX: Zuzuun dooon (zaboom boom)
129.4——FX: Bolololololo (bwrtttt)
129.5——FX: Guoooo (gwhoooooh)

——FX: Puchi puchi (pop pop)
——FX: Zazaza (zshhaa)
——FX: Puchi puchi (pop pop)
——FX: Puchi puchi (pop pop)
——FX: Shuu shuu (fwoosh fwoosh)
99.2——FX: Hou (bwoff)
99.3——FX: Shuu shuu shuu (fwoosh fwoosh fwoosh)
99.4——FX: Uooon (wrooon)
99.5——FX: Oooo (ooooooh)
99.6——FX: Uoooon (wrooom)
99.7——FX: Unnnnn (wnnnnn)
100.2——FX: Doka doka (stomp stomp)
100.5——FX: Goon goon (gwoom gwooom)
100.6——FX: Chika chika (flash flash)
100.7——FX: Oooon (oooomh)
100.8——FX: Shaka shaka (click click)
101.1——FX: Goon goon (gwommm gwomm)
——FX: Uooon (wrooom)
101.3——FX: Zazaa (zshha)
101.6——FX: Chapun chapun (slosh slosh)
102.9——FX: Hyu hyuu (hwooh hwooh)
104.1——FX: Hihihi (hee hee)
104.6——FX: Pita pita (ptwch ptwch)
104.7——FX: Pita pita (ptwch ptwch)
104.9——FX: Piiii (fweeee)
105.5——FX: Ba (bwap)
105.6——FX: Bota bota (whud whud)
105.7——FX: Doka (crack)
105.10——FX: Ton (tump)
106.2——FX: Gobo gobo (glub glub)
106.3——FX: Piku piku (twitch twitch)
106.4——FX: Bau (blam)
106.5——FX: Chiiin (kachiiin)
106.6——FX: Do (dwoh)
107.8——FX: Chi (chik)
108.1——FX: Ba (pounce)
108.2——FX: Su (swoosh)
108.3——FX: Kiiin (klaaang)
109.3——FX: Hyun hyun (hwip hwiip)
110.1——FX: Jili (gash)
110.3——FX: Tsu (glint)
110.5——FX: Buuun (vwooosh)
110.7——FX: Kachi (kachik)
——FX: Da (dash)
110.9——FX: Kiiin (klaaaang)
111.2——FX: Ta (vash)
111.5——FX: Gyuuun (vwooosh)
111.6——FX: Ka (vwak)
111.8——FX: Doba (dvwooosh)
112.1——FX: Dooo (dwoooosh)
112.4——FX: Zuka (zachok)
112.5——FX: Goon gaaan (gooong bang)
——FX: Bushuuu (bwshhhh)
112.6——FX: Bouuuun (booom)
112.7——FX: Gaaan gaana (gonnnk gooonk)
113.1——FX: Ba (boof)
113.3——FX: Pyulululu (bweeeeep)
——FX: Dadadada (dash)

74.7——FX: Kasa kasa (rustle rustle)
——FX: Sala sala (sha sha)
74.8——FX: Zazaza (zshzshzsh)
——FX: Bufwa bufwa (Ohmu calling)
75.4——FX: Kaan kaan (klaaang klaaang)
76.1——FX: Uooooon (hwroooon)
76.2——FX: Hiiiin (hweeeen)
76.3——FX: Guooooo (gwrooo)
76.4——FX: Ooon ooon ooon (wrooom wrooom wrooom)
76.6——FX: Uoooon (wroooom)
77.1——FX: Vooo (vwroooh)
77.2——FX: Kikiii (skreee)
77.3——FX: Shuuu (fwoosh fwoosh)
78.1——FX: Uoooo (wroooh)
78.5——FX: Zazaaa (zwooosh)
81.2——FX: Zawa zawa (murmur murmur)
85.8——FX: Yulali (wobble)
86.2——FX: Waaaa (crying)
86.3——FX: Oooo waaa oooo (crying)
86.7——FX: Shiku shiku (sob sob)
87.3——FX: Waaan eeen aaaaan (crying)
89.8——FX: Do (dash)
90.1——FX: Hiiin (hweeeen)
90.2——FX: Kuu (coo)
90.5——FX: Ta (dash)
——FX: Hiiin (hweeeen)
90.6——FX: Vuolololo (vwrmwrm)
91.1——FX: Dodooon (dwoooomsh)
92.1——FX: Kaaan kaaan kiiin kakaan kaan kaaan (klaaang klaang kiiink kl-klaang klang)
93.7——FX: Gashaan (craaash)
94.2——FX: Pala (scatter)
94.5——FX: Zawazawa (murmur murmur)
95.2——FX: Boka (bwak)
——FX: Gya (aagh)
——FX: Bishi (vwip)
95.3——FX: Bashi (vwap)
——FX: Hii (aiee)
95.4——FX: Pishi bachi (whack vwip)
95.8——FX: Doka bishi (whack vwip)
95.10——FX: Bishi boka doka (vwip whack crack)
96.5——FX: Ga ga (chomp chomp)
96.6——FX: Mogu (grmph)
97.5——FX: Tata (dash)
97.6——FX: Bou (bwoof)
——FX: Shlululu (shwrrrr)
97.7——FX: Ton (pounce)
97.9——FX: Gooo (gwhooooh)
98.1——FX: Gololololo (gwrom gwrom gwrom)
——FX: Ooon ooon (wrooom wrooom)
98.3——FX: Dooo (dwooooh)
98.4——FX: Chapun chapun chapun (slosh slosh slosh)
98.7——FX: Uoooon (wroooon)
99.1——FX: Salasalasala (shashasha)
——FX: Salasalasala (shashasha)
——FX: Zaa zaa (zwoosh zwoosh)
——FX: Salasalasala (shashasha)
——FX: Puchi (pop)

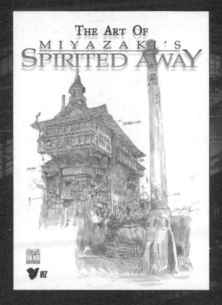